IMAGINARY HAND

Essays by George Bowering

Volume I
The Writer as Critic Series
General Editor: Smaro Kamboureli

NeWest Press

Edmonton

First edition

Canadian Cataloguing in Publication Data

Bowering, George, 1935-
    Imaginary Hand

(Poetics and critical writing by Canadian authors, 1)
Index
ISBN 0-920897-54-1 (bound). — ISBN 0-920897-52-5 (pbk.)

1. Literature — History and criticism.
2. Canadian literature (English) — History and criticism.*
I. Title. II. Series.
PN511.B69 1988   809   C88-091503-X

Credits

Cover design: Bob Young/Bookends Designworks
Editor for the Press: Smaro Kamboureli
Printing and binding: Hignell Printing Limited, Manitoba
Financial assistance:
    Alberta Culture
    The Alberta Foundation for the Literary Arts
    The Canada Council

Manufactured in Canada

NeWest Publishers Limited
Suite 310, 10359 - 82 Avenue
Edmonton, Alberta
Canada   T6E 1Z9

Acknowledgements

I would like to acknowledge the magazines that first published some of these essays, in earlier forms.

Room of One's Own
Open Letter
Essays in Canadian Writing
Canadian Literature
Line
B.C. Studies
The Review of Contemporary Fiction
Epoch
The Antigonish Review
Kulchur
Ellipse

Some have been reprinted in anthologies. Thanks to the editors of them, too.

for Brian Edwards

Contents

General Editor's Preface

The Writer as Critic series invites readers to read criticism as literature. If the essay, as Maurice Blanchot, Jacques Derrida and Jean-François Lyotard have argued, is an intellectual poem, then surely a writer's artistic signature is inscribed in her/his critical work in ways that expand our understanding of the function of both literature and criticism. This is particularly true of the criticism produced by many Canadian artists.

Reading a writer/critic is, almost invariably, an act of remission. Whether we begin with the creative work or the criticism, one genre sends us back to the other, thus revealing its own otherness — its separateness from and its correspondence to the other genre. But a writer's criticism, in its erratic relationship to the critical tradition and to the writer's imaginative work, goes beyond the secondary function assigned to it.

A writer's criticism does not simply constitute the absent other of a creative text; nor is it the residue of a creating and creative desire that could not be contained in the literary work proper — the critical work as surplus or parasite. It is a critical discourse, critical in the double sense of the word, for it is an *other* discourse, a discourse about the other, an act further and otherwise verifying the writer's ongoing engagement with language and culture.

It is within this context that *The Writer as Critic* series sets out to present the writer as reader of her or his own writing and of the work of fellow writers. Such a concentrated focus, I believe, will help readers identify the shifting boundaries and intentions of the artist creatively writing criticism.

It is more than a happy coincidence that *The Writer as Critic* series begins here with George Bowering's *Imaginary Hand*. Bowering, a novelist and poet, and one of the most aleatory and controversial figures in Canadian literature, has already published five books of criticism. Not only a novelist and poet, he is also the writer as critic, the critic as writer. And we should be thankful for that. For, in spite of what a number of academic critics and non-academic writers have dismissed in his work as something too playful or even verging on the meaningless, Canadian literature wouldn't be the same without this

writer who is "too busy bowering, I mean writing. You do see what I
mean. It is writing and I am reading, and so are you. What is your
name? Whatever it is, I hope you keep on doing it." (Bowering 1987,
8)

The essays in *Imaginary Hand*, in addition to making an important
contribution to Canadian criticism, disclose Bowering as a reader —
that creaturely state always preceding the writing act, be it creative or
critical. Bowering, the writer reading other writers (writers as dissimi-
lar as Anne Bradstreet and William Eastlake, bpNichol and Ethel Wilson, Michael Ondaatje and Matt Cohen, Leonard Cohen and Jack
Hodgins), is already active in the dispossessing, precipitous act of
self-reading. He fictionalizes and historicizes his critical endeavors; he
reads in the feminine, as he does when speculating about Emily Dickinson or Nicole Brossard; he reads as a westerner when he tries to
fathom what "home" means in the writings of Grainger and other B.C.
authors; or he reads as a baseball fan when he wants to show that he
too knows how to read thematically, and yet with a difference.

As a reader/critic, he dons many masks. He can be academic in
some essays, while in others he defies the strictures of academic criticism; he can be personal and anecdotal and at the same time speak in a
voice that claims objectivity; often, he doesn't write essays but mani-
festos, polemical pieces meant to elicit much-needed arguments. A
great master of occasion, he frequently lets his written word document
his own voice, the cadences and notations of his speech patterns.
(Compare his use of punctuation, the length of some of his sentences,
to the way he sways from the waist up, legs tightly brought together,
when he delivers a reading or a lecture.) This lack of uniformity, this
persistent elusiveness, has become Bowering's literary trademark, and
also the writerly signature his own readers must learn to decode, read
and reread. . . .

"Of course any text is an intertext" (1987, 6), he said once, pointing
both to his own reading practices and to those of his readers. The intertextuality of his fiction, poetry and his criticism demonstrates how coy
he remains in his relationship to history, including the history of his
own writing. Bowering's readings of Canadian and American writers,
of older and contemporary figures, reveal him to be not only an assidu-
ous reader, but also a writer who writes "against the grain" of history
while acknowledging his great concern with tradition and with what
tradition constitutes. His reading/critical act is the very act of *his-
torein*, a kind of ongoing (auto)biography that complements his writing project that began with *A Short Sad Book*.

A public critic? A cultural critic? A postmodernist? A writer who
loves to risk what he's gained? Perhaps. And perhaps not. For as long
as George Bowering "bowers," he will continue to defy our definitions

of him while still trying to come up with his own:

> I want to deconstruct everything I've said until now and from now on. . . . One thing I do like to do. I've been going to conferences for the last two and a half years with the main aim, besides that of getting four hours of sleep a night, of coming away with a made-up term, or a term I think I've made up. I've seen how successful people like Derrida and Barthes are when they do it, so I hope nobody else has already got the word I fell upon yesterday morning. The word is *"décriture."* Is that new? Okay, I got it! (1987, 241)

As a writer and a critic, an academic who parodies academic discourse, a reader of others and of himself, Bowering is already unwriting himself, inscribing into his texts the very paradox of what he knows how to do best: writing (as a definition of otherness forever remaining incomplete, wanting more words (reading), wanting to undefine itself).

Smaro Kamboureli
August 1988

WORKS CITED

Bowering, George. 1987. "Writer Writing, Ongoing Verb." George Bowering, Robert Kroetsch. Ed. by Betty A. Schellenberg. *Future Indicative: Literary Theory and Canadian Literature.* Ed. John Moss. Ottawa: Ottawa UP: 5-24.

———. 1987. "Present Tense: The Closing Panel." Stephen Scobie, George Bowering, Linda Hutcheon, Robert Kroetsch. *Future Indicative: 239-245.*

Author's Preface

These essays are not meant to cover the field, whatever the field may be. They are rather discussions of works written by the poets and fiction writers who have meant more than others to my thinking and writing over the few years that I have been doing those things. I like to think of the authors of those works as my superiors, predecessors, and companions in the tasks of the linguistic imagination.

When I look around at the essays of Canadian writers, I do not see many pieces about writings by non-Canadians and pre-Modernists. Yet I want to observe the shaping of our esthetic. So I have looked at my own, for instance. I reason that if my fellow writers can invoke the names of Derrida, Lacan, Bakhtin, Cixous, and so forth, one of us should be able also to call up Williams, Dickinson and Hawthorne (I managed to edge him into an earlier collection of essays).

A reader might also notice here a kind of geography. The works I look at tend to show a history full of holes but moving westward. From Europe to Australia, let us say, and let us note that North America, filled with holes, lies in the middle of that path. North America itself is moving westward, and so of course is north North America. But writers such as I look to the east when we are speaking. Our words walk toward the right-hand margin, and always fly to the left-hand margin to start again. As Robert Kroetsch says, there is a lot going on at the margin, and we in the west are in the middle of that.

George Bowering

1

A Great Northward Darkness

The Attack on History in Recent Canadian Fiction

> History is a world supported by the word "history," and not by an existence which is history.... The conditions for observing history are the conditions for creating history, and it is on this unstable ground that we invent the word "history."
>
> Hideo Kobayashi, Introduction to *The Life of Dostoyevsky*

A little while ago I saw a photograph in a magazine called *Science*, and it made me think about Canadian history and Canadian fiction. It was a composite photograph taken from space and showed the faces of the earth at night. It showed lights — no coast lines, no international boundaries, just artificial light. Still, one could see the familiar contours of Europe, for one instance, and the United States for another. But where was Canada? After another look I could see a slight extension of the lights of the United States, up from the Great Lakes, along the St. Lawrence River, presumably, and a millimetre up the West Coast. Otherwise all there was was a great northward darkness. That made me think about the necessity for Canadian history and Canadian fiction.

Canadians do worry about being invisible. Americans dont seem to know that we are here, and Europeans think that we are just some more Americans. Aware of the great darkness, and not having the resources to put lights everywhere, we write books against the obscurity. We write books in two languages brought here from Europe, and wish they would be read or turned into movies in the United States.

But mainly we write books for other Canadians across the domestic darkness. We know how critical it is to make us visible to each other, to ourselves. In the nineteenth century we built the railroad across (or we hired American engineers and extra-continental labourers to do it); that was the invention of Canada. Really, there wasnt any Canada before the nineteenth century, and considering our affection for historical literature, it is a charming irony that the country was tinkered together out of spare parts, that it was made by a group of inventors.

So we have been all this time a profoundly nineteenth century country at heart, that is at the heart of our writing. The nineteenth century is our golden age and our epic. Older nations of writers can look back on fables and sagas peculiar to their living space. But literary realism was developed in the nineteenth century, and so for our fiction writers the realist text is the fount or the bedrock of the fictive deed.

In Canada our most popular prose writers write popular history. Our readers prefer it to fiction. When they read fiction they like to read fiction that obeys the rules of historical narrative, the sense that character and setting and event combine to lead to a conclusion, that there is a force something like necessity, that language is the normal link between pre-linguistic history and drama. They have been encouraged to like anecdote in their history and realism in their fiction. Thus, while pre-realist fable, fantasy, myth, and the unnatural narrator have re-emerged in the literatures of the older world, Canadians intent on discovering themselves and exploring their time have been slow to welcome the unreliable and the capricious in their writing, to respect the author who invents rather than obeying.

It may be that Canadian immigrants, retreating from various losing causes elsewhere, are convinced victims of forces in history. It may be that they are expecting history to look kindly on them in some future; so it would be rash to scoff at the destiny that may decide to feed one.

One hundred years before this essay was begun, and one year before the last spike was hammered into the trans-Canadian railroad, Henry James made an argument for a positivist fiction:

> the analogy between the art of the painter and the art of the novelist is, so far as I am able to see, complete. . . . as the picture is reality, so the novel is history. That is the only general description (which does it justice) that we may give to the novel. But history also is allowed to represent life; it is not, any more than painting, expected to apologize. The subject-matter of fiction is stored up likewise in documents and records, and if it will not give itself away, as they say in California, it must speak with assurance, with the tone of the historian. Certain accomplished novelists have a habit of giving themselves away which must often bring tears to the eyes of people who take their fiction seriously.
>
> ("The Art of Fiction," 5)

Henry James sounds so Canadian to me. Twenty years later his former countryman, Henry Adams, took an even more deterministic view of the relationship between history and science. In "A Dynamic Theory of History" he saw man as a creation of outside forces, a creature who "can know nothing but the motions which impinge on his senses, whose sum makes education." Think of the fiction based on historical principles, and history resembling science, in a world in which "science always meant self-restraint, obedience, sensitiveness to impulse from without." Truth persuades through consistent facts.

But Clio was the muse of history, and she was not nature. There were historians who were not happy to see their occupation pass from literature into science. One year before Adams's essay the young George Macaulay Trevelyan wrote: "The last fifty years have witnessed great changes in the management of Clio's temple. Her inspired prophets and bards have passed away and been succeeded by the priests of an established church." (*Clio, A Muse*, 140). Trevelyan's complaint could be leveled today at French-influenced literary criticism. History, he went on, is "proclaimed a 'science' for specialists, not 'literature' for the common reader of books" (140).

Perhaps the argument can be traced to the common confusion regarding just what history is: is it what happened, or is it what the historians have written? Determinists, among them "progressives," tend to think that history is an inevitable force in which human groups are caught up. Ironically, Soviet historians are always making drastic revisions to their national encyclopaedia. On the other hand, people on the fringes of history tend to believe (to reverse Henry James) that history is a kind of fictional narrative composed in the centres of power.

Novelists who believe that history is a force or a law tend toward realism and naturalism — Zola, Dreiser, Hugh MacLennan. They believe that history speaks and teaches. Fiction writers who believe that history is someone's act of narrative tend toward myth and invention — Conrad, Borges, Robert Kroetsch. History comes from an old European word meaning possession of knowledge. Fiction comes from an old European word meaning the act of shaping. Our artists and critics are engaged in a dispute regarding which comes first.

• • •

Once there were two kinds of imaginative narrative, both making literature. They were history and fiction (including verse), and they were siblings. In the nineteenth century history went to live with science, and fiction, trying to stay with its sister, adopted the ideals of continuity, unity, and expectability. Now characters populated novels where figures used to walk. Now one could study character and setting and confidently predict event. Now the idea of conflict became the constant of serious prose. Now the author was advised not to give himself away, to keep, in fact, himself to himself, like an objective scientist.

In the twentieth century Stephen Dedalus found history a nightmare from which he tried to wake. The Modernist movement said to science that history could be shared but that literature belonged chiefly to art, to myth, that it was more like a religion than a science; that it was not the daughter of time. The only way we can really make contact with things and events, said the Modernists, is to imagine them. Not obedience but dream.

In Canada we were too young, too new for international Modernism. Nature was right outside the window. History had just recently put us here. Instead of the Imagists our poets copied the Georgians until the middle of the twentieth century. Our novelists were not interested in the Modernist game of stray fragments falling into patterns in the imagination. We had a land to people and a half-continent to name. We wrote well-constructed novels and moved in.

Thus when a writer energized by Modernism submitted an ahistorical and anti-realist text to the publishing centre just after the middle of the century, it took several years for those 125 pages to get through the house and into print; and when it did it was greeted as a delightful oddity, not a sign of things to come. The writer was Sheila Watson, the book *The Double Hook*. Watson had done what the Modernists but not the Canadians did — chosen a tradition rather than obeying her destiny. Speaking of it years later, she said that she wanted to prove that you could write a text that was not regional. In other words, history is not a fate that writes through the novelist. *The Double Hook* became the first and last Modernist novel in English-speaking Canada, and the text that would be honoured as a holy book by the few postmodernists of the following period.

• • •

At the moment in Canada we are observing, with appreciation of the irony entailed, the formation of a kind of canon of postmodern fiction. This is happening because in the 1980s we are at last hearing from critics who have little regard for the sociological concerns of the thematic critics. Thematic criticism was a discipline that worked best with realism because finally it was more interested in the society referred to in books than in the books themselves. The contemporary critics — Stephen Scobie, Shirley Neuman, Barbara Godard, Pauline Butling, etc. — are interested in writing as linguistic invention. They direct our attention to the fictions of Michael Ondaatje, Timothy Findley, Robert Kroetsch and Nicole Brossard. They almost always make reference to a 1966 novel that scandalized nineteenth century Canada, Leonard Cohen's *Beautiful Losers*.

The story takes place in the nexus of Canadian history (where lights shine bright in that photograph from space), in Montreal and Ottawa. Its two main male figures are a historian and a history-making member of parliament; its two main female figures are a historical saint and the historian's mythicized wife.

In the first and longest part of the novel, entitled "The History of Them All," the historian writes in the first person, his title suggesting the old literary use of the word "history" to mean story. The narrative is accumulated in short numbered passages, suggesting that the narrator is recording daily entries in a kind of confessional journal, very subjective. This is the only kind of writing he is capable of. He cannot write his history of a gone Indian tribe called the A⎯⎯s, and he cannot void his bowels. He is the "hater of history crouched over the immaculate bowl" (38).

The word "constipation" means crowded, narrowly enclosed. Cohen suggests that the historian's ideals and methodology are the reasons for his painful problem in health, both physical and psychological. The historian means to bring order to chaos, to ascertain facts and to arrange them into an incontrovertible theory, to change story into system. Thomas Babington Macaulay said in the nineteenth century (*The Romance of History*) that history begins in novel and ends in essay.

The writer of a realist fiction emulates the objective attempt at order prized by the historian. He is devoted to understanding of cause and effect in time. He tries to remove, or to seem to remove, the opinions and feelings of the author (so that he will not, in Henry James's California term, "give himself away"). He makes clear the relative positions assumed by text, author, narrator, character, and reader. And he seeks unity of presentation, a plainness of style, a persuasive comprehensibility.

But history, as we have often been told, is written by winners, often ugly ones. Cohen's narrator at one point gives himself away to address the reader directly: "O Reader, do you know that a man is writing this? . . . a man who hates his memory and remembers everything" (102). Reader cant help noting that he is being spoken to by author as well as narrator. Anti-realist Cohen intrudes, as they say, into the reading of the book, his personality and his poetry not so much woven as stirred into the text. He fuses and confuses characters, makes his character inconsistent and suspect, and even pushes the reader around. He employs severe disjunctions of style, so that it resembles fireworks in a night sky more than a highway of meaning alongside the St. Lawrence River. He punches holes in time. In other words, he does not seek Reader's belief, does not try to persuade one of his knowledge, *historia*. If he has any consideration for the nineteenth century it is for Chapter fourteen of Melville's *The Confidence-Man*.

Cohen's historian has a childhood friend, F., who in adulthood has turned into his guru, a parliamentarian whose task it is to save his companion from his constipated historicity. He tells him not to organize the past and its people, but to "fuck a saint." The saint, as Gertude Stein said in her discussion of her opera, does not live in time, but has been lifted out of history into legend, into immortality, in the sight of mere people, a reminder to them that, as F. says so often, "magic is afoot." Not a head, but afoot.

So, says the historian:

A saint does not dissolve the chaos; if he did the world would have changed long ago. I do not think that a saint dissolves the chaos even for himself, for there is something arrogant and warlike in the notion of a man setting the universe in order. It is a kind of balance that is his glory. He rides the drifts like an escaped ski. (95)

So does Cohen's novel. Beautiful losers do not write history; they are humble and peaceable, and would never think of setting the universe or a novel in order. Presumably their bowels move. When the narrator feels a moment of resentment toward his mentor, he asks: "Who was he after all but a madman who lost control of his bowels?" (34). Yet when he comes to prayer rather than arrogance he implores: "Saints and friends, help me out of History and Constipation" (111).

Despite the argument by naturalist writers that non-realists preach individualist escapism, it is easy to see that Cohen's concern is for a revolution of health in terms literary, physical, moral and political. Unlike the social realists, he knows that it is at best hypocritical to espouse social revolution through conventional and authoritarian aesthetic means. Hence *Beautiful Losers* is everywhere self-referential, and ironically is one of the most decisive novels in our history. It is with relief that at this moment, while writing about it, I feel that I must go to the bathroom before I begin the next paragraph.

Cohen's narrator reports that F. often speaks in what critics have called Cohen's koans, mesmeric phrases of truth with no history of argumentation. The most provocative one for the historian (or writer, or critic) is "connect nothing." It is a usefully ambiguous command, one that challenges the historian; because though the historian seems only to be documenting the past for present consideration, we all know that he is intent on answering a question that starts with the word "why." History, as Macaulay said, was often called "philosophy teaching by examples." F. said: "we are part of a necklace of incomparable beauty and unmeaning. Connect nothing ... Place things side by side on your arborite table, if you must, but connect nothing!" (17). Leonard Cohen, or his F. anyway, prepares the way for Robert Kroetsch, who would complain of the "tyranny of meaning." The trouble with historical writing as a model for fiction is just that rush toward meaning. On the way the historian did not study what people are, but what they did; he privileged time over space and even place, and perhaps content over form. I think that Paul Ricoeur goes far enough from nature toward meaning when he says that narration requires that "we are able *to extract a configuration from a succession*" (278).

Cohen demonstrates that that configuration need not rely on a succession involving dramatic suspense. He favours, in his 1960s-bliss, eternity over time, immortality over work, miracles over facts, and magic over history. So all the major plot elements are announced at the beginning of *Beautiful Losers*: the suicide of the historian's wife Edith, the fate of F., the sexual relationship of F. and Edith, etc. There is no need for beginning, middle and end. The plot elements are returned to and expanded rather than extended. They open and spread, like saint Katherine Tekakwitha's spilled wine at the Christian feast. Characters, or rather figures, do not have to be restricted conventionally to what they know. Any going back and forth is done in the text, not in referential time, and Reader is made to be constantly present. Only when we try ourselves to be historians of the text are we thwarted, as when we try to get the chronology straight. Reality, we should be persuaded, does not lie in the connecting of facts but in the imagination's pouring itself into the world, there to surround facts.

The second section of the novel is called "A Long Letter from F." In it F. relieves the narrator's constipation with an alarmingly detailed and personal history of Katherine Tekakwitha's last four years, invoking history (188-89) while admitting fiction (195) and advising forgetfulness (211-12). Most important is F.'s koan: "Watch the words, watch *how it happens*" (186). That means stay at the text, stay in the present, and remain part of the fictive action.

The last section of the novel is called "Beautiful Losers, *An Epilogue in the Third Person*." I have always wondered whether the Third Person is the Holy Ghost; certainly that person is omniscient, an odd point of view after the highly idiosyncratic voices of the first two persons. Here now Isis appears, her name a repetition of the ontological present, appears in our lowest dreams. Her appearance is a sanctified burlesque of the Jesuits' internal dispute "about to which they had the deepest obligation, History or Miracle, or to put it more heroically, History or Possible Miracle" (207). Cohen favours the last, and says that "The end of this book has been rented to the Jesuits" (242). Finally, he speaks as an apothegmatic Learned Cohen in the last paragraph of the book, not in 1966, but on whatever day that Reader reaches the place: "Welcome to you who read me today." Then he ends in a couplet, making the words not an earned meaning but an invitation to the last: "Welcome to you, darling and friend, who miss me forever in your trip to the end" (243). It is also a sneaky way of using the last two words that children like to finish their stories with.

• • •

Herodotus, Charles Olson said, used history as a verb, to find for oneself. Olson himself went further, saying that history is what a person does, not what he has done (in *The Special View of History*, 1970). To me that resembles a distinction between European classical music and Afro-American music, jazz for instance. The document of Josef Haydn is the score of his symphony. The document of Charlie Parker is the tape of a Los Angeles club performance in February, 1951.

Now how do you write the story of Storyville? How do you tell about jazz in the first place, and how do you tell about a legendary jazz trumpeter who could not write notes and who never went on record or made one? That is a very appealing problem for a postmodernist writer. How can you write a historical novel with no historical documents? Having produced a book about Billy the Kid out of sources that were mainly frontier lies, Michael Ondaatje essayed *Coming through Slaughter* (1976), about Buddy Bolden, "born" at the dawn of the twentieth century, nothing saved from the multiplicity of chaos except one group photograph in which Bolden is holding a cornet in his left hand, as lots of people wish Billy had held his six-gun.

Ondaatje loves photographs, especially when they disrupt one's settled notions of composition. In an important poem addressed to Victor Coleman, he ended:

My mind is pouring chaos
in nets onto the page.
A blind lover, don't know
what I love till I write it out.
And then from Gibson's your letter
with a blurred photograph of a gull.
Caught vision. The stunning white bird
an unclear stir.

And that is all this writing should be then.
The beautiful formed things caught at the wrong moment
so they are shapeless, awkward
moving to the clear.

(1973, 74)

So the picture for Ondaatje is not the deadly clear representation in a bird portrait by Audubon. It is rather something like clear sailing, to be free of time as a ship may be free from limiting land mass. The jazz soloist is not kept by time, nor does he forever keep it; when he is free of his dutiful ensemble work, he is on top of time. He is improvising for a breath muse, and history, including his own, is behind him, invisible below the horizon.[1]

As Cohen's book often mentions the word "history," so does Ondaatje's. In the first few pages, introducing Storyville, the crib of the music, it tells us that "here there is little recorded history," and that "History was slow here," that Bolden's homes remain, "away from recorded history" (1976, 8-10).

But the first two words of the text (not counting the italicized notes to the preface's three sonographs of dolphin messages) mark a pointed refusal of a favourite pun among young writers. Instead of the usual "his-story" (or the common successor, "her-story") we are offered "His geography." It is a signal that narrative will try to cover the ground rather than configure the time. The phrase is also an alternative to "his biography." It lets us know that we are to begin, in the present, in Storyville, fiction town.

So the text begins, then, as a magazine travelogue might, and in the imperative, perhaps: "Float by in a car today and see the corner shops" (8). It is clear that we are getting a glimpse of the author's research (and hence the author), a research represented in terms of place, as if the story of the present is of first importance, as if it is a story about, say, a Canadian poet-novelist rather than a dead American musician. But I am getting ahead of myself, arent I? Let us, he and I, simply say that here in the first pages Ondaatje's method of narration is presaged by a reported method of research, or first search: "Circle and wind back and forth in your car" (10).

Ondaatje's use of the second person pronoun here is unsettling for the reader who wants to be an anonymous consumer of a well-made book. It begins to confuse the conventional positioning of author, protagonist and reader. The reader accustomed to the realist mode wants to remain invisible, and he does not want to see much of the author; he wants a good look at the central character of the story in question. But if there is one thing we can readily discern from the plot of this short novel, it is that Buddy Bolden was always disappearing, running away, going out windows, escaping through holes in the fabric of the real world's text. And every time Buddy Bolden vanishes, there is Michael Ondaatje making an appearance. One is reminded of Clark Kent — every time Superman showed up, the reader knew that Clark Kent was not around to observe the action, even though Lois Lane never quite saw the connection.

If you were a bookstore browser rather than a reader, you would see, riffling the pages of *Coming through Slaughter*, that it is the text that is always disappearing, as white spaces appear here and there. On reading you become aware of the continuous beginning-to-make by the writer, as he puts together pieces, riffs, perhaps, as he tries occasion by occasion to assemble a thing made of words and getting a couple of centimetres thick. It is unlikely that the pieces were written in the order that they appear in the book. You become delighted, if you are not fully addicted to escapism, with what Robert Kroetsch called in regard to it, "the book-ness of book" (1983, 104). You do not regret the "consolation of narrative." You see a writer on the edge of the multiplicity of chaos, laying side by side on his table some interviews, first-person Bolden narrative, lists, lunatic asylum chronicles, and so on.

You see a travesty of documentation as the sole hope of truth. If it does not work for you, at least you are aware of the strange: if you dont know what jazz is, he cannot explain it to you.

If Ondaatje the poet finds himself becoming Bolden the trumpeter, he also finds Bolden putting together a publication much like his. The barber/jazzman was also the editor of a periodical called *The Cricket*, which for six years "took in and published all the information Bolden could find. It respected stray facts, manic theories, and well-told lies.... Bolden took all the thick facts and dropped them into his pail of subhistory" (24). In other words, no authoritarian structure, which F. called "arrogant and warlike."

Bolden rejects the authority of description as well. Called on to describe the famous hunchback photographer Bellocq to the conventional detective Webb (another aspect of the author Ondaatje), Bolden says, "I can't summarize him for you." Instead he says, "I want to *show* you something. You come too. Put your hand through this window" (91). I have to suppose that the second "you" is the one implied at the beginning of the book, the reader, the only other one there. The novel works by recurrence rather than progression: earlier we had read of Bolden's enjoining a conventional instrumentalist in his band: "'Cornish, come on, put your hands through the window'" (14).

Windows, and other kinds of glass, such as mirrors and camera lenses, are always useful for writers. For realists they make it possible for their characters to look out through transparency at the real world, into a mirror when they have to reflect on themselves, or through a lens when they want to focus a problem. People who espouse the usefulness of history rather than its artistic delight often call it a window onto the past or a mirror of our times. In *Coming through Slaughter* glass is usually something to be broken, generally by Buddy Bolden. He jumps through windows, or breaks them with his hands. He says that photographs are like windows, and wont hold still for them. At one point he describes referential narrative as a forbidding window: "When Webb was here with all; his stories about me and Nora, about Gravier and Phillip Street, the wall of wire barrier glass went up between me and Robin" (86). A trumpet note, blown hard enough and high, will shatter glass. But when Buddy's horn is gone, and he is on the prison train to the State Hospital the other side of Slaughter, he can only hold his head leaning against the inside of the closed window, riding away from music into history. He becomes a random entry interpolated by Ondaatje into "Selections from *A Brief History of East Louisiana State Hospital* by Lionel Gremillion" (143).

If fiction or history is a window through which a reader may get a clear view of a world during some time, and yet remain in his own, that reader must be unsettled a little by a figure who threatens to come crashing through that window (or the author he glimpses climbing through in the other direction). Hands off, we usually say to the author, hands off; hands off those characters and hands off me! Another aspect of Ondaatje is the photographer Bellocq, who is generally thought of as a historical figure whose passion was to make a pictorial history of Storyville. He is reported here to have made knife cuts in some of the pictures: "you think of Bellocq wanting to enter the photographs, to leave his trace on the bodies" (55). To deconstruct, some people would say, history.

Inside the window of the barber shop Bolden's boss liked to keep ice, which made a mist on that glass in the hot southern sun. When the window gets smashed the ice melts on the street. Ice is disappearing glass, and Buddy Bolden knows in his love and music that he lives a melting life, "As if everything in the world is the history of ice" (87).

But Buddy Bolden is a jazz artist, his work disappearing into the air, and he has to make his art in that condition. He speaks of searching for it when things get too regular, of wanting "to find that fear of certainties I had when I first began to play" (86). The detective Webb acts as a kind of reverse F. Whereas F. had told his friend to put things side by side on his arborite table, but to "connect nothing," Webb "came here and placed my past and future on this table like a road" (86).

But when Buddy was blowing, he "tore apart the plot" (37), according to one of his interviewed listeners. In "The Narrative Function," Paul Ricoeur makes the simple point that plot is the link between the work of the historian and the work of the fiction writer. Furthermore, says Ondaatje's interviewed Lewis, Bolden was "born at the age of twenty-two" and "never spoke of the past." He was "obsessed with the magic of air" (14) and knew, however hard time might be to him, that living in the absolute present would be to disappear from history, like the negatives Bellocq bleaches out when he drops them into his alchemist's acid tray. We have a new angle on the white spaces spreading through Ondaatje's text.

That is to say that Ondaatje did not come to the novel to "bring his characters to life" or to tell the story of a representative black horn player because he loves jazz. Ondaatje is trying to save his soul as a writer, and he knows that he has to rip up his book the way Bolden could rip it up blowing his brains out through bent brass in a parade through New Orleans. To do that he has to blow faster than time, higher than history. It helps to blow notes of anachronism around the story, to sound in the secret names of figures from his other books and of literary critics of them too, and of his life. It means "The beautiful formed things caught at the wrong moment."

It means attacking fictional-historical narrative where the latter had thought itself strongest — at the climax of the story. The climax of

Ondaatje's book comes on pages 133-134, shortly after the magnificent scene of the parade during which Bolden blows himself blind on the street. For a realist the climax is the logical consequence of conflicting characters and events. It is the apotheosis of the plot. In *Coming through Slaughter* it is the author's direct address to his "protagonist," and his declaration of a desire to become his creation's soul. "Did not want to pose in your accent but think in your brain and body," he confesses; the writer desirous of utterly closing the rational polite "distance" required of a responsible scientist. After Bolden's last fantastic parade, he never plays again, is shipped to the hospital for what Ondaatje calls "the rest of your life a desert of facts. Cut them open and spread them out like garbage." In another word: analysis. Without the horn player his geography becomes a scene of static chronicle: "The sun has swallowed the colour of the street. It is a black and white photograph, part of a history book" (134).

• • •

In one of the best essays yet published on the work of Robert Kroetsch, Ann Mandel constructed this news item:

> Moose Jaw, Sask. — At a recent meeting here of the Saskatchewan Writers' Union, Robert Kroetsch, discussing Canadian writers' obsessive investigation of history, offered this comment: "Fuck the past." Some participants at the conference objected to his language. (54)

What a nice ambiguity we are handed; and what a good marker of Kroetsch's ambivalence regarding the temptations of meaning. His phrase signals defiance at the same time that it suggests fertility, and it is formed in the imperative, like F.'s "fuck a saint."

Remember that Kroetsch was responding, with that ambiguity, to a post-1967 centenary fashion in Canadian writing, the trainloads of poems, plays, essays and novels that delved into our documents and past lives, as if bringing Louis Riel onto the stage again would tell us how we are living today while assuring us that the newly seen density of our history, if we just spread it out like a grid, or entrails, will guarantee our national substantiality. It is a pre-Modernist idea. One thing the Modernists discovered was that in the global community the artist has to *choose* his tradition. One is not any more automatically a product of cultural history. Sexual congress with history is not incest.

You cannot get history in your book. You can get only the child of history and yourself. If you could get the world of space and time right in your story, you cannot do it any more because the world now contains that story. History is impossible. Fuck it. Pardon my language.

Of all our fiction writers Robert Kroetsch is the one who has had most to say about literary theory, and the one who has most thoroughly discussed the conundrum of historical thought. While overly generous to all sorts of writers, he has nevertheless become the hero of the contemporary formal critics who are ridding our country of the thematic obsession that came along on the social-scientist ride of post-centenary nationalism. He is seen to stand against that determinism as André Malraux stood against the Stalinist realists: "And then comes the hoax of historical perspective," said Malraux in 1948. "I repeat: it's time to substitute the question 'What *is*?' for the constant desire to explain the hidden significance, preferably historical, of what is" (191).

In other words, art speaks to the listeners of art. You do not have to spend a lifetime of winters with snow up to your buttocks to understand Canadian books. You do not have to shovel snow or Louis Riel into your book to write a Canadian text. If you want to do something about the past, you do not have to record someone's recording of it and trust to some collective true voice; you can resurrect it, or raise it for the first time. As if it were the landscape you can hallucinate it and fill it with the pestiferous bugs you remember from your Alberta childhood. Arguing against reproduction of the world, Melville wrote in Chapter 33 of *The Confidence-Man* about good readers: "though they want novelty, they want nature, too; but nature unfettered, exhilarated, in effect transformed" (206-7). He felt the same way about history.

When I was a school boy the only Canadian history I was offered took place on a magical faraway planet covered with a forest dotted with log forts and occasional clearings such as the Plains of Abraham. It was peopled by French-speaking immigrants in florid uniforms and by Indians in some kind of animal pelts. The brown hills outside my house had no such glamorous fiction to make them significant — they were totally empty. Being west of history, we folk could find the absolute ground for myth, if we had only known it. I suppose something like that was possible elsewhere in Canada. The often-interviewed Robert Kroetsch told some people in Manitoba, back east in what they call the west:

> we are intrigued by history, by our past, and sceptical about it. There is a terrible scepticism about it, especially on the Prairies, where there was a kind of renunciation of the past by the people who came out here as immigrants. The landscape itself denied a repetition of earlier experience. Then in the '30s the past seemed to betray the immigrants even further so that they became "next-year people."
> (Cooley, Enright, 25)

Where Cohen's F. called historical order "arrogant," Kroetsch calls it "coercive" (Neuman, Wilson, 133). He sees it as an Eastern Canadian mode of narration and distrusts it because it begins from meaning instead of discovering it. Myth persuades us that time does not calibrate truth but that certain places, if we can but find them, will offer prophecy. Hence a writer such as Robert Kroetsch replaces history's paradigm with that of archaeology, an account made by the seeker who has found the story in place, and in fragments that encourage the seeker to dig and see the pieces and the gaps between the pieces together. In this model no reader need expect to be treated as victim or passive recipient of history.

Determinists who think of history as something that happens before the writing of it see us governed by unfolding events. Westerners, perhaps, see eastern written history as an attempt to manipulate them, who do not think in that language. Kroetsch:

> No, the West doesn't think historically. If the West accepted history, then its whole relationship to the country would have to change radically. I don't think that the West wants to move into a historical role, or to accept history. Myth is more exciting.
>
> (Neuman, Wilson, 134.)

(Croce of the east *vs.* Kroetsch of the west?) The rejection of history could be considered a postmodernist tactic, or habit. The Modernists, whether they liked it or hated it, felt that they were involved in the very centre of history, that they were a theophany of it. They worked to locate myth inside and *through* history.

> The enormous tragedy of the dream in the peasant's
> bent shoulders
> Manes! Manes was tanned and stuffed,
> Thus Ben and la Clara *a Milano*
>   by the heels at Milano
> That maggots shd/ eat the dead bullock
> DIGENES, Dijovos, but the twice crucified
>   where in history will you find it?
> yet say this to the Possum: a bang, not a whimper,
>   with a bang not with a whimper,
> To build the city of Dioce whose terraces are the colour of stars.
>
> (*Pound, Canto LXXIV*, 425)

Robert Kroetsch's lifelong poem is not called Cantos, or Annals, or Chronicles; it is a comedy but far from divine. It is called *Field Notes*, the writer having in mind the unobtrusive little note book the archaeologist can keep in the back pocket of his dusty work-trousers. In his fiction, Kroetsch's most obvious archaeologist is William Dawe in *Badlands*, whose expedition went west looking for dinosaur bones in Alberta's badlands in 1916, a year in which history was being written with a vengeance to the east. For a would-be historian we have Anna Dawe, his daughter. She comes west and enters the badlands in 1972, aged forty-five, with a cardboard box of her late father's field notes, trying "*to set straight the record*," knowing though that "*There are no truths, only correspondences*" (1974, 45).

The notebooks, like all written or painted artifacts mentioned in Kroetsch's fiction, are symbols; they point, though, not at character or eternal verity, but back at the text one is reading. I am reminded of the painting in *Heart of Darkness* by Joseph Conrad, a writer Kroetsch loves. It is a sketch in oils, "representing a woman, draped and blind-folded, carrying a lighted torch. The background was somber — almost black. The movement of the woman was stately, and the effect of the torchlight on the face was sinister" (36). Aware of the way paint-ings and dreams work in Romantic literature, we are alert to the picture's representation of the conscious and subconscious mind of Kurtz, its painter. But we also notice that it somehow resembles our voyage as readers into a very dark world of writing, where we cannot quite see the environment. *Heart of Darkness* is finally a story inside a story inside a book, and so is *Badlands*.

So we have to tread blind and careful. Anna Dawe sees the field notes of her father (who was nearly always away from his Ontario home) as "his way of communicating with his unborn descendants." Yet his day's entry is likely to be "*I despise words*" (34). We should read Kroetsch as curiously as Anna has to read Dawe, a man with a name that means crow.

Kroetsch has a chronology (time order) at the front of his book, as Ondaatje has one at the back of his, but this one is preceded by a retold coyote story, of the trickster fooled by illusion. The chronology is a guileful bit of irony, an aid to the historically mindful, but as an order-ing principle only a system the writer can hate. It is complete and skeletal, dead as a dinosaur. Remember what Anna says about the field notes she will eventually throw into the water at the source of the river: "*he was busy putting down each day's tedium and trivia. Shutting out instead of letting in*" (269).

In Kroetsch's novels the men are impulsive fools, and the women suffer the responsibility of keeping the world together. The men fall off horses and cliffs, while the women get the crops in before the first frost. As Anna Dawe sees it, women are fated to be hosts of time while men go looking for some magical place. (The men see women's time as a trap. See "World's End," earthwoman Bea's house full of clocks in *Gone Indian*.) As a host of time, Anna can look at Dawe as if she were an indulgent or rueful mother:

> *Total and absurd male that he was, he assumed, like a male author, an omniscience that was not ever his, a scheme that was not ever there. Holding the past in contempt, he dared foretell for him-self not so much a future as an orgasm.*

But we women take our time. (76)

Dawe was after immortality: he wanted to unearth an ancient animal and show it to the present; and he wanted fame that would last as long as calcium. Digging for bones while Europe was burying its young, "*he removed himself from time*," says his daughter (139). And his success made him what he wanted to be, a phenomenon like those he located, "*a man without a history. . . . Failure might have ruined him back into history*" (138).

In some usages history is a way of remembering things; in others it is a way of consigning them forever to a completed system, to a well-made story. Of the dinosaurs Dawe says to Sinnott the photographer who loves disappearances: "No! . . . Not vanished. Here. Now" (245). Sinnott sees all his pictures as "Future Memory" (125). He is one of the legion of photographers in Canadian fiction, of course, but for Kroetsch he is the forerunner of Karen Strike the photographer in *Alibi*, called by the narrator "a lunatic on the subject of history" (1983, 8). It is pretty clear that Sinnott represents the documentarist aspect of the Canadian mania for history. Dawe might be having a literary dispute with him when he says, "'I recover the past. . . . You reduce it. . . . You make the world stand still. . . . I try to make it live again'" (128).

Kroetsch commonly casts one figure in each novel as a kind of chronicler, a historian or biographer who tries to enclose the irrational behaviour of the central figure inside a conventional discourse, usually emerging with a Melvillean compromise we might call legend. That result could be said to bespeak the dilemma of Robert Kroetsch, who has admitted in various ways that he is drawn to both wild loops and familiar story telling. Most tall-tale aces and rural bullshitters, after all, depend on shared familiarity of their audiences with the details of common life.

But the chronicler is always suspect: he is a madman or a liar, maybe just a crank. When he is the narrator he is what academic critics call an "unreliable narrator." One is persuaded that Kroetsch takes that phrase to describe the historian. He never forgets that the characterization must resound on his own tale. As long as one is writing English sentences one is promoting historical order. As any reader will know, Kroetsch does not always rely on conventional sentences, for just that reason. "I think there's a danger in not learning new models of sentences," he has said plainly, in a discussion of our redemption from history (Twigg, 116).

In *The Studhorse Man* (1969) the historian/biographer is writing his narrative while reclined in a bathtub in a mental hospital. Hazard LePage, his subject, is interested in history as located in *The General*

Stud Book, wherein he depends on the two-hundred-year-old genealogy of his proud stallion Poseidon. His own last name should have told him where that might end. But the final insult to his sense of priapic continuity comes when old Poseidon's semen is used to make mares pregnant so that chemists can use their urine in the manufacture of birth-control pills.

In making a travesty of history one might be said, in Canada, to be mocking tragedy, making light of the seriousness of losers. In *The Words of my Roaring* (1966), Johnnie Backstrom rejects historical necessity and makes himself into a legend. During the 1930s Drought and Depression in an Alberta populated by folks who are convinced that they are history's losers, he fakes an apocalypse and invents himself. If people believe that he has made it rain they might learn to prefer invention to cause and effect.

Tragedy is usually presented in solemn language, as if inevitable loss must sound more important than momentary survival. The comic inventor, free from the simple machinery of loss, must steer clear of the tragedian's special pleading. Kroetsch chose a third-person narration for his most spectacular departure from realism, *What the Crow Said* (1979). It begins with a woman's ravishment by a swarm of bees, and her orgasmic cry that sounds over the prairie like a coming steam locomotive. Peter Thomas suggests that "The logic of what follows depends upon accepting its absolute ficticity, while simultaneously recognizing the matter-of-fact manner of the telling" (101). We do or did like to relate myth to the ancient, pre-historical world. Kroetsch sees it as continuous creation by card-players, horse-dealers, rodeo clowns, and novelists.

In *What the Crow Said* the chronicler is the small-town newspaper typesetter Liebhaber. He is a drinker and a lovelorn suitor. He uses a "twenty-six" of rye whiskey to fight the tyranny of the twenty-six guards of the alphabet. As a compositor he has always had to read type backward, thus having a special, sceptical view of the logic in history's weekly sentences. Then, according to his story, after the night that he got frozen and the salubrious Tiddy Lang thawed him out, he began to lose all memory of the past. Thereafter he can remember only the future. But Gutenberg, he also says, made all memory of the past irrelevant; print made the creative mind of the human story-teller redundant, as the past could with it be framed and preserved from the multiplicity of chaos. Only the future was free of Gutenberg's design, so Liebhaber remembers the future. Jacques Derrida would see what is happening in Liebhaber's conversion through love: "It is because writing is *inaugural*, in the fresh sense of the word, that it is dangerous and anguishing. It does not know where it is going, no knowledge can keep it from the essential precipitation toward the meaning that it constitutes and that is, primarily, its future" (cited in Neuman, Wilson, 44). The tyranny of meaning looms, but the writer does not begin as tyrant or satrap. Even the historian, when he is writing beautifully, does not know what his next sentence about the past will say.

In *Gone Indian* (1973) the chronicler is probably a conscious liar. Professor Madham writes a long letter to Jill Sunderman, with a transcription (and comments) of Jeremy Sadness's audiotapes sent back to the university at Binghamton from their miraculous survival in Alberta, where Jeremy faked a new life and maybe a death. Envious of his student, concerned about his own reputation, and finally considering the possibility of seducing Miss Sunderman, Madham has probably edited the tapes drastically, and also provided some original fiction of his own. The text is a lie within a lie — in other words the stuff of history, as a cynic would say. And the author, Robert Kroetsch? If he seduces the reader, it is not only the past he is fucking.

Jeremy Sadness is the most obvious among Kroetsch's figures who have trouble with the printed word. His namesake, Jeremy Bentham, may have challenged completion by having his body preserved for his successors to view. But Sadness's problem occurs far before the "Terrors of Completion." He is supposed to be writing a PhD. dissertation, but he never gets beyond a title, many of which he suggests in a comic fashion in his messages to Madham. Madham, who had left the west for a bookish life in the east, contrasts Jeremy's "perverse dreaming" with what he calls "my careful accounting for his end" (101), that is his craft of continuity and completion.

So that though the reader, along with Jeremy's wife Carol, looks on the spectacular disappearance of Jeremy and Bea from the High Level Bridge (and especially the survival of the tape recorder) with a jaundiced eye, Madham, whatever his reasons, looks for a traditional and realist denouement. He scoffs as Miss Sunderman's term, "the mystery." "I am certain," he writes, "that Jeremy and Bea were killed" (150). Then in a travesty of documentationism, he recites a list of facts and figures, having gone to "the original records of the now defunct Grand Trunk Pacific to get the exact details" (151). For several pages he marshalls logic and fact against Carol's "imagination," finally using the techniques of fiction (as F. did regarding the end of Katherine Tekakwitha) to "re"create the dramatic final scene of the runaways' story. It is told in the terms of approved Canadian naturalism: "The water below is indifferent; through a labyrinth of rivers and lakes, it falls off and down, to Hudson Bay, to Baffin Island, to the drifting Arctic wastes" (157).

Yet it is totally unlike a scholar, a historian, a custodian of the past and the recorded word, that Professor Madham disposes of the documents. Note this portion of a sentence: "in ordering his fragments of tape (and I had to destroy them, finally; they were cluttering up my office) ... " (154). Ordering of fragments is the job of a Modernist and/or a historian. Destroying them is the rejection of evidence. The cluttering up of his office is an unlikely story.

Jeremy's story, on the other hand, whether seen by Madham or not, is the story of the present myth-loving west, the deconstructing of a life and making of a legend, the opting for space over time, the choice of silence over the continuous talk of history. Making his epic lonely trek across the snow, Jeremy identifies with Scott of the Antarctic, surrendering language: "You are right to make the last entry and close the notebook, let the pencil slip from your hand. You have only to listen now. Say no more. Listen to the fall of silence ... " (40). When Jeremy was the child of a disappearing father, the little tailor across the hall would lend him the books of Grey Owl, hoping that the child would grow up to be a professor. Instead, Jeremy, whose name means uplifted by God, took Grey Owl as a model of the man vanished from his historical imperative into an invented life. Stepping from the United States with its Jeffersonian illusion that it had been selected as the stage of history, into the snow carnival of western Canada, Jeremy says: "This whole damn country, I thought to myself, they're all trying to vanish into the air" (91). As Michael Ondaatje told us regarding the testimony of the trumpeter, it is no easy task writing "the history of air."

• • •

Life in the west, where the layers are layers of earth rather than tiers of written records, is lived in metonymy rather than metaphor. Here is what Kroetsch said in conversation with a younger western writer involved with place:

> The notion of transference that's involved in metaphor moving from one place to another And I think it's that moving that we distrust That's why we aren't historians we're archaeologists We want to see the thing in its place what we want to do is record exactly where it's sitting where it's found and not make any assumptions not disrupt the ground and then read from there And that's why it becomes one hell of a task in reading because you have to read so bloody hard because the text hasn't been manipulated ... We leave things where they're found (46-47).

Connect nothing, said F., to his unhappy historian.

If, as the dramatic necessitarians say, history is a ship we are all sailing on, then literature might be a stowaway on history. If it succeeds it owes nothing to history. If it fails, if it is found out, it is the prisoner of history. Some of our novelists, at last, are finding out that they are not necessarily wanted on the voyage.

They might tell the rest, including the readers of the rest, what *Alibi*'s narrator Dorf tells Karen, who is loaded down with her cameras, notebooks, and watches: "'Get with it ... Speak our language. Forget about history. Make do'" (102).

1984

₁For further treatment of this key poem, see "Ondaatje Learning to Do."

• • •

WORKS CITED

Cohen, Leonard. *Beautiful Losers*. New York: Viking, 1966.

Conrad, Joseph. *Heart of Darkness*. Penguin Modern Classics, 1976.

Cooley, Dennis and Robert Enright. "'Uncovering Our Dream World': An Interview with Robert Kroetsch." *Essays on Canadian Writing*, 18/19 (Summer/Fall 1980): 21-32.

James, Henry. "The Art of Fiction." In *The Art of Fiction and Other Essays*. Intr. Morris Roberts. New York: Oxford UP, 1948.

Kroetsch, Robert. *Gone Indian*. Toronto: New Press, 1973.

_____. *Badlands*. Toronto: New Press, 1975.

_____ and John Marshall. "from The Remembrance Day Tapes." *Island*, 7 (1980): 35-50.

_____. "For Play and Entrance: the Contemporary Canadian Long Poem." *Open Letter*, Fifth Series, No. 4 (Spring 1983): 91-110.

_____. *Alibi*. Toronto: Stoddart, 1983.

Malraux, André. "Afterword." *The Conquerors*. Trans. Stephen Becker. New York: Holt Rinehart and Winston, 1976.

Mandel, Ann. "Uninventing Structures: Cultural Criticism and the Novels of Robert Kroetsch." *Open Letter*, Third Series, No. 8 (Spring 1978): 52-71.

Melville, Herman. *The Confidence-Man: His Masquerade*. Ed. Elizabeth S. Foster. New York: Hendricks House, 1954.

Neuman, Shirley and Robert Wilson. *Labyrinths of Voice: Conversations with Robert Kroetsch*. Edmonton: NeWest, 1982.

Ondaatje, Michael. "'The gate in his head.'" *Rat Jelly*. Toronto: Coach House, 1973.

_____. *Coming through Slaughter*. Toronto: Anansi, 1976.

Pound, Ezra. *The Cantos of Ezra Pound*. New York: New Directions, 1981.

Ricoeur, Paul. "The Narrative Function." *Hermeneutics & the Human Sciences*. Ed. and trans. by John B. Thompson. Cambridge, London: Cambridge UP, 1981.

Thomas, Peter. *Robert Kroetsch*. Vancouver: Douglas & McIntyre, 1980.

Trevelyan, George Macaulay. "Clio, A Muse" (1904; 1913). In *Clio, A Muse, and Other Essays*. London, New York, Toronto: Longmans, 1949.

Twigg, Alan. *For Openers: Conversations with 24 Canadian Writers*. Madiera Park, B.C.: Harbour, 1981.

Home Away

A Thematic Study of Some British Columbia Novels

In *Survival* (1972), her popular "thematic guide to Canadian literature," Margaret Atwood began with what she called a "sweeping generalization," that "every country or culture has a simple unifying and informing symbol at its core," and that it will be discoverable in that culture's literature. She suggested that for the U.S., or as she called it, "America," the symbol is the Frontier, that for England it is the Island, and that for Canada it is Survival. Leaving aside argument that these assignments might be acts of fiction themselves, that Survival, for instance, seems as important to Australian literature as to Canadian, I would like to take up the amusement for a while, and say something about my choice for the unifying and informing symbol for the culture (dare we say country?) of British Columbia. The symbol is Home, or more specifically, the attempt to find or make a home.

Home, of course, means family, means a place where people have inter-personal rather than societal rituals, means, literally and etymologically, a place where one may lie down. The common way to symbolize it in art is to construct the picture of a house. The main livelihood of the province of British Columbia is the harvesting and processing of house-building materials. But the houses that the families of the harvesters and processors live in most often seem temporary and unstable.

In *Survival*, Atwood has this to say about the literary meanings of families: "If in England the family is a mansion you live in, and if in America it's a skin you shed, then in Canada it's a trap in which you're caught" (131). Like a lot of the things in *Survival*, this notion is likely feasible in the imaginations of central and eastern Canada, but not easily applicable to the situation in B.C. and its literature. People in B.C. are less likely to feel trapped in their families than to be several thousand miles from them, or working with them on a patch of land out of sight of the next family.

A typical home in eastern literature might be stone Jalna, built in 1850 and named after a British enclave in India, or one of Timothy Findley's family mansions, hoary with gothic family history. British Columbia novels often offer tents, brush shelters, shacks and boats for their characters to pass short times in. Most towns (or should we say settlements) in the province are not much older than the writers who have built novels here.

Adherents of thematic criticism, of course, propose that conditions of territorial living will be reflected in the arts of the territory in question. Perhaps the predominant condition for people brought up in the territory of British Columbia is that they are brought up all over the territory, or that they were brought to the territory to be brought up. Fiction writers here do not often tell the story of the youth who feels impelled to escape the old home town, because the youths' parents were always hauling them from home town to home town.

Workers in B.C. have tended to be the kind who move around for their work — loggers, miners, fishermen, cowboys, fruit pickers. B.C. has since it became a province had Canada's highest rate of internal migration along with other indicators of instability — suicide, family breakup, lunacy. In addition, B.C. has Canada's highest numbers for immigration from other provinces and other countries. Net migration here easily outpaces natural increase; in fact B.C. has Canada's lowest rate of natural increase and highest rate of population increase. Since 1921, at least, sixty percent of B.C.'s population increase has continued to be due to immigration. In the quarter-century after World War II, ten thousand families per year moved to British Columbia.

So B.C. families are not really traps in which protagonists are caught. Traps sit still. We do not. I am probably a typical case, having been brought up in or near several towns in the B.C. Interior. When people ask where I'm from, I reply, "Which year?"

Looking for a home. I can think of two reasons why our writers write about it. One: that is why most of our people are here. Two: so far nearly all our novelists have come here from other provinces and countries, and have written about people who have done likewise. Some of these novelists, such as Hubert Evans and Audrey Thomas, have stayed. Others, like Margaret Laurence and Alice Munro, have gone back east. In most recent times we have been seeing novels by writers who were actually born somewhere in the province, as for instance Jack Hodgins and Robert Harlow. But most of the time our native novelists are abjuring Northrop Frye's famous Canadian question, "where is here?" in favour of the B.C. question, "where can I lay down my head?"

• • •

The question of home has been handled in most of the manners that have been used to handle other questions in fiction, at least those we have witnessed over the past century: cause-and-effect naturalism, romantic myth, psychological realism, propagandistic documentary, existentialism, and postmodernist illusionism. We have seen immigrant writers trying to bring their myths or their images of B.C. with them — the forest as magic, the island as Eden, the Coast as a realm of weird fads. But the serious writers have usually come to show the people on the land (and water) in continual motion, trying to come to rest.

M. Allerdale Grainger, born in 1874 in London, travelled around the world, taking jobs on various continents. After spending some time among the logging camps of the B.C. coast, he found himself getting married in England. There he wrote *Woodsmen of the West* (1908) to raise passage money for his wife (first class) and himself (steerage) on a ship bound for Victoria, where he would eventually become Chief Forester of British Columbia. Thus we see a tidy relationship between biography and literary composition; in a reversal of the usual procedure, a book is the resource used to create a life.

The novel is the work of a gifted amateur. Description of turn-of-the-century logging life, and dialogue among the immigrants who partake in it, are deft and amusing; but readers will be aware that there is no satisfying balance in the overall structure of the story. Chapters veer away from the mounting conflict, and main characters disappear just when we need them. But the moment-by-moment observations of the narrator, Mart, are satisfyingly real, both as to things observed and as to the attitude of the observer.

The strengths and weaknesses of the novel are related to its purpose. It was intended to be both a divertissement and a documentary, a report to English readers on daily life at the edge of the Empire. For our purposes it does something else — its structure shows the narrator moving gradually from his position as observant outsider, to participant in the forest industry, to settler. In fact the story ends with a little bit of gentlemanly doggerel that does not fairly represent the quality of the book, but nicely insinuates my theme:

> Farewell, then, to wrenching and tearing and intensity of effort; to great fatigues and physical discomforts; to sweaty work with simple tools; to trails in far-away mountain places; to rest and warmth beside log-fires in the woods!

> Farewell to loggers and my youth!
> Farewell to it all: marriage is better.
> And now I must go and scrub the kitchen floor of
> The cottage next to Mrs. Potts',
> in (what will be) Lyall Avenue,
> (outside the city limits of)
> Victoria,
> B.C.

(146-47)

Such pioneer domesticity describes the settled role of the changed Brit, and suggests the future of a changing land. All the way through *Woodsmen of the West*, wherein "West" is not a space but a concept, Grainger compares English city life unfavourably with the coast forest, where people work with "visible result" and "obvious importance," where "by the light of Nature," they meet problems head on; and where a living place, a camp, is made quickly from cedars at hand, upon which the sunshine then produces a "homelike gleam."

But Grainger returns often to the theme of loneliness, or rather isolation, the opposite of home-life, and introduces us to a concern felt in many of the novels and stories written about existence in British Columbia. For Grainger it is an ambivalent feeling; he is fond of a kind of Darwinian self-reliance, but in one of his evocative descriptions of life in the woods, his narrator says, "I hate isolation. . . . Making camp by oneself in bad weather, in a bad country, is a dismal thing to look forward to" (119).

Looking back on it is a different matter; rugged settlement, in a huge tract of primary resource, is a necessary precursor to suburban settlement. In B.C.'s logging history, communities grow from logging camps all the way or part of the way to metropolitan districts. Logging camps are isolated, almost totally populated by male employees of the logging outfit. If the camps last long enough they become company towns, with road links, doctors and schools. (More recently industry and government have made instant towns in the bush, serviced by air.) Sometimes company towns become real towns, like Powell River. Sometimes towns grow out of unincorporated communities, clusters of outgrown camps and volunteer development. Somewhat older than company towns are single-industry incorporated communities, with government and business services, but in times of industrial flux, these are in danger of disappearing. More secure in this regard are multi-industry incorporated cities. When they get large enough they contain "skid roads," where loggers and others pass weekends or lifetimes that are the dark holes of their camp life. In all these communities it is possible to encounter isolation and feel loneliness. Logging is only one of the primary industries that know such development.

• • •

Mist on the River (1954) by Hubert Evans has been, like *Woodsmen of the West*, praised as "an historical document as much as a work of art" (William H. New, "Introduction," NCL edition, V). Whereas Grainger wrote a realistic account of Canadian logging for the people back in England, Evans wrote a piece of social realism for Canadians, and especially readers in B.C., to show to them the problems for Indian villagers whose habitat is being encroached upon by White industry. The story employs as its central character a young Native man, Cy Pitt, who encounters a conflict between the pull of culture, security and spirituality in his village up the Skeena River, and the temptation of opportunity, progress and deracination at the fish cannery in Prince Rupert. Put another way, the choice is home vs. isolation. Almost every page of the novel contains the word "home," and almost every kind of home and house is described. Usually, as the title of the novel would suggest, the conflict and its integers are portrayed in terms of what is called in realism landscape:

> His feeling of being out of place came partly, he supposed, from the contrast between the surroundings here and those he was accustomed to. At home there was the wide and sunny freedom of his valley, with birches and white poplars between the belts of jackpine. The woods were stippled through with shifting light, while here the hemlock and cedar forest was dark and choked with undergrowth. These mountains, towering above the bay, lacked the soaring, shapely grace of those at home, where one could travel through many summer days or over the dazzling snow and never feel shut in or limited. (19)

Thus isolation for Cy, as for other Natives, is dangerous. The isolated individual can be picked off, on the White man's temporary payroll, or on the streets of Vancouver's skid road, where Cy's sister Dot is doomed. Even at home, when Cy feels called upon to defend the wisdom of taking a seriously sick village boy away to a modern hospital, he is assailed by the gloom of isolation, described by Evans in terms of landscape: "His hints and attempts at persuasion would not help; they were no more use than piling stones to overcome a mountain. Now he stood under its shadow and he felt himself in a dark and lonely place" (143).

The central fact of White-Indian relations has been, historically, that the Whites came here, and before they came here the Indians were here. The Indians were not in a new land; in a way of speaking (a way that Evans speaks) the Indians were part of an old land being threatened with change by a new people: "Not a stream or mountain, pond or draw, which does not have its ancient name and its ancient story. We are a part of this valley and it is a part of us. Separate the two and the life sickens and goes out" (152). Thus while newcomers to the coastal province came looking for a home, what they came looking with, a sense of change, was to the Natives a threat to their home. Home, as a mind's archetype, suggests a refuge from change, the opposite of change. The Whites, with a humanist religion, a resource-oriented expansionist economy, and transportation as freedom, wanted the Natives to redefine home.

So two major symbols in the novel. Cy, who wants to go "my own way" between the cultures, plans to get hold of an old truck, to gather wood at a distance: "The grounds had been held by his family for many generations, long before the first whites came, and it was hard to imagine never seeing them again; but more and more the truck was becoming a symbol of liberation in his mind" (179). But there are the salmon you do not have to go distant for. Somehow they elude the canneries on the coast, and swim home, up the Skeena, where Cy's people join them at the river. "His people were like the run of salmon. They were strong because they stayed together; they did not scatter and die out" (202). The salmon are our most amazing home-finders, nonchangers: "The salmon were born here, the people were born here, and no matter how far they travelled they always came back up river when their natures called them home. They had to; that was the way it was" (229).

It is a joining of fish and villagers that begins to settle the question for Cy. The young Miriam, an old-fashioned girl, takes Cy to the river, and in a scene that would make mythic D.H. Lawrence smile, they plunge into the coursing water to grab fish out of the nets. When a twenty-pound salmon tries to escape, "she threw herself astride of it, squeezing it between her knees to capture it. Its thrashing tail showered her with spray . . . As he turned to cast off his line, his hands were trembling" (215). That night Cy moves to her family's house, and eventually to the chair at the head of the meeting room, where he will be at home, agreeing to seek change in his people's ways only when it will ensure the preservation of their community.

A later generation of White people would, rather than trying to make Indians redefine home, go to them as teachers on the subject. Matt Cohen, like Evans an Ontarian, published *Wooden Hunters* in 1975. Its setting is an island not far from Prince Rupert. All the Whites on the island have run away from home for various reasons. They are what John Moss, in his introduction to the novel, calls "urban fugitives . . . in an intimate alliance with native people." The central figure is a young woman named Laurel, whose parents were killed, leaving her as a teenager in the home of an insufferable aunt. She escapes northward, meets an older Indian man named Johnny Tulip, and lives for some time in his family's house. Johnny introduces her to sex, and more important, perhaps, to a confidence that she can make a home in the forest, without a market nearby.

In the first chapter she demonstrates to Calvin (a nice inter-religious pun on Cohen), with whom she now lives, how to shoot a deer at night, and how to hang it, gut it, and pull its skin off. On her first arrival in the north she had been unable to light a fire beside her tent, but Johnny Tulip showed her how to do everything, especially how to make a home.

Why did Laurel leave Victoria for the rainy island in the first place? Laurel is a big drinker, a dope-user, in pain with an injured back, but Calvin says that there was "something she needed that she couldn't eat or drink or smoke or even get from other people" (58). The need led her to the accidental finding of an "abandoned cabin with a lock that was easy to break" (58), a kind of second-growth pioneer home.

Meanwhile, the old Indian village, including its burial ground (the word "home" shares an etymological history with the word "haunt") is being threatened, as in Evans's novel, by White industry, this time logging. In contrast to Laurel's home, the logging management people live in an instant suburb of the nearby town, in bungalows ferried to the island and set at the end of a street, in a circle like a wagon train garrisoned against the Indians or the forest.

That sense of confrontation is offset by the non-technological attempt by the young Whites to live Indian-like in the setting that does not look quite the way it did before trucks and saws arrived, but which disresembles the successor to Grainger's Victoria even more. As in *Mist on the River*, a choice of home is joined with informal, symbolic, natural marriage. In the last chapter of *Mist on the River*, we are told this:

> The smoke-houses on the river flat were closed, the hay and potatoes in, wild berries gathered, cured salmon stored for winter use. The fattening snow was on the mountains and when the last families returned from fall fishing, the cycle scribed by thousands of years of communal living would be rounded out. (268)

In the last chapter of *Wooden Hunters*, Laurel has this thought:

> It would be good to get home wet, the cabin cold and wet too, so they would have to start a fire to dry out everything. And by the time they were warm, by the time they had eaten and cleaned the dishes, the cabin would smell of smoke and dry cotton, and they would sleep to the sound of rain and burning wood. (217-18)

Besides peacefulness and security, there is hope, perhaps hope of redemption, as Laurel is pregnant. She may be carrying the child of Johnny Tulip, or she may be carrying the child of Calvin. The most hopeful thought is that it doesnt make any difference.

A child half-White, half-Indian, grows up to become a legend with no home but the grave in our most respected novel about Indian-White relations, Howard O'Hagan's *Tay John* (1939). Unlike Grainger, whose novel began as letters to his fiancée and became a documentary of daily life among the timber, O'Hagan perceived a legend of the Yellowhead and wrote the story of a myth as it meets the reality of the White advance on the mountains of eastern British Columbia. Tay

John's father was a White man from Alberta (as was O'Hagan), who burned his possessions and moved in with a band of Shuswap Indians, where he was accepted as the foretold flame-headed man who would lead them to a new home. But the newcomer is eventually executed by the people for taking to his brush-house a woman who belonged to another man. The pregnant woman dies, but soon her child emerges from her grave.

This is Tay John, whose resurrection is seen as a sign that he will take the Shuswaps home. As he grows up, he lives slightly apart from his people, going away and returning at intervals. As Cy Pitt wished to do, he goes his own way, and is fated to both isolation and a bond, never a redeeming marriage. It is said that "'Other men must marry. The woman of Tay John is the people. He is a leader of the people and is married to their sorrows'" (67). When he is prevented from repeating his father's sin, he divorces his people and leaves home.

During the rest of the novel we see Tay John as he appears at the edge of the White man's world. The White men have come west for exploitation, seeing the mountains not as home but as opportunity, even as access to markets in Asia. There are the usual trappers, loggers and prospectors; but the most ominous of all is an American named Dobble, who wants to build a tourist (and immigrant) trap in the form of an imitation Swiss town, which he will name, according to his posted sign: "Lucerne — in the Heart of the Canadian Rockies; Alf Dobble (formerly of Colorado) Proprietor" (175). The narrator of the novel, a remittance man named Denham, tells us that "Possession is a great surrender" (113). Throughout, he lets us know that those who stay closest to nature are better than those who try to impose their will over it.

O'Hagan is not, therefore, much in sympathy with human ideas of progress and personal advancement. In a recent interview with immigrant writer Kevin Roberts, he said, "I believe in the doctrine of eternal repetition . . . I think man has eternal life now whether he wants it or not." In other words, we are not passing through this world on our way to a heavenly home. Tay John, born without a shadow, born from the earth itself, is a true chthonic god, or at least a chthonic hero in a tragedy that foresees the eviction of his own people from their estate. Born of the earth, he returns to it, not after his death, but as his death. Or so, at least, is an eyewitness's legend-making report that ends the novel: "He had the feeling, he said, looking down at the tracks, that Tay John hadn't gone over the pass at all. He had just walked down, the toboggan behind him, under the snow and into the ground" (264). He did not take his people home, but he showed them where they lived.

Tay John's story is told again in the life of Donal Kenneally, the mad Irish pilgrim of Jack Hodgins's first novel, *The Invention of the World* (1977). Kenneally, a demi-god, magician, despot, hypocrite spiritual leader, was reportedly sired by a bull and born out of the earth on a hilltop in Ireland. After leading a gaggle of impoverished peasants to his communal Eden in the forest near Nanaimo, he satisfies his giantific appetites, both spiritual and physical, till his overthrow and finish. Just before the latter he begins to dig his way back into the earth, and is imagined drilling his chthonic body deeper even after his putative death.

It is common knowledge that Kenneally the "messiah-monster" is based on Brother Twelve and other charismatic leaders who have led cults to idealistic homes on Vancouver Island and the nearby Gulf Islands. As wildly imaginative as Hodgins's story-telling is commonly said to be, it is also generally considered to be related to pretty peculiar versions of community on that lunatic fringe western edge of the country, so far from the United Empire Loyalist graveyard in Saint John, New Brunswick. In recent times, and indeed currently, the island is the setting for unusual therapy camps, wacko diet enclaves, and hideaway family experiments. In *The Invention of the World* Hodgins tells about some of them, too, as (dis)harmonic accompaniment to the saga of the Revelations Colony of Truth or, as it has become, now that Maggie Kyle has taken it over, the Revelations Trailer Park, run for those latter-day colonists, the U.S. tourists with their fish-canning machines.

"World" literally means the age of the earth's occupation by human beings, the time that a place has been settled, made a people's home. So invention of the world means, literally, the coming in of home-making. Strabo Becker, the writer-historian Hodgins-figure of this novel, "has chosen to nest on a certain piece of this world and to make a few years of its history his own" (viii). Maggie Kyle, her childhood spent with brawling parents "in one shabby gyppo logging camp after another," her adult experience a series of abandonments by men and her children, fixes up the ruined Colony and collects odd refugees who now live in its cabins. Why? Because "there was something *home* about it all" (21). Meanwhile her boyfriend Wade Powers has built a phony tourist fortress cum museum, a bit of Dobbletry in what Hodgins has called Canada's hillbilly country. The novel is wholly concerned with attempts to find a home, to make a world. One of the questing figures is Madmother Thomas, an old woman who drives a donkey-pulled manure-spreader with a tiny shack on it, searching for the vanished village of her birth. No one has ever accused Jack Hodgins of restraint when it comes to pursuing a theme.

There is another fine novel that is wholly concerned with the search for a home and tells the story of pilgrims coming to the Nanaimo area in hope of finding an Eden. (The first Eden, one remembers, was for a while the only world.) That is Malcolm Lowry's *October Ferry to Gabriola* (1970), published thirteen years after his death. Lowry teachers usually speak of it as a flawed book, and some of them say that it should never have been published. But it is my favourite Lowry text; in fact I have come to think of it as the apotheosis of B.C. fiction, not only because of the subject matter, but also because it was written by a world-roving immigrant to our coast, and written in defiance of the principles of the well-constructed novel admired in London and Toronto and most university departments of English.

October Ferry is the longest telling of a story that obsessed Lowry in his writings after *Under the Volcano*, a story of a married couple in penury being evicted from their tenuous domiciles, or burnt out of them. Here the two wanderers, Ethan and Jacqueline Llewelyn, who "from the first" were "completely at home with one another" (14) have to leave homes in various parts of Ontario, to take up temporary havens in Vancouver's west end and the squatters' beach on the north shore of Burrard Inlet. In his usual manner, Lowry knits a busy fabric of images and symbols to wrap around his theme, filling the text with images of evictions encountered in the movies, books, music, newspapers, street signs, and classical mythology. When, as he often does, the protagonist goes to a beer parlour, he sees "a lonely home from home" (42). He is pursued by the memory of his suicided school roommate and his own feelings of guilt, memory kept alive by associated billboards offering Mother Gettle's soup as a bringer of "Homes to the Homeless" (46).

In a 1951 letter to his agent, Lowry had this to say about the theme of his novel: "it deals with the theme of eviction, which is related to man's dispossession, but this theme is universalized" (*October Ferry*, "Editor's Note," 335). It may be universalized, but it is attended by a story of westward movement. The Llewelyns move constantly toward the west, hoping to leave behind the corruption of modern mercantile order, but the latter follows them, westward too. At the end, when the couple is arriving in the falling darkness at Gabriola Island, Ethan feels the pessimism provided by the continual earlier dispossessions, but also a (perhaps desperate) hope that this Canadian western edge will furnish a lesson in living to redeem the world east of it:

> Quite against his better judgment he believed that some final wisdom would arise out of Canada, that would save not only Canada herself but perhaps the world. The trouble is, the world never looks as though it's going to be saved in one's own lifetime.
> — In Gabriola perhaps. (202)

It is a fugitive hope that is expressed by the quasi-autobiographical figure in other Lowry fictions. In "Through the Panama," for instance, he espies the hope under the

> appalling sights of despair and degradation to be met with daily in
> the streets of Vancouver, Canada, where man, having turned his
> back on nature, and having no heritage of beauty else, and no faith
> in a civilization where God has become an American washing
> machine, or a car he refuses even to drive properly — and not pos-
> sessing the American élan which arises from a faith in the very act
> of taming nature herself, because America having run out of a sup-
> ply of nature to tame is turning on Canada, so that Canada feels her-
> self at bay, while a Canadian might be described as a conservationist
> divided against himself — falls to pieces before your eyes. Report
> has nothing to do with navigation. Instead of ill this very extremity
> in Canada probably presages an important new birth of wisdom in
> that country, for which America herself will be grateful. (95)

Curiously, or for my purposes, happily, Lowry's protagonist always
accompanies such observations with attacks on realist prose, calling
for a new invention from west coast writers who have been evicted
from the parental house of fiction. "The only haunted house," says
Ethan, "is the human mind."

British Columbia may not be Heaven, but as a dwelling place it was
haven, for a time at least, till it became a new Pompeii under the fires
of "development." Lowry's refugees have constantly to sift through the
ashes of their previous homes, whether ancestral mansion or waterside
shack, and to listen to fire engines in the night. Which brings us to
another of Margaret Atwood's remarks in *Survival*: "English Canadian
literature is not overly-disposed towards fires" (228). Atwood mentions
The Double Hook as one relative exception, but I would like to point
out that most of the books I am here looking at treat of house fires or
the fear of them (as do books by prairie novelists, Kroetsch and others). As houses in Ontario are generally not made of wood, I rather
expect that Atwood's remark expresses again a central-Canadian
viewpoint.

• • •

That house fire in Sheila Watson's *The Double Hook* (1959) is, as
Atwood notes, redemptive. Watson's book satisfies Lowry's call for a
non-realist fiction, for a mode of creativity that would itself resemble
the elemental story of renewal it has to present. The events occur
largely in an isolated valley of the southwest Cariboo, among a few
families whose houses are scattered along a creekbed. In the preamble
to a first public reading from the text, Mrs. Watson said: "there was
something I wanted to say: about how people are driven, how if they
have no art, how if they have no tradition, how if they have no ritual,

they are driven in one of two ways, either towards violence or towards insensibility. . . ." (1974-75, 183). She is talking here, it seems to me, about a condition of homelessness; home is a place in which one feels less individual and isolate, where without consideration one participates in the tradition.

The figures in *The Double Hook* are puzzled by one another, each feeling isolated and thwarted, as if the sense of community were something lost in the inadequate usages of time. One of them, Felix (Culpa?), remembers but does not understand fragments of the Catholic liturgy. The native spirit figure Coyote is a ghost whose purpose is forgotten. But the landscape is intentional, and the domicile is elemental. It is the human imagination that is missing, the spirit of polis. Most severely cut off is the dreadful arsonist Greta Potter; of her brother James "She could not imagine the life he lived when the door closed behind him" (30). This is a place in which for all surviving memory a livelihood has been cutting hay and fencing horses.

As if looking for some bond, the narration of the text, our borrowed eye, goes paragraph by paragraph from house to house. Over and over we see them in their separateness, and between them we see the aridity of the cursed earth. The varieties of domestic failure are spread before us, and their rapid succession is proof of an abiding absence.

In a paroxysm of violence, James Potter slays his fearsome mother, blinds the young witness Kip, flails about with his whip, and abandoning all, rides down out of the hills to the railway town. In his absence his mad sister burns their garrisoned house down, her naked body inside it. As the girl Lenchen nears the hour when she will give birth to James's child, almost all the community converges clumsily to attend. Unlike Tay John, James destroys his chances in the mercantile world, gives his horse its head, and returns to his people, as for the first time, thirteen pages from the end of the book, the operative word is allowed: "Freed from the stable, it [his horse] turned its head towards home" (121). I am saying that in that action of turning his attention back to Lenchen and the rest, James Potter is inventing the concept of home. His decision is like that of Cy Pitt in *Mist on the River*, but its taking is not a statement of faith in the human heart; it is a glimpse of hope in the universal order.

Thus it is attended by magic. On his way to the birthplace of his issue, James passes a field grown moist, and later he sees a spring of water oozing from the ashes of the Potter house. He vows to build a new house, holds the baby Felix in his hands, and stands surrounded by a community that without thinking has converged, as if for a cultural ritual. "By some generous gesture he had been turned once more into the first pasture of things" (131). The gesture is grace, and the pasture is a new world, of nourishment. The place is not British Columbia —

Mrs. Watson has insisted that she is not interested in regionalism. But the book was written with this place under Coyote's eye. The imagination converged here. Many eastern critics, whose sense of home runs otherwise, say that this book is set in the Rockies. Mrs. Watson said that she was not offering characters in a landscape but figures in a ground. The figures are in the art and the ground is your imagination, wherever you are reading, isnt it?

• • •

The idea of grace is more homely in a realist novel or a romance. In the former it is usually related to human character, and in the latter it is generally bestowed by a relenting author who has made her central figures go through enough punishment. Patricia Blondal's *From Heaven With a Shout* (1963) is a romance about a London widow who strikes a deal with a wealthy man from southern Vancouver Island. He will see that her son is provided a comfortable home with her relatives, and she will come to the Pacific Coast as the new Mrs. Alex Lamond, where she will be condemned to a life of luxury and family intrigue. The Lamonds are timber barons, and their home is a mansion among the trees, though the Lamonds go sometimes to Victoria on shopping sprees.

Arden, the young wife, finds herself among the usual gothic romance family — her cold husband with his physical and psychic wounds, his twin brother who has given his life to literature rather than lumber, their flinty mother, their libertine sister, and Alex's ex-wife, a lawyer in the nearby town. So Arden has to come to terms with the new place and work her way through the twisted past and violent present of the family, before she is able to call her place home. Hope is held out in one early conversation with matriarch Avis, who allows that she has not "been home in twenty years." When Arden asks whether England is her home, Avis replies, "No, it's just an archaic way of talking" (53).

The Lamonds, Arden is told, treat their dwelling at the Big Place as a destiny. A turning point for Arden comes after a sordid night in Victoria with her sister-in-law. When the latter urges that they go back to the Big Place, Arden asks whether it is an instinct for the Lamonds. Nona replies simply that it is home. When Arden says that she has "never felt that way about a place," Nona predicts that she will. And indeed it is only a few pages later that Arden first calls the place home. Destiny is important to romance.

Arden's pursuit of a home is related here to a theme of the hopelessness of postwar England and the necessity of remaking a life on the frontier of the Empire: "where hope is stifled youth must go" (133). But the focus is on the elements of romance. Arden, of course, is fascinated by her husband's twin, George; and after the grand guignol of her husband's suicide, the death of the old lady, and Nona's fortunate marriage, Arden wins her place:

> two men walk, one on either side of me, now where none walked before, one is death and the other is life and both desire me. And when I die I shall rest in Brynton where I found a home. Up past the Meadows where the cliffs overlook the sea I shall lie like this, my husband to my right, my husband to my left. (180)

We are reminded that the word "home" can be traced to the Sanskrit and ancient Greek words meaning "he is lying down."

A less gothic romance is Ethel Wilson's first book, *Hetty Dorval* (1947). It tells of the teenage years of a girl named Frankie Burnaby, who leaves her home on a ranch near Lytton, and goes progressively to Vancouver, London, and Paris. Each place she goes she has a chance encounter, such are the ways of romance, with Hetty Dorval, the exotic and mysteriously scandalous woman who had aroused small town feelings by taking up genteel residence in a bungalow just outside Lytton.

Hetty and her enticing bungalow are, naturally, important to the innocent girl on the edge of her small-town teens. Frankie spends only her weekends at her secure ranch house, because she has to go to school; she boards in town, a long way from other towns, her weekday world the confluence of the Thompson River and the Fraser River, which is always described as "sullen," which means solitary. She thoroughly enjoys the local environment, but is entranced by the idea of Paris, where her mother was educated, and where she is expected to go to finish her schooling. But she first follows the Fraser River to Vancouver, to another boarding school. We are reading the story of a girl's maturing, and that story involves her growing knowledge of Hetty Dorval's nature. Finally, as Frankie becomes a woman, that story will be told in the confrontation of the two females in Europe, as Frankie learns that an adult's home must be earned or lost with effort.

Hetty is a drifter, crossing the world, gathering men, from China to Vienna, in search not for home but for comfort. She can leave situations with equanimity, a foreign element passing through, even through a place such as Lytton, a life such as teenage Frankie's. Called "The Menace" by Frankie's parents, coincidentally appearing and disappearing in Frankie's expanding world, she is something more than a single exterior figure. She is something the girl has to assimilate into her experience and then let go. She is the opposite to another influence (literally, the Thompson River influences the Fraser) that holds Frankie back from a similar drift: "The *genius loci* is an incalculable godling whose presence is felt by many people but certainly not by all. . . . The thing goes deeper than like and dislike. It is the genius. To some the genius of place is inimical; to some it is kind" (55). In the climactic scene Frankie throws off the spell of the enchantress, fights with her for a young man, allows her one last night of comfort in Frankie's London bed, and stands looking at the sleeping female. She wonders, "What is Hetty?" — a critic's question, and is called to again by her source:

I remembered the yelling of the coyotes in the hills, and the moon shining on the hills and on the river; the smell of the sage; and the sudden silence as the coyotes stopped for a moment in their singing all together. I remembered the two-coloured rivers. And my home. What a strange Hetty, after such an evening, calling up this magic — for it was a disturbing magic to me, the genius of my home — ... (88)

It is a genius that Frankie will carry within her, "as real as ever in British Columbia while we looked at each other in London." Having come from a country wherein the pioneer's fence posts are still standing, Frankie Burnaby cannot think of the words about home as "an archaic way of talking."

• • •

A romance allows itself to invoke the genius of place and talk about magic. The realist's novel has to find the details of interplay between environment and a human mind; what is it in the environment that causes the mind to react as it does, and what is it about the mind that makes it see the environment as it does?

In *A Jest of God* (1966) Margaret Laurence entered by way of the present tense into the mind of a thirty-five-year-old Manitoba virgin who has stayed home with a mother who will not allow her to grow out of adolescence. She resents her sister, who abandoned her to her mother's care and went to Vancouver, to freedom and the raising of her own children. In *The Fire-Dwellers* (1969), we see that sister, Stacey, as she approaches her fortieth birthday (these milestones are always important to Laurence's system of examining life). Laurence the realist wanted to show an ordinary person, a middle-aged salesman's wife, trying to cope with a world that seems to her increasingly "violent and indeed lunatic." Those words recall Sheila Watson's discussion of violence and insensibility.

The book begins with a rime present in Stacey's mind:

Ladybird, ladybird,
Fly away home;
Your house is on fire,
Your children are gone. (3)

Stacey is living in the place that Malcolm Lowry saw as hell. Like Lowry's novel, this story is haunted by fires, real house fires, imagined ones, and fiery images carried by the television's Vietnamese war. In the late 1960s British Columbia, or at least the southwest corner of it, can be reached easily by the sickness and horror in eastern places. In fact the fears of the present, whether sexual or mortal, are countervailed by memories of innocent lakes in central Manitoba youth. It is too late to dream of finding a home on the coast; Stacey feels her home, and the idea of it, assailed from all sides: "It's all I can do to cope with what goes on inside these four walls. This fortress, which I'd like to believe strong" (15).

The theme of armageddon, fitted with Stacey's images of the city charred by nuclear flames, is joined by the old theme of solitude. Here we see every adult lonely, the single and the married; so it is not the landscape's fault, and parenthood is not a salvation. Self-reliance is not the key to survival and living on the edge of the nation. Stacey's husband is failing. His best friend is a suicide. Hometown acquaintances are whores and charlatans, Stacey's sexual fantasies are set on other planets. "I live alone," says the ordinary housewife, "in a house full of people" (169). And a house full of guarded secrets and protective verbal formulae. Realism is usually sad. Stacey comes to understand middle age as a time to cope with an unsatisfactory world: "Why did I ever once feel that to tell the truth the whole truth and nothing but the truth would be a relief? It would be dynamite, that's all it would be. It would set the house on fire" (282).

So she learns to accommodate herself to the real, to see not her house, not even the city, as home. One lies down in one's mortal imperfect body in a trap called the world. One makes the best of the worst, hoping to communicate with one's family a little more than one does, when "Temporarily, they are all more or less okay" (308). Home is not a dream; it is a place in which you lie down to close your eyes and hope that you dont wake up to a nightmare.

The time of the American-Vietnamese war was characterized by the wandering away of American and other youth from their family homes. Refugees from the military situations in the United States have always formed an important part of Canadian immigration. In Jane Rule's *The Young in One Another's Arms* (1977), American refugees join some Canadians to try to invent a new order of home for survival of the times suggested in the visions of Lowry and Laurence.

In a conventional anecdotal realism, the novel tells the story of Ruth Wheeler, a woman like Hodgins's Maggie Kyle, who has suffered homelessness in her childhood and her relationships with men, and who attempts to assemble similar home-losers into a new kind of unit. Into an urban commune made of her house she gathers various evictees and runaways, trying to overcome their various isolations. There, and later at their island retreat, she wants to "invent a world for them all to live in again" (124). Thus Rule employs the term that Hodgins used in the same year, and perhaps described the main preoccupation of British Columbia fiction.

The fictional conflict is the usual one: trees against bulldozers and concrete, home versus real estate developers; here the idealist argument of the time when incomers have proven their ability to dominate the land — home versus ownership. The sexual plane of that conflict is shown often, for instance during the visit of Ruth's estranged husband, a bulldozer man: "he cupped a hand under her buttocks and squeezed, the sureness of ownership in his gesture" (50). Throughout, the threatened refugees are identified with trees, and that makes a lot of sense for people in this province. In real life as in fiction, one understands people's values concerning the meaning of home by observing their treatment of trees. B.C. people have always known this. In the novel a black American youth called Boy comes to join the commune, and speaks of his refuge as a kind of Cheetah tree: "this here is a tree I can swing in. They cut all that kind down by now in my native land, and that's the truth" (86).

The city haven is violently defeated by the urban redevelopers, so the commune moves to that refuge common to the imaginations of people who perceive loss of a battle on the mainland. They go to one of the Gulf Islands, as Lowry's couple hoped to do, and they set up a working commune there, gradually winning the trust of the islanders. As in other novels we have looked at, a baby born into the community brings it together and offers at least a literary kind of optimism to the situation. The island's fragile ecological balance will make people live thoughtfully with the environment and each other.

But of course history suggests that what has happened to Canada's remotest province can happen to the islands just off its coast (as citizens of those islands have been trying to tell the provincial government). "Urban sprawl might not be permanently daunted by the twenty-mile barrier of water, but it could be postponed," thinks Ruth (131). That sentence proposes the kind of holding-action resolution in the last-page thoughts of Laurence's Stacey Cameron. But it also holds out a little hope, that there may be time for the birth of Malcolm Lowry's faintly hoped-for alternative society. Jane Rule is not a visionary, though. She will not be apocalyptical because she is interested in reform, or at least recovery of original innocence still flickering in us as we are. Throughout her novel runs the idea that we must live by choice rather than accident, that home is something people must decide to make. As Tom, one of Rule's Americans, says when asked whether he wants to go home after the war: "No. This is home now, and there's plenty to do here" (173).

• • •

There are probably American refugees in Australia, and middle-aged housewives fearful of armageddon, aborigines caught between village and industry, evicted dreamers looking for Eden. Surely in Australia there were legendary pilgrims and remittance men hoping to change fearsome wilds into dwelling places. To learn that home-seeking is the preponderant theme in British Columbia is not to deny that it might also prevail in the literature of other edges of empire.

Even in Nova Scotia and Quebec and Ontario there are probably novels written about people with a longing or an expectation of finding or inventing a place to lie down. But when I think of the homes in eastern fictions I think of the operations of memory, the importance of the collective past and its influence on the present in those books. I think of the family chronicles of Hugh Hood, Timothy Findley, Robertson Davies, Charles Bruce, Ernest Buckler, Alice Munro, Graeme Gibson, and of Matt Cohen. I think of family farms and the ghosts in their fields and upper storeys. When I think about home in an eastern novel I think about weight and memory, about chronicle and gothic plot. I think that the paradigm of eastern fiction might be Anne Hébert's story, "The House on the Esplanade," in which a dessicated old woman barely holds on to life in the ancestral home, where the rooms have been closed as family members died. Her brother, coveting the place and hoping bitterly for his sister's last thin breath, comes ritually to her table:

> Perhaps he sensed the presences that were hidden in the shadows, the invisible spectators at this singular repast, and feared to discover, at any moment, that the spectres haunting the upper rooms would come down and take the empty places at this great table, over which presided this little old maid. No bigger than a kitten, and as white as linen, she seemed already to belong to the world of the supernatural. (84)

It is no Eden that the brother desires to enter and own, but rather a stone monument to death. It is the past, where ancestral dust evades the hand of the sister's gothic servant.

British Columbia's fiction may come to this sometime, after the human beings outnumber the trees. For the present the figures of our fiction, literary and nonliterary, are restive, desirous, like Ethan

Llewelyn smart enough to know that the bulldozers and lawyers are just the other side of that stand of Douglas fir; but like Ethan Llewelyn they entertain a sun-shaft of hope that a people who have left their ancestral plots may invent a new way to make a home west of the Rockies.

1983

WORKS CITED

Atwood, Margaret. *Survival: A Thematic Guide to Canadian Literature*. Toronto: Anansi, 1972.

Blondal, Patricia. *From Heaven With a Shout*. Toronto: McClelland & Stewart, 1963.

Cohen, Matt. *Wooden Hunters*. Toronto: McClelland & Stewart, 1975.

Evans, Hubert. *Mist on the River*. Toronto: McClelland & Stewart (New Canadian Library), 1973.

Grainger, M. Allerdale. *Woodsmen of the West*. Toronto: McClelland & Stewart (New Canadian Library), 1964.

Hébert, Anne. "The House of the Esplanade." In *The Torrent: Novellas and Short Stories*. Montreal: Harvest, 1973.

Hodgins, Jack. *The Invention of the World*. Toronto: Macmillan (NAL), 1978.

Laurence, Margaret. *The Fire-Dwellers*. Toronto: McClelland & Stewart (New Canadian Library), 1973.

Lowry, Malcolm. *October Ferry to Gabriola*. New York: World, 1970.

_____. *Hear Us O Lord from Heaven Thy Dwelling Place*. New York: Lippincott-Capricorn, 1969.

O'Hagan, Howard. *Tay John*. Toronto: McClelland & Stewart (NCL), 1974.

Roberts, Kevin. "An Interview with Howard O'Hagan." *Event*, V, 3 (Fall 1976): 42-48.

Rule, Jane. *The Young in One Another's Arms*. New York: Doubleday, 1977.

Watson, Sheila. *The Double Hook*. Toronto: McClelland & Stewart (New Canadian Library), 1969.

_____. "What I'm Going to Do." *Open Letter*, Third Series, No. 1 (Winter 1974-75): 181-83.

Wilson, Ethel. *Hetty Dorval*. Toronto: Macmillan (Laurentian Library), 1967.

Baseball and the Canadian Imagination

When I was a student at the University of British Columbia I got involved in all the arts I could, and for that reason I had a crush on myself, hero of the green room, the newsroom, the muse room, the art gallery, the concert hall, and especially the caf. In the caf you could sit at the special arty-farty table up front, half a scrawled poem in front of you, a mickey of cheap brandy weighting down your benny pocket, cigarette butts spilling over the edge of the gummy ashtray, and impress the newcomers, if you and your friends permitted them a chair. Realizing that there were other esthetes there, I needed something to mark myself apart from even them. So I would sit with the sports pages in front of me.

"Afgh," I would mumble, "Drysdale pitches a two-hitter, and *still* he loses."

They rose to the bait, the actresses, poets, columnists, dancers. They would always pull sour faces and ask me what the hell a poet was doing looking at the baseball scores. I expected them to be naive because they were only college students after all. I had been out in the world, an air force station in Manitoba, mainly.

Baseball is poetry, you coddled future-dilettantes, I would think behind my serene or more likely goofy smile. I had what I wanted, a kind of uniqueness inside the uniqueness. But I also knew that a great number of the writers I admired shared with me a lifelong interest in baseball. You wrote about it once in a while, as William Carlos Williams did, or you wrote about it all the time, as Grantland Rice did. You also read the scores and knew something late at night as you remembered them. I rather believed that if some raglan-clad semi-Brit campus poet did not know anything about baseball, did not like it, in fact, he probably didnt know that much about poetry, either.

Things havent changed much. Even though the fashion-conscious are leaping on baseball and baseball books in recent years, I still get lots of writers and especially reviewers tut-tutting me for mentioning baseball in everything I write, whether it is a novel about eighteenth-century mariners or a "translation" of Rilke.

I have finished another historical novel recently. It will be published early in 1987, ninety-eight years after the actions it depicts. It has baseball in it.[1] Let me tell you why.

The setting for the novel is the Thompson Valley in 1889 and 1890. While doing my research, one's favourite part of writing a novel, I found that a Kamloops team, fortified with some American players, won the British Columbia baseball tournament in 1889. Even though the villain of the novel is an American who shot a French-Canadian ranch hand near Kamloops, I resisted temptation. Then I found out that New Year's Day of 1890 was preternaturally warm and that the Kamloops team played the CPR team in a game that day, and that the game had to be suspended in the fifth inning because of an eclipse of the sun! What was I supposed to do? Refuse a gift from a muse who has been watching over me since my teenage days when I reported the doings of the Kamloops baseball team for newspapers in the South Okanagan?

In any case, I dont really feel that I have to defend the appearance of baseball in my poems and fiction. As everyone knows, I have been overly-influenced by American writers, and many of my favourite American writers — Fielding Dawson, Joel Oppenheimer, Tom Clark, Jonathan Williams, Jack Spicer — pepper their writings with references to the diamond game. Even the writers I dont particularly like but always read — Philip Roth, Bernard Malamud, etc. — find that they have to pay attention to the great American game, too.

Well, I have always thought that it was the great Canadian game, too. That reflects, in all likelihood, the fact that I was brought up in a part of Canada that was not cold enough for hockey, and too poor for football, games that were popular, I heard from immigrants, on the prairies. Some of my friends got baseball scholarships to U.S. colleges, a few signed minor league baseball contracts, and one left-hander who used to strike me out with a terrifying curve ball went 3-0 against the Yankees after being brought up by Boston late one season while I was toiling in Manitoba, where the people I knew were already sharpening their skates.

So I am not patient with a certain kind of letter I have seen in various newspapers during the recent hullabaloo about the Toronto Blue Jays, the letter from some unknowledgeable malcontent, probably an ex-Brit, who complains about our press leading the excitement about an "imported" Yankee game. Maybe he is the same guy who spent the seventies trying to keep American poets out of the country. I would direct him to a lovely picture book entitled *Cheering for the Home Team* by William Humber.

Humber points out that in Southern Ontario they were playing baseball a year before the legendary Abner Doubleday was supposed to have invented it down farther south. That was a century and a half ago. It did not take it long to get into the hands of Canadian writers.

Humber quotes Nellie McClung, writing about a game in 1882, from

Clearing in the West (1936): "The seats from off the wagons were set around the place where the baseball game was played. The ball was a homemade yarn ball, and the bat a barrel stave, sharpened at one end, but it was a lovely game, and everyone got runs." Humber also quotes this, from Ralph Conner's *The Sky Pilot* (1899): "He evidently regarded the exchange of the profession of baseball for the study of theology as a serious error in judgement, and in this opinion every inning of the game confirmed him" (cited in Humber, 11).

Several years ago I went through all the Canadian poetry books I could find at home and at the UBC library, collecting poems about baseball by Canadian and other poets, including the Cuban and Japanese ones I had found. There were enough to fill a thick volume, and I thought of trying to interest a publisher in such a thing. A.J.M. Smith told me I should call the book *Cobb Would Have Caught It*, apparently a piece of doggerel he had long favoured. I dont remember the name of its author, probably American, but I wish I did. Even the baseball poems by Canadians would make a nice hefty and representative anthology.

The first Canadian poet to have any appreciable influence on my own work was Raymond Souster, who has published many fine poems (and some light hitters) about the game. We have even seen pictures of Souster in baseball garb (check the last issue of *Combustion*, a special issue of its successor, *Is*, edited and published by Victor Coleman, a well-known basketball fan). Most of Souster's recent books have baseball titles — *Change-Up, Extra Innings*, etc. — an acknowledgement of his sky-pilot-like regret that he switched lineups.

One of my favourite Souster poems has always been a joyful fancy from the fifties, called "The Opener":

From where I was sitting
it looked like an easy double-play.

But at that precise moment
a sloppy-looking freighter
slipped through the Western Gap
with a clothesline of washing
half the length of her deck,

and the runner going into second
took one look at the ship
and yelled: "Hey, look, they got
my old lady's black pants
flying at the masthead."

And when all the infield

turned around to get a gape,
he made second, stole third,
and scored standing up
the winning run in what otherwise
was one of the cleanest-played openers
in a Toronto ball-park. (38)

Souster has always looked for moments of irrational delight that will
ease one's necessary observation of normal mortality. He knows that
for baseball aficionados opening day is not only the proof of the end of
winter (and should thus be made a Canadian national holiday), but a
defiance of the end of things.

George Stanley, a poet who lives in northern British Columbia, and
whose poetic is much different from Souster's, understands that
defiance. In his book entitled *Opening Day*, the title poem ends this
way, saying of "every fist, mouth, mother/ and mother-to-be down the
first base line":

& I knew they triumphed

not over me, not over my, mine

mind

not over mind

but over darkness, iso-
lation, as the staring
of windows, the eyes of cars
& streetcars

& most of all the Victorians,
crouched in jealous rows on the hills

tall dark rooms we had stayed in
too long

now out in the sun! (29-30)

Of course not only opening day, but any game at all is surcease from
grim reality. But baseball is not all escape; it is not all phantasy or
marvel. Dwight Gardiner, a poet from the prairies, who moved first to
Montreal and then to Vancouver, in search of minor league ball, has in
his latest book, *The New York Book of the Dead & Other Poems*, a
serial poem called "Double Header," which, among other things, flicks
a note at the condition nearly any fan can glimpse in his own condition:

Max Venables'
single
first news
from Phoenix
the pathetic leagues
the almost got close
enough leagues.

But in baseball we can say what we have learned not to say in our lives: wait till next year! Now in the last innings of the nineteen hundreds we have come to realize that there is not much time left for the twentieth century to belong to Canada.

Baseball, however, is not life, except for a few hundred substitute players in the majors and minors. Baseball is postmodernism. It is just about all signifier, very little signified, at least in a metaphorical sense. We know that football is referential as can be — to war, to business, to sex life, to the years filled more and more with injuries and failing health.

In Canada, most of the poets are baseball fans. Even some of the women poets are playing softball and writing baseball poems. Judith Fitzgerald is already at least a chapbook ahead of Marianne Moore. The only two football fans I know among the Canadian poets are Eli Mandel and John Newlove. A moment's reflection will remind you that they are both from Saskatchewan, the province most often associated with novels of grim naturalism.

In Canada, a lot of the poets are also ball players. If the poets were to play a game against the fiction writers, they would win 10-3. In Montreal in the early days of the Expos I played on a team called the York Street Tigers, and we played a double-header every Saturday against the Domtar All-Stars. The All-Stars used to beat us two games out of three, but I think that was because we had so many fiction writers in key positions. On return to Vancouver I joined the Granville Grange Zephyrs (Zeds, it said on our headbands), one of the founding teams of the famous Kosmik League. We were very successful, made up as we were entirely of poets and painters. Now I play for the Bad Backs, an amazingly successful team with poets as its majority. We clean up on the opposition, formed of teams whose rosters are filled with newspaper reporters and booksellers.

Canada's baseball-loving fiction writers are more famous than its poets, at least for loving baseball. But it has been my experience that they are not as good at playing the great Canadian game, by which I mean, in this context, fastball. In *The Crow Journals*, Robert Kroetsch records this observation, Saturday, July 10, 1976, Qu'Appelle Valley,

Saskatchewan:

> Hugh Hood here to teach prose writing. He knows by heart all the
> statistics about baseball and quotes them without provocation. He
> comes equipped with seven pairs of expensive sneakers, colors vari-
> ous, many sweat suits and baseball caps and a couple of gloves. We
> went out to play ball. He can't catch or throw or hit. The novelist as
> amateur. He'll probably write a great sports novel. (59)

In Montreal, we gave a three-game tryout to Clark Blaise, another
writer who can quote baseball statistics at the drop of a popup. We put
him at first where a guy who cannot run will do the least harm, but we
found out that he could not hit the curve ball. Or the fastball. Or the
slowball. When W. P. Kinsella, prize-winning author of *Shoeless Joe*
and other baseball fictions, announced that he was moving from Calgary to the west coast, we extended him an invitation to come to our
beloved Section 9 for the AAA games at Nat Bailey Stadium, and to
the sandlot for a tryout. We have not seen him in either place. Well, we
know that he goes to big league parks on his summer rambles, but we
wonder what his excuse is for not coming to a Bad Backs practice. Of
course Kinsella is also famous for his stories about Indians; and we do
not expect him to be good at being an Indian, at least not when we find
out that he is not.

Of all the Canadian fiction writers I know, the ablest ball player I
have seen is Hanford Woods, and his best-known fiction is a novella
that won the Fels Award for the best novella in an American little
magazine that year. It has since been published with another long piece
of fiction in a book, but its title is *The Drubbing of Nesterenko*. That's
right — a hockey story.

A few years ago I edited a book of fiction about sports for Oberon
Press, though, and was delighted to find out that Canadian novelists
and short story writers seem more interested in baseball than in
hockey. Every fall and winter the department store book shops are
filled with new hockey books, but they are almost always written by
newspaper hacks. Baseball attracts the novelists. Blaise has covered
the game for *TV Guide* and other slicks, and so has Kinsella. Mordecai
Richler has written with his characteristic high-low humour about
baseball in and outside his novels.

With few exceptions football does not animate the imaginations of
our novelists or poets. Only the reporters try to make the CFL into
some kind of national mucilage, and tout the Grey Cup weekend as a
national holiday. That says, I think, something about football. Let the
Americans have football, says the poet. Canada has not been in a
shooting war for over thirty years.

Hugh Hood has written two non-fiction books about hockey, and a novel about politics that uses touch football as a motif. He has written more stories with reference to sports than any other Canadian fiction writer, even Morley Callaghan. But in recent years he has referred to baseball more than to any other athletic and esthetic play. One marvelous story tells of old Jarry Park fans taking their portable radios there rather than attending the game at the Big Owe, until there are bigger crowds at the phantom game than at the corporeal one. Another relates the dream fiction of a middle-aged man who goes to a major league training camp as a walk-on, and enjoys one magical season as a premier pitcher. In his most recent collection of short stories, *August Nights*, the opening story tells of a woman who listens to Expos games on the radio as she follows the adventures of wild birds around and in her summer place, and the title story relates the giddy activities of a couple of female Expos groupies. That first story, "The Small Birds," has a nice moment that offers a kind of theological, anti-utilitarian defense of baseball. Some swallows have nested under the porch, and by mid-July the miraculous young have grown so large that they are in danger of crowding one or another out of the nest:

> On Saturday, 19 July, she was lurking near the nest, thinking she might anticipate some infant attempt at flight, catch the creature if the attempt should go badly. She might retrieve some squeaking Icarus before he hit rock, a basket catch like those the outfielders kept making in National League play as described in the summer-long sequence of Expo broadcasts going on in the swallows' sky. In a bird's mind, the account of the game would seem like the voice of God, superior to the visible order, coming from elsewhere. Something given, a part of pure life. (17)

Those readers familiar with Hood's cycle of novels know that he is interested in the details of earthly life, but that his vision is spiritual, that he sees Wordsworthian spots in time as epiphanic. Referential meaning is converted by a special energy of attention into pure radiated meaning, regard into love. Even when Hood pokes nimble fun at his own religious and literary belief, he means that a most mundane event can hold the news of redemption and grace. It is no wonder (though it is for wonder that he is there) that Hood will be in the grandstand, looking for a perfect game.

Kinsella, too, is after wonder when he looks at baseball, and like Hood, he has an optimistic view of the world. But while Hood is after vision, Kinsella is after magic, the sort of thing Malamud wanted in *The Natural*; and no wonder — Kinsella came up to the majors from the Iowa Workshop. One of Kinsella's stories bears a remarkable likeness to Hood's story about the radio fans in old Jarry Park. In Kinsella's story, "The Thrill of the Grass," the fans take advantage of a baseball strike to sneak into a stadium night after night, gradually replacing the artificial turf with real grass. Kinsella does tell nifty and dreamy stories about baseball players and especially pure-hearted fans. But one aspect of his prose does not really suit the game. Kinsella loves similes, the easiest of tropes. He seldom lets a thing or event go by without inventing a lush simile. Baseball, though, is not like anything. Similes would work admirably with football.

Baseball is not like anything. But it does seem to be various things for writers. For many writers, as for many fans, it is a stadium for the play of memory. Clark Blaise, at the heart of the North American tradition, has always been interested in telling stories about (his) childhood and youth. Nostalgia, and what in lesser places is called trivia, pervade his fictions. What could be more useful, and in view of his upbringing, more natural than a first-person recollection of boyhood fascination with baseball statistics or the (temporary) home team? Here is Richard Durgin, the epistolary narrator of Blaise's *Lusts*:

> The first time Pittsburgh became entirely mine was when I walked out of the house one summer Saturday and pieced together the various transfers and streetcar routes that would drop me at the Forbes Field parking lot. I was eight. Bliss, when you're eight, is sitting in the bleachers and pitting your knowledge against the beer-swollen platitudes of laid-off steelworkers. The sweetest words in the world come from some hunky downing his Iron City and nodding, "Think so, kid? Yeah, maybe yer right." (32)

Of course he is right. I mean in saying that those are the sweetest words in the world.

(By the way, have you noticed how often the quotations I have made mention Saturday? Do you remember how you felt about Saturday when you were a schoolboy or schoolgirl?)

One of my favourite short stories is a piece called "Losers," by Brian Fawcett, who is also the catcher for the Bad Backs. Fawcett made his reputation as a poet, but in the past four years he has published three books of fiction. I have noticed that since he became a fiction writer his playing skills have diminished. "Losers" is a story about the earlier days of the Kosmik League, and treats the relationships between that (dis)organization and the rest of the Revolution as it altered consciousnesses in the early seventies. In the Kosmik League it was considered politically incorrect to give way to ambition or to steal against a lefty. Fawcett's story relates the difficulties of a former Little

Leaguer who still wants to knock over the second baseman, but who has become socially educated enough to despise aggressive competition.

In the first year the narrator's team has fun, and occasionally a little stylish victory. But:

> The next season, unfortunately, the team began to win. For me and a few others, it signalled that The Revolution was over, and that our side had lost. Our baseball skills had grown, which meant that we were all now *good* sandlot ball players, and that if we were willing to go to work for the telephone company or something like that, we could be playing Senior B softball. It got to some of us. (172)

Some of us baseball fans have wondered for a long time how we can admire someone like Ted Williams, who flew U.S. Marine Corps fighters in Korea, and probably voted for Barry Goldwater and Ronald Reagan. But we do admire Ted Williams. He was the Ezra Pound of baseball, an epic maker who would not wear a necktie. In "Losers," Fawcett's narrator says:

> But The Revolution was in trouble too, and it was in trouble with baseball for the same reasons it was in trouble with a lot of fairly basic laws of behavioural physics. For one thing, if people practice anything, they'll get better at it — unless, of course, they get bored with it, or become afraid of it, and quit. Skill has its own unique set of demands, one of which is that it breeds ambition. (170)

The trouble with The Revolution is that it thought baseball was like something, or about something. Since the Kosmik League has gone and been replaced by a bunch of older guys who like to play ball with each other, the softball has got to be more fun, and there is no more competition to see who can be more revolutionary. Not on the field, anyway.

There are still those who think that baseball is a "slow" game because players do not bash one another. To them, I suppose, "survival" is still the main theme in the Canadian character. There are still those who think that we will be polluting the Canadian imagination by playing and following the game usually associated with the Imperialistic Power to the south of us. There are probably still those who think that an interest in baseball is frivolous and therefore not in keeping with an essentially puritanical Canadian ethos. One thinks of the scorn directed Lester Pearson's way when it was reported that he watched the World Series in his office when he might have been meeting with his cabinet members. In that instance, Pearson, a one-time ballplayer with skills resembling those of Raymond Souster, was probably receiving the tut-tutting of both puritans and chauvinists (if they are two distinct groups).

But it would be hard to find anyone more recognizably Canadian than Lester Pearson or Raymond Souster. It should not surprise anyone to look into the trunk of a Canadian writer's car and see a ball and a bat, a glove and some turf shoes, perhaps some elastic knee bandages and *Cheering for the Home Team*.

1985

---

[1] See *Caprice*. Markham, Ontario: Viking, Penguin Books Canada, 1987. (Editor's note)

• • •

WORKS CITED

Blaise, Clark. *Lusts*. Garden City, New York: Doubleday, 1983.

Fawcett, Brian. *My Career With The Leafs*. Vancouver: Talonbooks, 1982.

Gardiner, Dwight. *The New York Book of the Dead & Other Poems*. Vancouver: Talonbooks, 1984.

Humber, William. *Cheering for the Home Team: The Story of Baseball in Canada*. Erin, Ontario: The Boston Mills, 1983.

Hood, Hugh. *August Nights*. Toronto: General, 1985.

Kroetsch, Robert. *The Crow Journals*. Edmonton: NeWest, 1980.

Souster, Raymond. *Selected Poems*. Ed. Michael Macklem. Ottawa: Oberon, 1972.

Stanley, George. *Opening Day*. Lantzville, B.C.: Oolichan, 1983.

Wiebe and Bail: Re Making the Story

I sometimes think that the great subtext of Canadian and Australian literatures is the escape from colonial status in our histories, or *vice versa*. Thus the unusual preoccupation with national identity, and thus the recent turn of our fictions against history. For two hundred years the serious writer has been expected to turn a rebellious face to authority, anyway. The writer in a post-colonial culture, it seems to me, is an obvious agent of deconstruction.

In western Canada, and in Australia, which is just about *all* western, the most interesting fiction writers have noticed that even the popular cultural myths, those folkloric signs that would seem to assure us of the singularity of our environments, are negatives of the British European self-regard. There on the pitiless outback or the bald-headed prairie the admirable yokels laughingly perform deeds of stoical legend that no caparisoned (and envious) Limie or Pommie could even dream of. Our lived epics were the stuff for Boys' Own Annuals in damp Sussex parlours. We were *allowed* to create our dryland otherness.

Thus it has become necessary for us grandsons of the pioneers to call into doubt our icons. To declare our selves we have to interrogate our Australiana and Canadiana. No decent intelligent Aussie I know sings Waltzing Matilda without savage inebriety; all sensible Canadians hope for an awkward unhorsing at the RCMP's musical ride. In New South Wales, Jean Bedford puts a subversive female centre into the saga of Ned Kelly. On the prairies, Robert Kroetsch refutes the garrison mentality regarding nature, encouraging his characters to fornicate merrily in the eye of a desert whirlwind.

Here I want to look at two short stories that reach with their erasers back to the late nineteenth century, and that write in the newly cleared space with post-historical irony. These stories are Rudy Wiebe's "Where Is the Voice Coming From?", title story of his first collection of short fictions, and Murray Bail's "The Drover's Wife," which became the title story of his first collection when it was retitled for republication ten years after it first came out. Wiebe's story, with the interrogative title, questions the authorized record of Almighty Voice's final stand against the Federal authorities on May 30, 1897. Bail's story seems to repudiate the very title of Russell Drysdale's famous

painting, while mocking the almost official national adoption of the
Henry Lawson story (1892) from which that title was taken.
The two approaches, the two kinds of irony, are quite different. Murray Bail's view is always comic, usually parodic. Rudy Wiebe, readers
often point out, has never cracked a joke; nevertheless it is not possible, I would suggest, that one could engage in literary deconstruction
without at least the trace (let us say) of a smile. Not Vonnegut's smile.
Not even Beckett's smile. But maybe the smile hidden behind those
defiantly expressionless faces we see in the photographs of famous
Indian leaders losing the rebellions at the end of the nineteenth century
in the Canadian west.

Wiebe's story is told in the first person, but that "I" does not, for good
reason, appear until the last two pages of a nine-page story. In this way
the reader is reminded that he might have been asking of the story the
question posed in its title. Wiebe's handling of the narrative strategy is
sophisticated in its irony, but it has a problem beyond its fruitful problematizing: we will see that the narrator naively rejects myth in favour
of the scientific approach, and that at the end of the story he represents
our national incapacity to understand the spirit of the Native voice; yet
the story begins with a literary adept's proposition that the story must
be "made" rather than retold. Further, it quotes Teilhard de Chardin to
the effect that our alienation is due to the fact that we act " 'as though
we were spectators, not elements, in what goes on' " (135).
    The narrator, who at first is rather an arguer than a story-teller,
describes the sites and relics he has seen in his pursuit of the actual
events of 1897. He is impatient with contradiction he has found in the
written accounts, the source materials of history. He suggests that, as
the "story ended long ago," things should have become more clear than
they are in the present (135).
    The first sentence of Wiebe's story is: "The problem is to make the
story" (135). Problematizing what seems to be received is, of course,
the first step in deconstruction, to make difference. Making a story, not
recounting one, is the problem, not the solution to it. A problem, in a
discourse of enquiry, is a proposition. Wiebe's narrator is a critic of the
official history, and the text he is examining is made up of museumized
weapons, bone fragments, printed proclamations, etc. He finds out that
the glass-encased or well-painted exhibits do not add up, that objective
distance does not calculate a "solution." In an essay called "Where to
Begin?" Roland Barthes said of the critic's activity: "it is not a matter
of obtaining an 'explanation' of the text, a 'positive result' (a final
signified which would be the work's truth or its determination), but
quite the contrary — that it is a matter of entering, by analysis (or what

resembles an analysis), into the play of the signifier, into the writing: in a word, to accomplish, by his labor, the text's *plural*" (79).

Wiebe's narrator, even though he has quoted de Chardin, seems to want to avoid the plural (though it is the plural, the contradictory descriptions of Almighty Voice, that will lead him to the personal encounter with the Voice at the end). He complains of the difficulty of "precision" (etym.: cut short). He tries to discredit the oral tradition and anything of the mythical. He refers to myth as "non-factual accretions" (135). Yet all the while we hear, or hope we are hearing, a sarcasm in this "objective" account. We are pretty sure that we do when we first hear a reference to something "national." He will compare the disrepair of Almighty Voice's museumized rifle with preservation of the Mounties' gun carriage. The kind of sarcasm found in some of Hugh Hood's stories: "the brilliant burnish of its brass breeching testifies with what meticulous care charmen and women have used nationally-advertised cleaners and restorers" (137).

So one becomes persuaded that the irony is a studied one, that the laconic voice and the talk of testimony and evidence are attributes not of privileged author but of Socratic narrator. He is trying to trick his audience into asking the title question, to help make the story, to problematize the museums. At the beginning of the story he also quotes Arnold Toynbee, our type of a historian: "For all we know, Reality is the undifferentiated unity of the mystical experience." Then he says that "that need not here be considered" (135). We know that this report could have been revised, of course, so we go on considering.

Mystical means silent, the unspoken. The Merriam-Webster dictionary offers "mystery" as the first synonym of "problem." Just as a light may be seen only if surrounded by something darker, the only place a voice can come from is out of silence. The writer's first job will be to produce that silence. Wiebe's writer begins his survey of history with an increasingly tiring litany of names, then follows it with A Proclamation that insists "Hear Ye," and is so long that it has to be cut off. Then, writes the writer: "Such hearing cannot be enough. The first item to be seen is the piece of white bone" (136), a mute piece of Almighty Voice's skull . . . maybe. The narrator-witness offers as exact as possible a description of the bone fragment, as if in this way one can begin to make the story; as if he hopes to be Ezekiel watching the connections, seeing breath bring life to assembled bones rather than being converted to speech. He is attached to the word "evidence," which means the things seen. If he has any remaining attachment to the idea of history, he models his procedure on that of Thucydides, who was not satisfied with the reports he read and heard, but went to the battlefields to see for himself. To see, since time before the Greek, is to know, not to garner knowledge from other writing but from the spirit of places and things themselves.

He ranges over the ground of Saskatchewan, preferring the land to the map, and brings us finally to the North West Mounted Police Museum in Regina, that old pile of bones. Inside that "small rectangular box of these logs" (138) there is the silence out of which one might expect authentic voice to come. But not yet: as soon as Wiebe's writer mentions the silence, these authoritarian and contradictory words intrude on the stillness of the text:

Hey Injun you'll get hung for stealing that steer
Hey Injun for killing that government cow you'll get three
weeks on the woodpile Hey Injun (138)

As history goes it is not an almighty voice, only the mean voice of half-comprehensible authority. Still, it speaks more openly the white attitude toward the Plains Cree than did all the printed proclamations. The oral tradition insinuates its authenticity.

In the museum there are many photographs, writing made with light. All are mere babble of black and white for Wiebe's writer, all but the last, a photograph of Almighty Voice himself. It brings about the "ultimate problem in making the story" (140). It differs from the two "official" written descriptions of the criminal-martyr, which vary from one another. But it differs most in that it bypasses history and cuts quickly (precisely) into the narrator's present: "It is a face like an axe" (141). In *The Pleasure of the Text*, Roland Barthes said of criticism: "its preferred material is . . . culture, which is everything in us except our present" (22).

Now Wiebe for the first time uses the first person pronoun, and moves from report to narration, in the present tense, invoking de Chardin. Because of the devastating effect of that image of a face caught in *a* present, "I am no longer *spectator* of what *has* happened or what *may* happen: I am become *element* in what is happening at this very moment" (142). The events of Almighty Voice's end become a middle, as the encoded past is made present, and photograph gives way to presence. The narrator is part of the living diorama of the assault on the few holed-up Indians surrounded by thirty-five soldiers, thirteen armed civilians, and fifty-six policemen. We then see that the scene becomes focus for a widening surround of a continent filling with white immigrants. There are guns and rifles pointing at the middle, human figures waiting in expectation this sunny Sunday morning — all in a brightened silence.

Then there is the rise of an "incredible" voice, the high strong call of Almighty Voice's death chant, which rises above the answering noise of the gun explosions. The surrounding guns are making the noise of authority. The voice is above authority now; it is the voice of the Great

Spirit. Both sounds are beyond meaning. To the defeated Indians the white authority "threatened incomprehensible law." To the narrator, now, of Wiebe's story, the beautiful spirit voice is a "wordless cry" because, as he says in his final ironic sentence, "I do not, of course, understand the Cree myself" (143). The deconstruction of authoritarian history, of the attempt, even, to find one's way along its contradictory traces, is surely to be made possible and likely by an hallucination of the loudest possible detonation out of silence of the oral tradition, even at the latter's death (though the present tense suggests that the spirit's cry makes the notion of such a death a delusion). The highest reach of the oral tradition might be called an almighty voice; it is above meaning, or at least understanding. In the *Tractatus* (at 4.121) Wittgenstein said: "that in language which expresses *itself* is not something that *we* can express by means of language." So Rudy Wiebe situates the event of his story carefully in place and time, the evidential argument of history, and then leaves a question mark at the end of his thereby unclosed title.

• • •

Roland Barthes, in *The Pleasure of the Text*, wrote: "the avant-garde is never anything but the progressive, emancipated form of past culture" (20). Murray Bail's "The Drover's Wife" tries to free the Australian imagination from the colonialized attempts at freedom in Russell Drysdale's 1945 painting (1945 being the year in which England's erstwhile dominions regarded their military independence as the sign of their cultural independence) and Henry Lawson's 1892 story.

Lawson did not have an artefact as subtext. He wrote, with dialect and local colour, to represent the typical, the Australian outback ethos. "Her husband is an Australian," he sums up, "and so is she" (49). The story is about the woman's loneliness and her prodigious battles against the ferocious agents of nature. It is in that way similar to many Canadian prairie fictions, though somewhat more extreme in its portrayal of hardships. However, there is a nearly mystical relationship between harried mother and harsh land: "As a girl-wife she hated it, but now she would feel strange away from it" (50).

This bush — it may be ugly, but it is ours. Such an attitude is likely to see a piece of early literature or art become a shibboleth, a cultural artefact, a national rather than esthetic treasure. This is especially true when the subject is treated successively, like Argentina's legend of the gaucho brigand hero Martin Fierro. Drysdale's painting does not illustrate a scene from Lawson's story, but it contains its elements, the flat land, the skeletal trees, the distance of the husband, and a woman just set down, a woman as tall as the picture of her world. She has a delicate head that can dream of what Lawson called "the 'womanly' or sentimental side of nature" (50), but the monumental legs and feet that will subdue while resembling the earth beneath her.

She is a monument. When art or writing becomes popular or otherwise institutionalized it becomes authoritative. Murray Bail's short story wants to topple the monument, the one in the Australian heart. His irony will mock the authoritative version of artistic-historical national identity, as Brian Edwards has pointed out in his article, "Alberta and the Bush: The Deconstruction of National Identity in Postmodernist Canadian and Australian Fiction." Of Bail's subversion, Edwards says: "Problematizing the field, the uncreating process promotes discourse and initiates news ideas about that which it deconstructs" (80).

The narrator of Bail's story, like the narrator of Wiebe's, is led into deconstruction in his looking at a public picture. But Bail's narrator is presented as a naive and insensitive dullard in Adelaide, who does not even recognize Drysdale's painting as icon, only viewing it as evidence concerning his wife's disappearance into the bush with a drover. His story, two thousand words long, is worth two pictures, one of them ours. Finding the bush a nuisance rather than a symbol of the Australian ethos, he cannot even imagine that art is anything more than reference to objects. (With this lack of difference, of course, he represents a post-colonial citizen who does not have to think in terms of negatives of the British.) Throughout we hear him trying to win sympathy for the wronged individual. Even his proffered diffidence is a stratagem fashioned to that end. He is interested only in the personal, unable even to imagine history or cultural identification. His description of the painted Hazel personalizes the peculiar form of the woman, so that the delicate head on the indelicate body is purely referential rather than a statement about discord between mental aspiration and environmental fate.

Symbolic and heroic survival in Lawson's story is diminished, too. His story centres on the wife's suspenseful war against a lethal snake. When the wife in Bail's story dispenses with a snake and chucks it into the incinerator, the narrator passes it off as a minor and slightly disgusting episode that makes her less attractive in his eyes.

But of course it would be to attend to the narrator's view rather than to Bail's, were we to care at all about the abandoned marriage. What matters is not the narrator's relationship with Hazel, but rather his relationship with "The Drover's Wife." His argument is simply put: that's not the drover's wife — that's my wife. He has never read Lawson's story.

Wiebe's narrator bends over a museum case, trying to focus through the glass on a triangle of bone. Bail's narrator takes magnifying glass to Drysdale's painting and naively stumbles, for us, upon the fact that on close examination, art is not representation but record of creation. Of the "drover" he says: "Magnified, he is nothing but brush strokes. A real mystery man" (57-8). Unable to pursue that point, he imagines Hazel posing for the painter, totally denying art as cultural statement. If he does not even know that the painting is famous, he cannot bow to its authority. Surely Hazel was justified in leaving this dullard and answering the call of the Australian wild. But is it then dull to have no sense of culture, to be a literalist and a personalist?

Bail's attitude toward his narrator's naivete is as much plural as is Wiebe's in regard to his narrator's naivete. Hazel's husband is no dupe of Australiana, but he is no hero of deconstruction either, because he is so fecklessly egotistical. There is a nice confusion of attitudes (ours) in this paragraph.

> To return to the picture. Drysdale has left out the flies. No doubt he didn't want Hazel waving her hand, or them crawling over her face. Nevertheless, this is a serious omission. It is altering the truth for the sake of a pretty picture, or "composition". I've been up around there — and there are hundreds of flies. Not necessarily germ carriers, "bush flies" I think these are called; and they drive you mad. Hazel of course accepted everything without a song and dance. She didn't mind the heat, or the flies. (60)

Henry Lawson, too, left out the flies. Outback survivors can be seen as legends, as agents of the national character, in a struggle against floods, snakes, fires and loneliness. Harrassed by flies, they might not be seen as much different from mute cows flicking their tales in the heat. Replacing nature's monsters with flies is the kind of deconstruction that Derrida calls "a positively displacing, transgressive, deconstruction" (66). The not-unreasonable comments on flies, placed next to the narrator's seemingly philistine remarks about painting, suggest that while we might not want to ally ourselves with such a dullard, we might be glad that he is around to make one question the value of conclusions made about national identity in air-conditioned coastal offices.

Hazel, having disappeared into the bush, "as if she were part of it" (61), might be well lost. But look at the poor narrator at the end of the story, at what his chance introduction to the painting has done to him: "it is Hazel and the rotten landscape that dominate everything" (61). We see that national culture is not just an expression of an ethos. It is the creator of one. It can problematize a previously unconscious individualism. It can start to dominate an inchoately unsatisfied personality.

• • •

The hope of a writer such as Murray Bail, or Rudy Wiebe, is that in an interrogation of earlier attempts to give us a particular national history, we will learn to be more perceptive than their narrators, that we will understand the voice we hear, that we will learn our power to make history rather than accepting it; not to "alter truth for the sake of a pretty picture," but to understand that "the problem is to make the story."

1986

WORKS CITED

Barthes, Roland. *The Pleasure of the Text.* Trans. Richard Miller. New York: Hill and Wang (a division of Farrar, Straus and Giroux), 1975.

_____. "Where to Begin?" In *New Critical Essays.* Trans. Richard Howard. New York: Hill and Wang (a division of Farrar, Straus and Giroux), 1980: 79-89.

Derrida, Jacques. *Positions.* Trans. and Annotated by Alan Bass. Chicago: Univ. of Chicago P, 1981.

Edwards, Brian. "Alberta and the Bush: The Deconstruction of National Identity in Postmodernist Canadian and Australian Fiction." *Line,* 6 (Fall 1985): 72-82.

Lawson, Henry. "The Drover's Wife." In *Short Stories and Sketches 1888-1922.* Memorial Edition. Volume One of Collected Prose. Ed. Colin Roderick. Sydney: Angus and Robertson, 1972.

Murray, Bail. *The Drover's Wife and other stories.* St. Lucia, London, New York: University of Queensland P, 1984.

Wiebe, Rudy. *Where Is the Voice Coming From?* Toronto: McClelland & Stewart, 1974.

Portrait of a Horse with Twenty-Six Artists

Literature is a matter of peace, not of war. A writer may take any number of complicated attitudes toward peace; he can take only one toward war. In a fight he must win.

Hideo Kobayashi, Introduction to *The Life of Dostoyevsky*

I should make it clear at the outset that for nearly three decades I have loved the books of William Eastlake. During his relative silence of recent years I have found other American fiction writers more interesting, perhaps, more adventurous. William H. Gass and Ron Sukenick have made serious inventions for the survival of our imagination. But I dont love any American's books the way I love Eastlake's. They most amply prove Roland Barthes's theory about one's desire for the author. I certainly wish there were more Eastlake novels. It is thus with a subjective personal history that I find *Castle Keep* (1965) to be one of the great novels in U.S. literature.

Castle Keep is woven of many rich fabrics and illuminated by many precious threads, and yet it is an "easy read." It is, like his six other novels, made up largely of dialogue, something we do not expect to find in the most serious of comic novels these days. Samuel Beckett and John Hawkes do not seduce us with that apparent ease. Ernest Hemingway did, and in this "war novel" Hemingway is often on our minds. Hemingway's artificial dialogue is pushed over the edge of the bizarre here. Major Falconer and the Countess Thérèse replay Colonel Cantwell and his European teenager lover in a mock Venice, and they recapitulate the situation of Lt. Henry and Catherine Barkley as they make a baby in the relaxation of attention to "the front." As the wounded youths in uniform lie bleeding near the end of their story, one says to the other, "'We're cutting out, Clearboy. We got a separate war'" (366).

Hemingway, though, was writing modernist war fiction, from the viewpoint of a disillusioned American whose mandate was to show his countrymen what the world was "really like," so that people might learn to live in it. *Castle Keep*, published during the U.S.-Vietnam war, is a postmodern novel, written from the viewpoint of an American artist free of illusions, whose ambition is to make a new world to replace one that nobody can live in. Thus he has to deconstruct the old world, including its wars; and as a novelist he has to start with its fiction. So his proper homage to Hemingway is a travesty of his work.

Eastlake goes on to deconstruct other American wars in his ensuing novels — Vietnam, the War of Independence, the mopping up against the environment in the Southwest U.S. — and in each case he employs all the devices of the postmodernist, including fictive discontinuity, authorial meddling, affronts against history, and especially laughter in the face of inevitability and its doorkeeper, death. No one is so solemn as a realist, and nothing unites the post-realists so much as their laughter.

Yet William Eastlake comes across as an old-fashioned man. He gathers together a kind of naturalism, black humour, and myth-making (or breaking) as does no living author I know. He arrives, unlike Gass, Hawkes, etc., as a humanist. Maybe that is why one loves him, even while one likes to call oneself an anti-humanist. At the lyrically violent climax of *Castle Keep*, we do not feel sad for the destruction of all the art objects because we have not learned to know them; but we have learned to love Alastair P. Benjamin, the obscene Rossi, and even Major Falconer, and we know we will miss them, those artists. The paintings are the prints and the victims of history, but the artists are in charge of making. Henry James called history the model for the mimetic fiction he saw as art. During the Great War in Europe, Ezra Pound's anger was not aroused by blasted cathedrals but by the killing of artists, the great hole in the present. Just before the publication of *Castle Keep*, William Eastlake made this statement: "If there is no future then the artist will make one" (Allen, 263).

• • •

On the same occasion Eastlake wrote: "The writer is a creator who has built things and cannot face the tragedy of their destruction." There are numerous ways to handle that emotional problem. If the destruction of his American soldiers at the end of Castle Keep saddens their creator as much as it does his readers, all can re-read *The Bronc People* (1958), wherein Alastair P. Benjamin,[1] later to die in 1944, heads off to an Eastern university in 1958. From there he writes home to New Mexico: "This is not an education, it's a war. This is not a school, it's a battlefield" (1961, 263).

Such comic reconstruction of his own work is a delight to the novelist's coterie of readers, and a way in which the artist may declare his creative freedom, his defiance of necessity. In *The Bamboo Bed* (1969) he undoes time by having the sun rise from the west over Indo-China. In *Castle Keep* he borrows Ralph Clearboy, an anachronistic cowboy, from *Portrait of an Artist with Twenty-Six Horses* (1963) (the number of horses, incidentally, that Eastlake ran on his own New Mexico ranch), and watches him die in wartime Belgium. Thus it is that I count twenty-six artists among the soldiers, evangelists, prisoners and whores of the spread around the castle, and one knight, who is figured as on a chessboard, as a horse.

Falconer's name suggests chivalry, of course, and we are not surprised (given the fictive rather than the military imagination) to find him riding a white stallion against an armored advance. He has raised thousands of horses in New Mexico, his previous feifdom. But he is more than associated with the nobility's steeds; he is identified as a horse. The Comte de Maldorais and his teenage niece/bride are the only remaining members of their thousand-year-old family, and whether for fear of an incestuously weak offspring, or because of his own impotence, Count Henri has chosen Falconer as a stud.

So the instructive scene in which Henri tries to shoot the stallion Leopold, and the pregnant Thérèse and her child's father Falconer prevent his doing so:

> " . . . you don't want to be always careful in your own house, careful of the wild animals. However," Henri says in a lower tone, "I knew he was dangerous when I got him, but I thought he'd be excellent for breeding."
> "Was it worth the risk?"
> "Yes."
> "But now you don't think so?"
> "Now I have finished with him. If he had behaved himself — "
> "Good," *le faucon* says. "When a horse has bred for you, you shoot him. That could be expensive."
> "Yes," Henri agreed. "But I must get on with it." (115)

Henri has never made any secret of his wish that Falconer should not survive after his use, and even tries to help the German seige. But in this episode, the Major silently and satirically removes the Count's cartridges and returns his empty gun. Then, says the narrating Thérèse, her lover enters the place of the mad horse: "*le faucon* talks to him in that horse language of gentleness, cajoling and calm" (116). On an impulse that would have met the approval of D.H. Lawrence (whom the lovers elsewhere parody), Thérèse leaps astride the liberated animal and goes for another husband-defying ride, "so smooth, so wild and smooth and gentle, like music rising and descending on bursts of a kind of joy, ecstasy, like part of the horse, secure and gentle in each terrific leap" (116-17). Eastlake's outrageous obviousness is part of the fun.

For Falconer's own thoughts on his role as breeding stallion, we go to the scene in which Henri has tricked him into entering the castle's dark secret passageway to what the Major thought would be the lady within:

The duke is not a monster and I thought I was doing him a service. It started out as a service to myself, being with Thérèse; then I realized from his attitude it was a service to the duke. He can't have a child. He was going to have a child. It was service. Service is rendered, and you thank the United States Army for supplying the soldier. The Service is pleased. Excellent public relations. The castle, the aristocracy, the name, goes on. Thank you very much, sir. Come back when your services are needed again, when there's another war, another castle to keep. I thought you kept a castle with guns. No, you do it in bed. You're a fine serviceman. That's why we're called servicemen, because we serve. I service the duke's wife with child. (220)

But something, Falconer tells us, has gone wrong. "Everything was perfect, and the complications developed. . . . when you're dealing with human beings, everything goes wrong" (220). Falconer is not only the stallion, but also the chivalric courtier. "Love is never supposed to happen in war" (221). The courtier, according to the code, is supposed to adore the noble's lady but never attain her. Here, where the husband expresses cynicism rather than *noblesse*, the courtier is supposed to do enough attaining to make the lady foal, but not to fall into love, courtly or otherwise.

• • •

All Eastlake's novels have horses in them, and horsemen. All of them present at least some men as artists, too. For Eastlake the artist is his favourite type of the human. The novels always display people as a society in small, and the presence of the artist among them as their hope. Society's frustration of the artist is sad (*Castle Keep* is peppered with remarks about hostility toward art and the artist in the U.S.), and the destruction of the artist is a tragedy waiting at the end of comic narrative.

Yet, says Eastlake, the artistic temperament lies unbidden and unrecognized in the ground of vulgar American life. His position is not unlike that of William Carlos Williams, who acknowledged the mean rube hucksterism of U.S. life, but maintained that the New World, if it were seen clear, would grow an indigenous art that would not have to conform to the splendid over-ripe culture of Europe:

for you have it over a troop
of artists —
unless one should scour the world —
you have the ground sense necessary
                    ("Tract," Williams, 129)

The wounded soldiers in the Belgian castle are a troop of artists. They also combine to make an enjoyable parody of the conventional platoon novel, a term I once invented to describe the kind of American war story in which we follow the adventures of a representative bunch of Yanks (a Brooklynite, a Southerner, a Black, an Indian, a guy in glasses who is called "Professor," etc.) through boot camp, into battle, to death. In the platoon novel we get American youths becoming men in the midst of a setting called combat. In *Castle Keep* we get American culture first wounded and discarded, then threatened by bad luck and German steel, in a setting made up of inherited European art and culture.

Throughout the novel European art is represented in objects, paintings, statues, maze hedge and moat, the castle itself. American art is represented as a spirit, a potential. The nearby oil portrait is an artifact from the Renaissance, but Alastair P. Benjamin is a boy who is saving up images to become a novelist. Captain Frank is a composer, and therefore "zero in America." Lt. Amberjack, an escapee from American religion, plays Bach on the Maldorais organ in order to avoid thought. The obscene Sgt. Rossi is a baker who stands before his adopted St. Croix ovens like a Vulcan, and his beautiful breadloaves stand as the alternative to death through the last violent scenes. He poses in his bakery "like some clown about to amaze the universe" (264).

So do all these artists. So de Vaca the cook is, says Alastair, "a very sensitive man with a *haute cuisine* in which he takes enormous pride; so proud is he of his art that he can't toss a salad unless he's stoned, can't look a potato in the eye unless he's falling drunk" (24). Clearboy the cowboy and Elk the Indian are actors in the American drama of cowboys and Indians (the European version was knights and Musselmen.) Elk improvises Indian dances and a bow and arrow, neither of which he is familiar with, for the edification of his captive audience. The other Americans are just as successful at portraying Indians when they have to dance naked and vulnerable past European eyes, after their clothes have been stolen by women who might be collaborators. As for Clearboy the laconic desert wrangler — he opines at one juncture that cowboying is not work. His suggestion is that it is rather fun, or a calling, that one feels about it as one feels about doing art, not for wages but as an unquestionable (a)vocation.

Among the inner circle of Americans there that leaves Captain Lionel Beckman. Beckman is, until late in the book, an atypical American. He is an art historian rather than an artist, an expert on European tradition, and a lover of objects and history. He received his wound on the roof of the first cathedral the D-Day invaders came to, trying to protect European architecture from U.S. bombers, from time and process. Since then he has been "at war with the United States," and spends his time lugging art treasures to the castle's wine cellar. He is portrayed throughout as the defender of art against arms, and in his sad frenzy about impending doom of the edifice, enjoys a moment of reflection for this lovely Eastlakian fantasy:

> How would it be if every twenty years the professional soldier was drafted into one of our professions, the arts? There would be a howling and gnashing of teeth, AWOLs and desertion, insubordination, mutiny, and rape of models. There would be suicide at the thought of having to write a poem. Some would be sent to music, some professional soldiers to the ballet, others to painting, some to sculpture. All would think they were going to hell. But they think we should take to the sordid and murderous job of soldiering with éclat. (330)

But Major Falconer, with the traditional comprehensive wisdom of the "Old Man," says to Beckman when the crucial decision has to be made: "'We're not playing art any more, Captain Beckman. Art is Dead'" (341). And in fact Beckman with his machine gun kills more Germans than do all the rest of the Americans combined. It is he who in his maddened condition most clearly makes the decision that artist is more important than art, and that making history is better than reading it. Eastlake, with the stones of the castle cascading, and the bodies of the soldiers bleeding, will not permit a one-sided feeling about the end of Beckman's thought or his life.

• • •

I dont know whether to call art the theme of the novel, or its subject, or a metaphor; but it is clearly a constant topic. All the characters comment about it. All the arts are introduced and burlesqued, and sometimes they offer painful creative alternatives to the destruction Eastlake will regret while he is detailing it.

Thérèse is first seen by Beckman and us on the third page of the text, among two Botticellis, a Delacroix, and three Fragonards; and on the last page the dying Alastair P. Benjamin tells the probably dead Thérèse that he can see "above the castle a flag painted there . . . Our flag painted there in the sky" (382). Love occurs in light transmitted through stained glass windows, and death happens in a shower of stained glass. Soldiers are often heard to quote old poetry that is mocked by their deadly situation, and obscenely though good-naturedly vilified by their fellows. To "keep the men occupied" (the kind of pun Eastlake uses throughout), they are ordered to compose and enact plays. Some are scatological, some fanciful. Beckman the art

historian creates an extravaganza of their actual situation. A chapter is
devoted to Beckman's disastrous lecture on the history of art, in which
he tells bored G.I.s that "The function of art is to disturb and to awake"
(148), a pretentious bit of academic twaddle in a place where distur-
bance and wakefulness are not in short supply. Music is heard
throughout the story, whether Thérèse's lute quieted by an airplane
engine, or the organ music pounded out by the dying Frank.

In ways too obvious to ignore, all the artists, and the horse-man Falconer, are projections of their author, who is by turns obscene and
academic, a New Mexico range-rider and a big-city esthete. But in
such a reflexive text one can expect the author's views on the nature of
art to be expressed most aptly by the out-of-time novelist Alastair P.
Benjamin. (One is tempted to call his writing not a line of development but an APB.) Whichever novelist speaks to us on page 101, he
reminds us of the anti-realist remarks of Thackeray in *Vanity Fair*:

> Being a writer, I can give all the good lines to myself. I can load
> the dice. I can make them all look bad. But this is not my intention.
> My purpose is madness. It's the only way you can tell what hap-
> pened in a war. By lying you can open the door a little crack on the
> truth, I lied when I told them I hated the army. I wanted them to feel
> at ease. Actually I like the army. It gives me a chance to write and
> smoke cigars. On the outside it's a jail. You go along step by step,
> but it's all arranged for you like a prison. The army, in spite of all
> the seeming orderliness, is chaos. All the precision is on the surface.
> The army is a giant freedom greater than any freedom if you go
> along with the surface nonsense. Yes, sir. No, sir. Right away, sir.
> Fuck you, sir. All on the polished surface. Underneath there is such
> madness it supplies the artist with the only refuge in the world.
> (101-102)

Whoever is speaking is offering advice on how to read *Castle Keep*.
Private Henry Three Ears of an Elk in his chapter offers a remark that
comes from the other direction to tell us something similar: "a lot of
strange things happen in war and by giving them a little twist, by making them absolutely true, you can make them funny" (67). In his harrassed lecture on art, Captain Beckman is tricked into stating a
ridiculous-sounding truth: "The painter heightens the perceptions of
reality by ignoring reality" (150). Eastlake the postmodernist is not
looking for our belief any more than tall-tale cowboy Aesop is, any
more than Lewis Carroll is.

There are several buildings in which the novel's action occurs, but
the most important number three: the church invaded by a huge tank,
the castle, and the latter's anti-type, the whorehouse named for (or
vice-versa) its proprietess, the Red Queen. In Eastlake's chain of

command, she outranks a major or a count. Her whorehouse can be entered by walking into a mirror rather than by seeing oneself reflected realistically in it. When one leaves one has not really escaped wonderland. During the scene in which the inexpert hunters on the island try to act natural in order to attract the inquisitive deer (described by de Vaca as "curiouser and curiouser"), Alastair P. Benjamin echoes Carroll's Alice when he says: "It's very difficult to behave naturally in the army. Maybe it's very difficult to behave naturally anyplace. Just try being ordered sometime to behave naturally and see what happens" (107).

The Red Queen herself, a pragmatic and friendly old doxie, a kind of phantom wife of the warrior Falconer in *his* crazy house, is life-affirming, the most level-headed figure in the novel. She is the only person in the region that one would never expect to say "Off with his head!" Rather, she always says, "Where do you come from, and where are you going?" Alastair P. Benjamin says she looks as if she were created by Goya, the anti-war painter (26).

Carroll's odd chessboard land is a sub-setting for all the adventures of Alice-stare Benjamin, as might be expected in a mad game of weapons, what the Countess calls "playing the war." The sanest or maddest pawns are the German prisoners who prefer to sit in their cellar prison and play chess when they are offered their freedom. My favourite touch is the figuring of Carroll's feckless but endearing White Knight, here accomplished with Major Falconer on his stallion, of course, but also travestied by the tank-stealing soldiers who are coated sequentially by bread flour, church plaster, and snow.

Chess is the European art of war, or its representation. Fiction is not.

• • •

I once heard *Castle Keep* described as a war novel. But why: because that is what pervades the scene and touches all the lives of its characters? Why not call it an art novel, or a love novel, or a work novel? In the 1960s most war novels were called anti-war novels, but there the basis for the classification switches from setting and incident to the author's attitude. At least here we can stay with the story, and call *Castle Keep* an anti-war novel. It is a novel about a large number of people trying to do something other than war, an absurd ambition near the Ardennes in 1944.

Before the German breakout in the Ardennes the castle appeared to be a refuge for these American casualties who no longer needed the hospital, or for whom there was no longer any room in the hospital. The Section 8 Evangelists in their swamp settlement have chosen camp-meeting U.S. Christianity over European war. Henri Tixier chooses collaboration over bulwark in order to defend his own line.

The German soldier on the other side of the bushes throws a flute rather than a grenade over to Frank and Amberjack.

If the war can be called reality, why not opt for fantasy, for fairytale, says the novelist Benjamin, twitting the vulgar Rossi: "'Doesn't it give everything another dimension? Doesn't everything seem to be once-upon-a-time? Can't you see it as once upon a time the American Army captured a castle and therein hangs this tale?'" (29). Alastair P. Benjamin is already looking forward to writing *Castle Keep*. But Rossi says no; his attempt to turn his back on war will come later when we find him obdurately fashioning the staff of life even while the gray uniforms of death are entering town.

The people of St. Croix, we are told, do not allow a periodical activity such as war to disrupt their continuous cultural activities, including lectures on Indo-European texts. Similarly, the whores at the Red Queen ply their ancient art, and for them the military advances and retreats act simply like the various tourist seasons to effect changes in their clientele. For them the castle is a place where a historical fantasy play is being performed — and they are not the audience.

Thérèse Tixier, the chatelaine of the castle, offers the naivete of her age and the wisdom of her position when she thinks of all the soldiers: "if you can get them lost creating something, then they don't have to kill" (343). So we see that it is no real paradox that she is so often naked in her bed or on the Prospero island with the warhorse Falconer. The Major believes in his role as combatant, but when he and the Countess are making love instead of war, he always thinks of it as "ending the war."

For the author, the alternative to war is this novel, both "a separate war" and a creation to replace the murdered art and men of World War II. "All else is the lies of history," says Alastair P. Benjamin in his introduction (23). If a town made by artists (25) can be deconstructed by artillery, a new city of words can be made from the human imagination; "If there is a future then the artist will make one." It may be, as Beckman says, that the old world survived because of the love affair between Christianity and art. Eastlake says that the American novelist has to build a new world out of love and an insane faith. It is stupid to try to rescue or capture American Christians in a fake Venetian gondola — better to head for Prospero's island on a craft of words.

So Eastlake's novel is largely dialogue, a war of words, fresh words that will not depend on a referential world to fix them. John Hawkes once said that his WWII fiction began when he saw an open book fluttering in the breeze as it lay in a street of a bombed-out German city. That kind of dislocation suggests that one cannot just write another platoon novel describing normal and representative people caught in an existential setting. One cannot just present the human window of history. One has to swallow history, perhaps, to absorb energy for the creation of fiction. Otherwise one is only applying a fresh exterior to the edifice of an old story. I take Count Henri's heraldic name, Maldorais, to mean "badly gilded."

Rather swallow the house of fiction. At the beginning of *Castle Keep* we see that the soldiers, most of them from the wide open world of the American southwest, are inside the castle (which means, etymologically, that they are "cut off"). By the end, as they all die in their roles as human artists, with the "drawn, death look" of saints, they have, like Alice, grown too large for keeping. The last words of any novel are, of course, the author's. Eastlake gives his to Alastair P. Benjamin: "We had the castle within us. We carried it away" (382).

1982

---

[1]His name resembles that of Alexander Bowman, the other young novelist, from *Go in Beauty* (1956). Alastair Benjamin is adopted by Sant Bowman after Sant kills Alastair's first father, in *The Bronc People* (1958).

• • •

WORKS CITED

Allen, Donald M. and Robert Creeley. Eds. *New American Story*. New York: Grove, 1965.

Eastlake, William. *Castle Keep*. New York: Simon and Schuster, 1965.

Williams, William Carlos. *Collected Early Poems*. New York: New Directions, 1951.

2

Three Ladies of Spirit in New England

The ladies are Anne Bradstreet, Emily Dickinson, and Denise Levertov. Why they should appear together in one essay is our business, but it is not necessarily clear at first sight. That they do appear together here is surely no more arbitrary than any other grouping of writers, be they even the Brontës. Anne Bradstreet and Denise Levertov share the experience of moving to the American northeast from England, and of being married. Anne Bradstreet and Emily Dickinson share the experience of living in Massachusetts, and of being studied in university courses on American literature. Emily Dickinson and Denise Levertov share the experiences of wonder in the natural world of the forest, and of making the stiff formalisms of poetry bend and fall before the personal voices of their lyricism. All superior poets experience deep insight into their worlds, and estrangement from their other worlds.

I feel that there is some purpose in looking at the poems of the three ladies (I hope that readers will have patience to see my usage of that term), the leading women poets of America in their respective times, and to see how each formed in verse her feelings and thoughts about things spiritual. Anne Bradstreet wrote in Puritan Massachusetts of the seventeenth century. Emily Dickinson wrote in Transcendental Massachusetts of the nineteenth century. Denise Levertov writes in New York and Maine, on the edges of New England of the twentieth century, in a time when American poets are suspicious of giving formal names to their beliefs. Levertov is now even hesitant to use her earlier description of her versification as "organic."

Anne Bradstreet's works are more interesting as records than as poems. In fact, it is questionable whether her verses would be read today if American professors were not so much interested in having a body of American literature that reaches as far back as possible. Canadian professors do that with material committed to ink in the nineteenth century.

However, it is fair to remember the nature of Anne Bradstreet's community, and the Puritans' attitude toward writing. The poem, they said, should provide pleasure, but a pleasure something like homely inspiration, the satisfaction of a job well done, an expression of the will of Calvin's God. The well-known conspiracy by Mrs Bradstreet's family and friends to have the poems published at the Sign of the Bible in London speaks for their approval of her piety and intelligence, for they would have had to ask themselves whether the poems would contribute to God-fearing moral industry of Puritan folk.

In that first book, *The Tenth Muse, lately sprung up in America* (1650), and in the additional poems added to the two later editions of her poems, there are indeed few lines in which Mrs Bradstreet does not mention her authoritarian God, however indirectly. In the prose pieces that accompany the poems she always declares her intent that her readers (in the first instance her children and grandchildren) may benefit in terms of strengthened piety, never delight.

So the poems are limited both in what they may say and in how they may say it. The touchstone of subject matter and vocabulary is Puritan dogma, largely the notion that the Bible is God's revealed word, and that images and arguments drawn from elsewhere are suspect (this despite the pagan title of the book). The verse forms, too, are no more venturesome than the Puritan ideal for style — that it should be plain, regulated, and without surprise. Surprise is the work of a dark and treacherous seducer. Prudish Americans learned to use the word to denote sexual success by males, human and livestock.

It is an understatement to say that the Tenth Muse wrote inside conventional frames. The very tight plan for her book, from the hymn-like stanzas of the short poems to the prescriptive historiography of the "Four Monarchies," makes for stilted expression; and as reasonable Ben Jonson has said not long before, that makes for stilted imaginings. Poets tend to construct their poems in ways that resemble their notions of the construction of the universe, while taking only such liberties as they see fit for the poem-maker in the cosmos, however ordered. The Puritan felt guilty about vanity, so he could not write in the Caroline fashion. In order to fit her plain arguments into a received form, Anne Bradstreet did violence to sentence rhythms and mangled more than the occasional word. This sort of thing was disliked by Victorian critics, and easily lumped by them altogether with Donne and other Metaphysicals of the seventeenth century under the name of Gongorism, or what eminent American critic Moses Coit Tyler called "lamentable rubbish."

But the Metaphysicals were in the business of giving testament to ecstacy. Anne Bradstreet's religious life hung more heavily on duties, piety, homely doings; not on speculation, nowhere near transcendence. Religious talk was likely to concentrate on the vanity of all wishes, on the shortness and unhappiness of life, and the humility and obedience needed to bear all that. For the Puritan, men were slaves of a God of their fancy. They lived in a kind of cheerful gloom.

Introducing the writing called "Religious Experiences," Mrs Bradstreet addresses her sons: "I have not studied in this you read to show my skill, but to declare the Truth — not to set forth myself, but the Glory of God" (4). Twentieth-century readers of Marxist and Feminist and Mattachine poetry will recognize the argument.

The intent of the "Religious Experiences" is, of course, that readers may benefit from their examples, whether of God's punishments or his benevolence; and to show the typical Puritan belief in the direct concern of God with the individual's punishment and reform. The usual signs of God's concern are illness and recovery. Anne Bradstreet suffered the smallpox at age sixteen, and that made her realize her vanity of the previous year. She confessed, rued, and was restored by God. A basic Puritan pattern is there set up. God is most presently realized with the nearness of woe, the fact that would cause other and later poets of spiritual bent to reject Puritanism, or try to.

A quick survey of the chronically ill Mrs Bradstreet's poems will show that a large number of them are in thanks for deliverance of herself and her family from sickness (she may have been persuaded by the fact that seven of her eight children grew to maturity, an unusually high ratio in Puritan New England), or self-assured consolation that God chose to receive unto him some other children in her less immediate family. One piece of intelligence she gave to her children was that she thanked God for covering all bets, granting some of her requests and setting her mind at ease about doing without the others.

The formula may be seen in the verses upon the burning of the Bradstreet house. It begins with the Puritan logic:

And, when I could no longer look,
I blest his Name that gave and took,
That layd my goods now in the dust:
Yea so it was, and so 'twas just.
It was his own: it was not mine;
Far be it that I should repine. (40)

Then it shows great feeling of personal loss as the poet lingers over lost comforts:

Here stood that Trunk, and there that chest;
There lay that store I counted best:
My pleasant things in ashes lye,
And them behold no more shall I.
Under thy roof no guest shall sit,
Nor at thy Table eat a bit. (41)

But it does that mainly to show how much a person must forego in laying up treasures in Heaven, as suggested from the Mount:

A Price so vast as is unknown,
Yet, by his Gift, is made thine own.
Ther's wealth enough, I need no more;
Farewell my Pelf, farewell my Store.
The world no longer let me Love,
My hope and Treasure lyes Above. (42)

It is the familiar pattern of temptation overcome. A similar thing happens during the few times that Mrs Bradstreet turns to nature. The poems begin to seem to adore nature, then are caught up short by the Puritan admonition against its hidden dangers. The attention then goes immediately to the stern Father who controls the sea and the land. Often it appears that Mrs Bradstreet exaggerates Satan's interest in her, in order to enforce the lesson her poetry should teach her children. In the "Religious Experiences" she maintains that she was troubled often by Satan and thoughts of atheism, but these writings are sermons to her flock, and Anne Bradstreet was thinking of her children's strength to forestall temptation.

I am not contending that Mrs Bradstreet was never tempted; just that her poems are not as heterodox as some late readers would wish them to be. Some readers have made much of her self-admitted questionings, such as the one about Roman Catholics:

When I have got over this Block, then have I another put in my way, That admit this be the true God whom we worship, and that be his word, yet why may not the Popish Religion be in the right? They have the same God, the same Christ, the same word: they only interpret it one way, we another. (9)

But these readers quote too little, not wishing to remember that this writing is a rigged dialectic, and that Anne Bradstreet sets up the questions to be knocked over by Puritan dogma:

This hath sometimes stuck with me, and more it would, but the vain fooleries that are in their Religion, together with their lying miracles and cruel persecutions of the Saints, which admit were they as they term them, yet not so to be dealt withall.

The consideration of these things and many the like would soon turn me to my own Religion again. (9)

Hers is a simplistic faith. One is either for or against her Lord, and a Puritan townsman or poet declared very clearly for the Lord all the time, so he would not be thought against Him.

Samuel E. Morison is one of those readers who want to see Mrs Bradstreet as a gentle rebel against the Puritan controls on thought and feeling. He feels that the fact that she was not at first writing for publication suggests that she was more personal, less doctrinaire, than most Puritan writers. He writes: "As I turn the pages of Anne Bradstreet's poems, and try to project myself into her life and time, I catch the merest hint of that elfin, almost *gamin* attitude of Emily Dickinson to God" (323). Perhaps Morison also catches a whiff of Mark Twain in Cotton Mather.

It is true that Mrs Bradstreet found herself able to praise Sidney's arcadian verse, but she also fancied a family tie between the poet and herself. It is true that she speaks often in her lines of sexual interests, over and again kissing God's rod, and once beginning a poem: "I had eight birds hatched in one nest," but such references, we must feel, are the Freudian revelations common to Puritan and puritanical writings. It is also true that a consistent theme in the poems is the warm love for her husband, but it never steps outside the Calvinist concept of marriage and duty. And it is true that in the dialectic of "The Flesh and the Spirit" we find not just personification to illustrate conventional Puritan war between the two parts of the human being, but actual dramatization of the poet's experience of her own inward struggle; but as in the poem on the burning house, the fight is fixed, the seducer is a sitting duck. Mrs Bradstreet offers very little romanticism or sentimentalism — her life is formed by the unquestioned will of God, to get on with the business of living in America. Any real comfort was to come in reading the Scriptures, "especially those places I thought most concerned my Condition" (4).

It is always possible that Mrs Bradstreet did write some romantic or sentimental or heterodoxical poetry. But we remember that her verses were preserved by her family, as too often happened in American literary history, and the Puritan family would likely suppress anything that seemed the littlest bit vain or heretical — to protect the reputation of the late poet, of course. (At least two hundred years later, Emily Dickinson's family concentrated on vulgarizing her rimes and punctuation, and seemed to leave her religious views alone.) In fact it is admitted by a note in the second edition of Mrs Bradstreet's poems, that some verses were left out of print.

But we may guess at the way Anne Bradstreet wanted to be remembered, if we read the gloomy and pious epitaph she wrote for her own mother:

Religious in all her words and wayes,
Preparing still for death, till end of dayes. (369)

The long posthumously-printed poem, "Contemplations," is by far her best writing, as it is not clogged by the cliches of excessive piety and the normal tortured phrases jammed into rime. Significantly,

though it is a pastoral religious poem, there is no personal supplication
or devotion to the Puritan God. It deals with the beauty of the Massachusetts countryside, and the frailty of all things beautiful and brave
in mortal earthly adventure. It is her *one* really good poem, and it is
least like most Puritan writing, the most like later pastoral American
verse.

Anne Bradstreet was the best published female poet in Massachusetts in the middle of the seventeenth century. We go to her not to
learn anything about poetry, but to learn something about the woman's
experience in the religious life of the Bay Colony. We learn something
about the way in which the human imagination was bound in Puritan
New England.

• • •

Turning to the poems of Emily Dickinson, we are likely to find as little
about received religious views of her time as the people of her time
found out about her. But she did exemplify one aspect of the American
nineteenth century's transcendentalism — she took personalism
further than did Emerson and even Thoreau, both in what she wrote in
her poems, and in the way she wrote them.

She was a young woman and a young poet during the United
States's great literary "coming of age," the time of the great books of
Emerson, Thoreau, Whitman, Poe and Melville. We know from her
biography and her letters that she was favourably impressed by Mr
Emerson and Mr Thoreau; but in things spiritual she seems to gather
up their thinking and add to it a fuller mysticism to go as far beyond
them as Melville and his voices of silence. Conrad Aiken, in his introduction to the Modern Library Dickinson, settled for speaking of her
"singular mixture of Puritan and free thinker" (xii). T.W. Higginson
early saw a quality more suggestive of William Blake than of anything
else; he saw flashes of wholly original insight in her work. Even now,
with our enormous weight of scholarship and critical theory, we sense
that Emily Dickinson, like Blake, was a prodigy, a human-poetic
anomaly.

Thoreau saw no feasible separation between living and writing, as
far as belief is involved, and in both living and writing, Emily Dickinson was the American extreme of individualism, of self-sufficiency.
She never married, and she became in her later correspondence quite
vain about her artistic role. We have something different from Anne
Bradstreet's duteous social commitment.

Not only did she spurn any demands made on her as a social
creature and as a versifier, but she also refused to accept the New England humble passivity before God. She called him the names of things
he has been made by men — "Burglar, banker, father." She had no

children to whom to leave her example. Anne Bradstreet, often playing the sacrificial mother, framed many of her writings as advice and example for her children, the scapegoats of any strict social control anywhere. Modern-day puritanical censors justify their controls in the name of the morals of their children. Emily Dickinson found a way to explode that deceit. In her poems she characteristically adopted the role of mischievous child of God the Father, hiding out in the upstairs bedroom instead of doing her chores. She was an indoors gamin. Her family tried to cover up for her by doing her chores after her death, revising her hundreds of poems for God the Editor.

Thomas H. Johnson eventually did one of the most graceful acts in the history of the American academy by making his effort to restore Emily Dickinson's real poems for her readers. The poems as read in the first published versions sound an originality or personal stance somewhat better than that of Mrs Bradstreet. But now, with the Dickinson rime and punctuation to observe, we may hear a voice re-creating discovery, and that is what her poems are:

Best Things dwell out of Sight.
The Pearl — the Just — Our Thought.
(# 998)

(Observe the ways that even that unremarkable line may be mortified by the intrusion of commas. Dickinson knew that sound does not echo sense, that it makes and delivers sense.)

In Anne Bradstreet's Puritan cosmology, all nature, the ground of the New World, the sea between worlds, the desires in the heart, all nature is dangerous. When her husband is to sail to England she prayed to God that he may not fall into the grasp of the sea, as she would pray to elude the grasp of the devil. But following German romanticism and American transcendentalism, Emily Dickinson is enchanted by nature and its mystical beauty, nature as a sign of the divine, if not something more immediate. So in the forest of words: Anne Bradstreet would never let argument and lesson become obscure; Emily Dickinson plucks on obscurity, to confuse, amuse, delight, and reveal part of the real. So in the face of death: death obsesses Dickinson as well as Bradstreet, but Miss Dickinson offered no panacea. No one was reading her poems (except God).

The Puritans, to be plain, thought they would apply man's reason to God's revelation, and in that way order social and spiritual life. It could, to an idealist, be exciting. But seventy-five years after the death of Jonathan Edwards, Emerson saw that the Puritan idea had become a dead dog, stiff in the American street. Emerson would not see the human sojourn on earth as a hopeless journey of the fallen who should spend it in supplication of God's mercy and expectation of the end.

The determinant for conduct of life on this world was to change from the obedience of the individual soul, to the vigour of the individual mind. The ordinary Puritan poet had private feelings but no real private expression. Private expression, or style, becomes apparent in the nineteenth century, minimally in Emerson, triumphantly in Walt Whitman and Emily Dickinson.

For Emily Dickinson that private expression, in poetry, was to a considerable extent a replacement for childhood's religion. She speaks of poetry, in one of her early adult letters, as "the lingering emblem of the Heaven I once dreamed" (Vol. I, 306). (Notice Emerson's language.) In fact, as she continued to write hundreds of poems in her sanctuary upstairs, they took on the appearance of daily devotionals, writing as religious activity; and the world of her dreams became for her an equivalent to what Anne Bradstreet was expecting in Heaven:

Some keep the Sabbath going to Church —
I keep it, staying at Home —
With a Bobolink for a Chorister —
And an Orchard, for a Dome —

Some keep the Sabbath in Surplice —
I just wear my Wings —
And instead of tolling the Bell, for Church,
Our little Sexton — sings.

God preaches, a noted Clergyman —
And the sermon is never long,
So instead of getting to Heaven, at last —
I'm going, all along.

(# 324)

That is an early poem, and not all that unconventional for a young idealist. Another poem, written a dozen years later (1873), shows how the poet came to worship at Home, how not to make eternal artefacts but poetry of process:

To pile like Thunder to its close
Then crumble grand away
While Everything created hid
This — would be Poetry —

Or Love — the two coeval come —
We both and neither prove —
Experience either and consume —
For None see God and live —

(# 1247)

All Emily Dickinson's poetry, when seen in the light of these quatrains, is seen to be religious, both by definition of function and understanding of subject materials.

In that religion, as in most poetry, there is a little paganism. Emily Dickinson's letters as well as her poetry show a young witch's fancy operating in the natural setting of the semi-rural woods. She goes for rides with the moon and makes the frosted grass into a poor old woman's gray hairs. The poet-advocate sees romantic phantoms and paradises in the woods, and the whole world as a dream. The gift God gives is a "glee intuitive," not a reason duteous. Nature in its beauty-mystery is the medium through which God or the Life Spirit touches men. For the Puritans the contact had been the Scriptures and personal fortunes, or too often, misfortunes. Following Thoreau, Dickinson was happy to replace thoughts of God's purpose with senses of his presence in all living and dying things, and the spooks that move among them.

All this indicates that Emily Dickinson arrived at a Keatsian feeling about the nature or merits of the spirit's home, eventual or otherwise. Something like paradise would engage the mind in a place of delight of or through the senses, to the highest possible degree. Dickinson seems to have moved as far as possible from the Puritan heritage, preferring delight in nature to prospects of the afterlife. "If God had been here this summer, and seen the things *I* have seen — I guess that He would think His Paradise superfluous," she said in one of her letters. And:

The Fact that Earth is Heaven —
Whether Heaven is Heaven or not
If not an Affidavit
Of that specific Spot
Not only must confirm us
That it is not for us
But that it would affront us
To dwell in such a place —

(# 1408)

In this heaven that is earth, awareness of immortality comes in flashes of exciting illumination:

The Soul's distinct connection
With immortality
Is best disclosed by Danger
Or quick Calamity —

As Lightning on a Landscape
Exhibits Sheets of Place —
Not yet suspected — but for Flash —

And Click — and Suddenness.

(# 974)

Spectral photograph. And the beauty seen is, as Blake said, Infinity:

Estranged from Beauty — none can be —
For Beauty is Infinity —
And power to be finite ceased
Before Identity was leased.

(# 1474)

In fact Dickinson went to the indicated conclusion reached by Blake, that the spirit of man or anything infinite is never at war with the flesh:

The Music in the Violin
Does not emerge alone
But Arm in Arm with Touch, yet Touch
Alone — is not a Tune —
The Spirit lurks within the Flesh
Like Tides within the Sea
That make the Water live, estranged
What would the Either be?

(# 1576)

But Emily Dickinson is a heretic, not an infidel. In the constructing of her poems she normally used Christian terms in her nature's metaphor; she is still looking for heaven, though not in the meeting house made of dead trees: "Some keep the Sabbath going to Church — / I keep it, staying at Home — " (# 324). She ejected Calvin, but not God; she chose to be nature's priestess, and let her poetry-making be her testament. She made an order something like Emerson's, but did not remove pain and evil from it, as he dreamed that he had done.

She often refers to God as Jehovah, the Old Testament Puritan wrathful God who was angry at men for being debased. But she does not petition him as the Puritans did. She enjoys the rhythm made by the name. She cajoles, flirts, calls him names. She acts, as I have said, like a child to a father, waiting to outgrow his authority. But one nowhere gets the sense that she is scoffing at his existence — rather that she would just rather be lost than plead to a heedless ear. She walks in the devil's traditional land, and finds it beautiful, pointing out, for image, the divinity in a beautiful snake. She knows what she is supposed to feel — on confronting this "fellow," she feels "zero at the bone." Then she counts.

In a very clear poem of 1862 (# 576) she tells of not being able any more to be a protected child of God as the Puritans would, that God is unknowable, his plan not revealed to any reader, though his beautiful works may be. God does not speak to man's slavish reason, but mumbles to his senses. His is "A Force illegible" (# 820). Jesus Christ, too, seems cut off from her, though she concedes that he is possibly active in the world, making earthquakes and storms, for instance (# 502).

John Keats wrote once to Fanny Brawne that he envied her her Christian God. When her corresponding friend, Dr J.G. Holland died, Emily Dickinson wrote to Mrs Holland: "I shall never forget the Doctor's prayer, my first morning with you — so simple, so believing. *That* God must be a friend — *that* was a different God — and I almost felt warmer myself, in the midst of a tie so sunshiny" (Vol.III, 713). But whereas such a death would bring versified Christian reassurance from Anne Bradstreet, it was only a part of the Mystery for Emily Dickinson. She would worship the Mystery, not the Word. Unlike the Puritan, she holds (see # 1126, 1651, 1668, 1700) that the Word, or words, cannot always be sought for reason's discovery of truth and ends. Magic and visions escape words.

But of course it is with words that she responds to the Mystery, or mysteries. That is the romantic's dilemma and strength. With the words, the church-disdaining child may regain a faith, altered and comfortable — re-arranged by herself, not prescribed by her family and town (1878):

To mend each tattered Faith
There is a needle fair
Though no appearance indicate —
'Tis threaded in the Air —

And though it do not wear
As if it never Tore
'Tis very comfortable indeed
And spacious as before —

• • •

In the two hundred years prior to the writings of Emily Dickinson there were no women poets of prominence in North America. Between the times of Dickinson and Denise Levertov there have been a few, though most of the great women Modernists wrote fiction. H.D. is the best female poet in the short history of the United States, but vital work came from Marianne Moore and Gertrude Stein. The highly overrated poems of Edna St Vincent Millay and Amy Lowell have long faded from sight except in the rose-tinted glasses of academe. Lorene Niedecker and Marya Zaturenska and Mina Loy helped to make the way for the many fine women poets working in the last part of the twentieth century.

But in the middle of the century, and into the sixties and seventies and eighties, Denise Levertov, who came to America in 1948, commands the grove. In what was to become known as the New American Poetry, she was only one among the leaders and champions, but her poetry, like Robert Creeley's, persuaded the new and common reader that it was accessible, while being at the same time in the post-Williams modern stream.

In addition, her work through the end of the sixties was all centered on the religious view, as I have described it in reference to Emily Dickinson's poetry. She extended the idea of poetry *as* religion, writing: "I believe poets are instruments on which the power of poetry plays" (1973, 3). But she says that poets are not thus passive; they are also makers, so that poetry comes from shared activities, human with hobgoblin, mind with mystery.

Denise Levertov's poetry shows a mind's activity far different from that of Anne Bradstreet. Mrs Bradstreet was surrounded by family and community thoroughly Puritan and powerful in the Puritan isolation of New England. Denise Levertov traces her descent on her mother's side from a Welsh tailor and mystic, Angel Jones of Mold, and on her father's side from Russian Hasids, the last of which, her father, experienced a conversion to Christianity and a desire to join Judaism with Christianity. That varied background or confusion may be taken as a representative determinant for the nature of American poetry in the last half-century, in which the names of the poets themselves indicate that spiritual considerations will be liberated from any mainline English Protestant domination: Levertov, Zukofsky, Ginsberg, Corso, Kerouac, Reznikoff, Rexroth, Oppenheimer, etc. There is something here that may be analogous to the situation in American music, where some of the names may be English, but the colours reflect truths that were not self-evident in eighteenth-century Massachusetts.

Denise Levertov is also confronted by the nature of spiritual unconsciousness among the whole community of people in the twentieth century — or rather, *we* are. *With eyes at the back of our heads* (1960) is the name of her first widely-distributed American book. The title poem is modernly elusive about the aims, chances, prospects, of mortal folk, but adds that elusiveness to Emily Dickinson's espousal of nature. In the poem we hear an interesting modern development of an image of clothing. Whereas Dickinson had imaged her faith as raiment torn and re-sewn to fit comfortably, Levertov writes of hers this way:

> The doors before us in a facade
> that perhaps has no house in back of it
> are too narrow, and one is set high

with no doorsill. The architect sees

the imperfect proposition and
turns eagerly to the knitter.
Set it to rights!
The knitter begins to knit.

For we want
to enter the house, if there is a house,
to pass through the doors at least
into whatever lies beyond them,

we want to enter the arms
of the knitted garment. As one
is re-formed, so the other,
in proportion.

(1958; 9, 2nd to 5th stanzas)

The eyes at the back of our head see that while we are walking toward the narrow, maybe deceiving doors of some indefinite palace before us, we are walking away from clear beauty and loveliness behind us on this earth.

A good portion of Denise Levertov's poetry is given to celebrating colours and flavours, the sustenance of the senses. One of her early books is called *O Taste and See*. She feels no guilt for these appetites, as Anne Bradstreet would, and she feels no need to be defiant about them, as Emily Dickinson would. The celebration of the senses is not done under the reproachful eyes of a paternal God. The modern poet does not often call God by that name except in irony or other rhetoric. Levertov seeks unstated spiritual significance in emotional honesty, precise attention to the natural, exercise of pity, mercy, peace and love. Not that God is dead, unless by that is meant that he no longer wears Talmudic and Mosaic disguises and fright-beards. Levertov uses images of nature's things to speak of more abstract feelings, but not with such consciously stated intentions as are to be found in Thoreau and Dickinson:

I like to find
what's not found
at once, but lies

within something of another nature,
in repose, distinct.

(from "Pleasures"; 1958, 17)

For Dickinson that would include the pearl, the just and our thought. Something like those might be the twentieth-century self:

. . . 'Are we
what we think we are or are we
what befalls us?'
(from "Seems Like We Must Be Somewhere Else"; 1958, 19)

That is going at least a step beyond Emily Dickinson's feeling that
God is knowable.

Many of Levertov's poems express and name the loneliness of the
human individual, so often a realization of modern writers that it may
be taken as true for us, at least to the extent that the Puritan world-
picture seemed true in Massachusetts in 1650. But it is that loneliness
that forces the imaginative act — the individual will fall down inside
herself or she will try to find some possible communion. In Levertov's
poem called "The Communion," the act is not made between a peti-
tioning servant and a superior god, but as "an accord" among things
living: the poet, a frog, a bowl of plums. In the act of communion the
poems tend to open moments outward, as do those of Emily Dickinson,
with the difference that here there is no talk of Eternity. Rather the
moment may teach the observation of the world as it is, even surprising, even irrational, even if the old values and meanings are violated:

The cat is eating the roses:
that's the way he is.
Don't stop him, don't stop
the world going round,
that's the way things are.
The third of May
was misty; fourth of May
who knows. Sweep
the rose-meat up, throw the bits
out in the rain.
He never eats
every crumb, says
the hearts are bitter.
That's the way he is, he knows
the world and the weather.
(from "The Sage"; 1958, 29)

One of Levertov's poems is called "Everything that Acts Is Actual"
(1986, 13). Her greatest debt as a poet is to William Carlos Williams,
the champion of what he called plain language and ordinary concrete
things as the materials of poetic reference. People have flapped down
on the kind of poem that results, saying that mundane materials do not
permit any flight of the imagination in the poem. But the eyes and the
other senses may be as close to the divine as any speculative brain, if

not closer. The shaman's sticks and bones are as much signs of human spiritual imagination as abstracted theology may be. The actual is in the act, and in the soul's music that emerges, as Wallace Stevens knew, plunking on his blue guitar. Denise Levertov may have had Blake's "Everything that is, is Holy" in mind when she made her above title, and the muse is watching not only at the inkwell:

The authentic! I said
rising from the toilet seat.
The radiator in rhythmic knockings
spoke of the rising steam.
The authentic, I said
breaking the handle of my hairbrush as I
brushed my hair in
rhythmic strokes: That's it,
that's joy, it's always
a recognition, the known
appearing fully itself, and
more itself than one knew.

(from "Matins"; 1983, 59)

With no expressed thoughts of afterlife, and hence no impulse to call this life either a vanity or a dream, the poet keeps eyes open and walks "deeper into Imagination's/ holy forest." She uses the Biblical image of Jacob's ladder as a title of a book (*The Jacob's Ladder*, 1961) and an image to show the nature of the imagination's ascent. Even the angels ascending and descending the steps depend on the mind that has reinvented that spiritual conveyance. The ladder is not "a radiant evanescence." Rather:

. . . a man climbing
must scrape his knees, and bring
the grip of his hands into play. The cut stone
consoles his groping feet. Wings brush past him.
The poem ascends.

(from "The Jacob's Ladder"; 1983, 39)

Continuing the movement of Emily Dickinson and Walt Whitman, Levertov denies all separation between the material and the divine.

Thus too the concept of death is here much different from the Puritan one. Death is not an alternative to humble life, nor is it a pathway to Eternal life. Life and death are inadequate and partial names for the process perceived in mercy and love:

The pastor
of grief and dreams

guides his flock towards
the next field

with all his care.
He has heard

the bell tolling
but the sheep

are hungry and need
the grass, today and

every day. Beautiful
his patience, his long

shadow, the rippling
sound of the flock moving

along the valley.

                              (from "A Cure of Souls"; 1964, 20)

Paradise is the endless movie of the world, perceived within the individual, perceived with a mystical metaphor in which the individual
apprehends that there is no final cosmic separation between the interior
history and the exterior forever.

In the seventies Levertov's poems tended more and more to express
popular protest against political targets, and to use the language of the
"movement," but in the mid-sixties they tended toward mystic-
romantic subjects, influenced as they were by the work of Robert Duncan (who was himself to turn to the Vietnam war and other political
issues); they may be said to be based on the early Hasidic sense of
mystery, and the devotion to "the actual." There is less direct talk to
the soul's experience than in the poems of the fifties, more making of
ritual, more arranging of the magic materials by one who functions as
a spell-binder or alchemist. Undescribed spirit-figures seem to be moving about the daily house and forest. In "The Prayer" the poet tells how
in Greece she prayed to Apollo, and was probably heard instead by the
goat-god.

The mysteries are never merely anterior to people. They are part of
them. In "Earth Psalm" the poet worships the mortal after saying that
she "could replace/ God for awhile" (1964, 80). (The fact that she puts
the word "replace" at the end of a very short line suggests the literal, as
re-place.) The mysteries are not something to be nervous of as they
were to the Puritan poet, just as reason is not now man's highest attri-
bute or gift on earth. Writing about H.D., Levertov mentioned an imaginative act that would have repelled Anne Bradstreet: "not to flood
darkness with light so that darkness is destroyed, but to *enter into*

darkness, mystery, so that it is experienced" (1973, 246). (Levertov's critical language is always simple.) Mrs Bradstreet would have called that a pagan step, over-asserting as always, but touching some truth. (I know that I sound unkind to Mrs Bradstreet, but think about the way her community would treat us.)

For Denise Levertov's views on reason and poetry, see her article, "An Approach to Public Poetry Listenings" (1981), in which she appeals against overrationalizing of an approach to or from poetry, and the damage done by the New Criticism and textbook poets. The poems in *The Jacob's Ladder* attend to diffuse divinity, seen in action between a human being (his body and all) and all things, none perfect, none theoretical. "Come into Animal Presence" is the title of one poem. The moon is not perfect and cold. It is flawed. The flawed human sight picks out intensities and unusual lights in the common world.

Emily Dickinson's image of a humanized God is remembered in Levertov's "absurd angel of happiness." In "The Novices" (from *O Taste and See*) the speaker watches communicants enter the woods to find a mystery which they neither fear nor try to explain. In this world the child and the primitive see eidetically, as Whitman would have it, without systems of abstract enquiry, and that is the way to encounter moments of illumination. While she is hosing dirt off an old brick wall (one with a history, presumably), Denise Levertov the poet sees an

    archetype
of the world always a step
beyond the world, that can't
be looked for, only
as the eye wanders,
found.
                (from "The Garden Wall"; 1964, 60)

:serendipity instead of doctrine. Or the doctrine of Duncan's wandering eye.

I think that what may have been coming clear is that Denise Levertov represents a twentieth-century American cosmos (poetical) quite different from those represented by the two earlier ladies. This is true not only because of her exotic origin. The American artist in the seventeenth century tended to draw from two places outside America — England and the Classical Mediterranean. The Transcendentalists added German romanticism, and flirted with their own peculiar notions of Brahmanism. After the middle of the twentieth century, through mass-print and super-electronics and jet-stream, the New England poet draws on eclectic nodes. Levertov's poems are made in Maine, but also in Russia, Mexico, Greece, and Egypt. She, like Bradstreet and Dickinson, has her important New England influences or associations — Charles Olson, Robert Creeley, John Weiners. But literary U.S. is no longer lodged in Boston, or Massachusetts, or New England. Those are unrealistic geographical and theological determinants. There is little doubt that Levertov's quasi-pantheism has some of its sources in New England thought (and she did use Emersonian language in calling her poetry organic), but it is part of an interior cosmos that also houses mysteries from further East. (See "A Ring of Changes" in *With eyes at the back of our heads.*) When Levertov says

> let the oranges
> ripen, ripen above you,
> you are living too, one
> among the dark multitude —
>
> (from "Under the Tree"; 1958, 46)

we hear of a process quite different from Anne Bradstreet's "Meditations," those rigid allegories. We see a development of poetic sensibilities, from simile to metaphor. Emily Dickinson made many poems in which she rides in angel-directed vehicles of the sky, and Levertov says:

> I in my balloon
> light where the wind
> permits a landing,
> in my own province
>
> (from "An Ignorant Person"; 1958, 50)

— which is not necessarily Manhattan or a county of Maine.

Religiously, if we are now using that term, Levertov seems to move especially to gods of fertility, of the natural cycle, of death as part and motive of life — the Mexican god of Spring, Xochipilli, for instance. One of the most frequently seen images in the Levertov poem is a seed. In the sixties the poems concentrated on the sexual nature of a woman in conjunction with the rest of the universe:

> The moon is a sow
> and grunts in my throat.
>
> (from "Song for Ishtar"; 1964, 3)

Levertov could take advantage of the twentieth-century consciousness of archetypes that speak from mortals' feelings about mysteries; not being constricted by Christian allegory, she could draw on mankind's whole world of magic and ritual. Modernism made it possible for the poet to choose her tradition. Levertov sees a snake, for instance, as good and beautiful, and not only with Emily Dickinson's pagan-like perversity. She hardly ever speaks of God, except as he appears in a painting, or folklore, as part of someone else's spiritual scene.

In her earliest poems she often spoke of poetry as religion in a Dickinsonian sense. "I long for poems of an inner harmony in utter contrast to the chaos in which they exist" (1973, 3), she once said. Her position there was similar to that of Yeats, whose eclectic spookiness always seemed to have a Christian base. In the poem "Art", she said that she wanted artists to work with "hard, strong materials," to strive for longevity in a flowing and malleable world (1973, 129) — art as alternative to the faults in the mortal world. Very Yeatsian.

But later, while not disposing of the concrete and homely materials, she came to a position in her "Three Meditations," a poem on the purpose of a poet, at which she agrees with the emblem she takes from a poem by Charles Olson:

> the only object is
> a man, carved
> out of himself, so wrought he
> fills his given space, makes
> traceries sufficient to
> others' needs
>
>   (here is
> social action, for the poet,
> anyway, his
> politics, his
> news)

         (from "Three Meditations"; 1986, 37)

That may correspond in her ethic to the Puritan idea of fulfilling God's purpose. Here we see something else about the poet's spiritual position in America. Anne Bradstreet was spokeswoman for the religious norms of her community. Emily Dickinson chose to worship God at home. In "The Grace-Note," Denise Levertov shows a Sabbath scene in which an underground artist stands in the shape of the Crucified while a cop frisks him, looking for a sacramental herb the community's lawmakers do not condone. "Nothing / is new to him and he is not afraid" (1983, 56).

There is a curious poem near the end of *O Taste and See* that seems to suggest the other two ladies I have been referring to. It is called "In Mind":

> There's in my mind a woman
> of innocence, unadorned but
>
> fair-featured, and smelling of

apples or grass. She wears

a utopian smock or shift, her hair
is light brown and smooth, and she

is kind and very clean without
ostentation —
                but she has
no imagination.
            And there's a
turbulent moon-ridden girl

or old woman, or both,
dressed in opals and rags, feathers

and torn taffeta,
who knows strange songs —

but she is not kind.

                (1964, 71)

In retaining the homely materials, and walking deep into the sacred forest of the imagination, Denise Levertov is looking for a way to be the complete woman and poet, spiritually whole in a world that looks fragmented in any intellectual or philosophical scan.

What seems to be required is an admission that there are no final certainties that remove the merest responsibility from the individual:

It could be what I'm waiting for is
not here at all.

            (from "Notes of a Scale"; 1958, 34)

— as well as complete self-reliance such as the Transcendentalists never dreamed was needed in a century nowhere as terrifying as this one. Twentieth-century man is irremediably alone in a world he cannot hope to justify, and his spiritual resources are called upon to make him brave with no theoretical rewards for bravery. Denise Levertov's model for that brave man or artist is the blind man of her poem, "A Solitude," which ends with these words:

and now he says he can find his way. He knows
where he is going, it is nowhere, it is filled
with presences. He says **I am.**

                (1986, 44)

Levertov would go on to give more and more of her attention to the politics of the peace-makers, but she would never give up the forest, and she would never give up the spirit that lives in it. Her 1984 volume was called *Oblique Prayers*. Its last section was called "Of God and of the Gods." The poet's sense of life's lightness and the endurance of the mystery are the frames and substance of a poem called "Of Being":

I know this happiness
is provisional:

the looming presences —
great suffering, great fear —

withdraw only
into peripheral vision:

but ineluctable this shimmering
of wind in the blue leaves:

this flood of stillness
widening the lake of sky:

this need to dance,
this need to kneel:
this mystery:
(1984, 86)

1967 [1987]

WORKS CITED

Bradstreet, Anne. *The Works of Anne Bradstreet in Prose and Verse.* Ed. John Harvard Ellis. Gloucester, Mass.: Peter Smith, 1962.

Morison, Samuel Eliot. *Builders of the Bay Colony.* Boston: Houghton Mifflin, 1964.

Dickinson, Emily. *Selected Poems.* With an Introduction by Conrad Aiken. New York: The Modern Library, 1924; 1948.

_____. *The Complete Poems of Emily Dickinson.* Ed. Thomas H. Johnson. Boston, Toronto: Little, Brown and Company, 1960. (The numbering of the poems in the text follows that of Johnson in the Harvard (variorum) edition.)

_____. *The Letters of Emily Dickinson.* Ed. by Thomas H. Johnson; associate ed. Theodora Ward. Cambridge, Mass.: The Belknap Press of Harvard UP, 1958.

Levertov, Denise. "A Testament and a Postscript 1959-1973." In *The Poet in the World.* New York: New Directions, 1973.

_____. *With eyes at the back of our heads.* New York: New Directions, 1960.

_____. *Selected Poems.* Newcastle upon Tyne: Bloodaxe Books, 1986.

_____. *Poems 1960-1967.* New York: New Directions, 1983.

_____. *O Taste and See*. New York: New Directions, 1964.

_____. *Light Up the Cave*. New York: New Directions, 1981.

_____. *Collected Earlier Poems 1940-1960*. New York: New Directions, 1979.

_____. *Oblique Prayers*. New York: New Directions, 1984.

Margaret, a Vision

a.

When a person was young he was interested in poetry, of course, but he never thought of the idea of a famous Canadian poet. Well, himself, yes, but that was a matter for the future, and then it wasnt Canadian. He didnt think of that. For the present, then, he never even thought of thinking of a Canadian poet any more than he thought of a Canadian astronaut.

If there was any Canadian poetry it was amateur stuff, stanzas made of convoluted attempts at imitating the debased English coinage, inverted syntax and gentlemanly rhymes, descriptions of landscapes that never existed in the New World. He was not sure there was such stuff but if there was any it would be such. Later he would find that he was right. In the first half of the twentieth century the Canadian poets followed the lead not of the Imagists but of the Georgians, those British gentlemen who chose to ignore the sound of pneumatic drills and pretend that Nature was still peacefully at hand and ready to enter the insides of any tender heart. Of course the images were not at hand, so one had to borrow their faint images from an earlier time, when Nature was an amazing discovery.

b.

So he got along with American poetry, in which the setting was not familiar to him, but at least it gave evidence of being familiar to the writer of the poems. That was until a friend brought some thin books back from Montreal and Toronto; there contact was made. Now he could believe that there were Canadian poets, real people writing in plain language, even though it was the language of Jewish and Polish and UEL eastern city-dwellers. What a pleasure to read a poem naming the streets of the city in which the recognized Habitants walked.

But once those poems were known, and imitated, their plainness seemed not enough. Yes, one could understand that the men who wrote them were making a point — and his own point — against the artificial formulas of sylvan glades and anapests propagated by their predecessors; but the plain language, fresh as it was, nourishing as it was, was transparent. It offered a picture of a world back there on the streets, and it offered a voice he wanted to hear. But it did not rime.

He was not looking for the old abab, or worse, the old abba. He was listening for the kind of musical self-absorption and release he could always hear in, say, Lester Young or H.D. The voice that belonged to the poem itself, it seemed, the sounds that felt around for spirit rather than earth and concrete. The concrete should be there, and the nouns in the poems should be "concrete," but they should delight more than your hands and feet.

He and his friends talked a lot about the senses, about poetry as a business of the senses rather than the discursive mind. But he had been a serious personal Christian a few years back, and had turned his Christianity into Poetry. He wanted to hear rime, even rhyme if it came to that. He knew that rime, as long as it was not plunked down doggedly at the end of eight syllables, spoke of mind delighted by spirit. For the poets who had stayed with his seriousness after their job was done on the survey courses he had sat through in college, rime had meant the enjoyment of God.

John Donne. William Blake. Gerard Manley Hopkins. William Butler Yeats. Emily Dickinson. Robert Duncan.

Thank you, he said to those eastern Canadian city poets. Do you have a poet who is in love with language because it is not just the poet saying it?

c.

They sent Margaret Avison.

Or rather it was not they who sent her; she came by way of the conventional literary apparatus, the University of Toronto, a few academic poet editors. But there she was. Her poems were filled with the streets and the street habitues to be found in the plain poets:

> The rushing river of cars
> makes you a stillness, a pivot, a heart-stopping
> blurt, in the sorrow
> of the last rubbydub swig, the searing, and
> stone-jar solitude lost, and yet,
> and still-wonder (for good now) and
> trembling:
> (from "July Man"; 1982, 116)

But (no, not but; rather and) the lines of her poems, often such portraits, sounded in his own mouth as he read, so that the city rubbydub was not only there but also here, significant not because of what the poem was saying about him, picked out from among the many, but because the music is intense, because it is filled with delight.

It is not too hard to sound filled with delight on patronizing a pretty flower or a lofty tree. If a bum on a street bench is part of the delight of a sequence of words, the reader knows that he is in the presence of spirit. He is not a point proven. He is a vision.

d.

When that first person got older and had been published a lot, and had landed some teaching jobs because of that, he was heard to say over and over that Margaret Avison is the best poet we have had. Whether he was asked or not, he said it everywhere.

She does not like to hear people say that.

Nowadays there are more and more poets in Canada who are very good. This would not have happened if it had not been for those plain poets in the cities back east.

But when it comes to making a canon, and wanting a figure to look to as the founder of excellence and the first name in the canon, the writers with regard for precise language and delight tend to agree. In fiction they tend to agree on Sheila Watson, and in poetry they tend to agree on Margaret Avison.

Sheila Watson and Margaret Avison do not like to hear people say that.

e.

People say why didnt Sheila Watson publish another novel. They say why hasnt Margaret Avison published more poetry.

Margaret Avison has a big pile of poetry that she has not published. Publishers across the country have written to ask her for a manuscript. This has been going on for years and years.

If she will not publish another book of poems, he said to himself and then to others, one will just have to go back and read the books we have. He often said that "Searching and Sounding" and the poem that rimes with it, "The Dumbfounding," are not likely to be equalled by any work that any poet will ever publish.

But a poet who wants to learn from someone in his own country, to learn how to make a poem as best he can, will be well advised to turn to those two poems. It is a great pleasure to be able to turn to a Canadian poet for such instruction and delight.

Thank you for sending her.

1986

WORKS CITED

Avison, Margaret. *Winter Sun / The Dumbfounding*. Toronto: McClelland & Stewart, 1982.

Language Women

Post-anecdotal Writing in Canada

1.

During the heyday of international Modernism women made up a significant part of the avant-garde, perhaps as much as half. That in itself was new, though we remember that in England at least three female novelists had leading roles in the great drama of the nineteenth century. In the early years of the twentieth century, though, there was a Virginia Woolf for every James Joyce. The languages of fiction and poetry were changed forever by the likes of Gertrude Stein, H.D., Dorothy Richardson, Marianne Moore, Djuna Barnes, and Mina Loy. These were not just prominent writers; these were artists who interrogated and overturned the architecture of literary convention as much as did T.S. Eliot and William Carlos Williams.

In Canada there wasnt any international Modernism. As Robert Kroetsch has pointed out, our writers went from late Victorian to postmodern without stopping to look around in between. The tradition of the avant-garde in Canada is pretty short. The canon of the avant-garde, if that is not an outrageous phrase, starts in the 1950s, with Sheila Watson's novel *The Double Hook* and Howard O'Hagan's rare novel *Tay John*, and remains pretty thin through the 1960s and the early 1970s, picking up Leonard Cohen's *Beautiful Losers* and some other lonely texts along the way. Only now in the 1980s does this marginal country begin to realize that the margin is the most fruitful place for postmodernism, generated as that is by an imagination that begins with decentering the text and the tradition.

There are probably two main reasons, among others, for our slow start, for the popularity of the conventional realist text during a time of Borges and Calvino and John Hawkes. In 1967 we celebrated the centenary of Confederation, the official version of nationhood. That birthday led to a government-encouraged flowering of nationalism, which in literature meant telling Our Story, and in criticism meant thematic studies, counting references to moose and snow. The most successful book was Margaret Atwood's *Survival*, which has sold 85,000 copies. Its whole argument about CanLit was based on references to the Canadian surround and psyche, with hardly a comment to be made about structure and language.

Which brings us to the second reason for representational realism and Canada's hermeticism. If you are going to have a decent avant-garde in this century you have to have women writers practising an affront to the manor house. Right after the surge of nationalism we experienced a surge of feminism, or more properly, women's consciousness-raising, with women's liberation as the goal. As in the late sixties the literati were looking for Our Story, so in the seventies, once again led by Ms Atwood, the women writers were intent on telling "Our Stories." They had forgotten, or perhaps never heard, Gertrude Stein's remark that there were already enough stories around, that what was required was some new writing.

In fact during the early seventies we began to see women's bookstores and women's studies programs appearing across the country, even in the Atlantic provinces. But in 1972 I was the only person at my university ever to have taught (and supervised special projects on) Stein and H.D. and Barnes, and Daphne Marlatt. I visited women's bookstores and found works by Sackville-West and Edith Wharton, but never a copy of *The Making of Americans* or *Palimpsest*.

To be sure, the late sixties and early seventies saw a remarkable rise to prominence of our women writers, especially among the fiction writers. In fact they took over. If we were going to be noticed outside the country it would be because of the books of Atwood, Margaret Laurence, Alice Munro and Mavis Gallant. The latter two were part of the stable at *The New Yorker*, after all. Inside the country the remainder of our literary space (reviews, radio, special issue of journals, etc.) was filled by Marian Engel, Audrey Thomas, Constance Beresford-Howe and Dorothy Livesay. Every six months there would appear a first book of short stories written by a not-necessarily-young woman who would be hailed on dust jacket and in newspaper notice as the new Alice Munro.

What were these women writing for us? They were telling the story of a teenage girl growing up sensitive and repressed, usually in a semi-rural climate, perhaps marrying unsatisfactorily and learning to speak of the world with irony. In other words, the same story that Stein had read often, the story told by the designated writers from all the other identifiable groups we have seen in North America — midwestern youths, New York Jews, Blacks, homosexuals.

With "Our Stories" to be told, there was no room for fooling around with language; the content would speak for itself. Something like this was happening in the U.S. and Britain and Australia too, anywhere that the male population could be seen to be significantly better off than men and women in the third world. In Canada the women were getting their stories told, and the men were heading for poetry and the small literary presses. People in the book trade started, ironically, to call

Margaret Laurence the Mother Of Us All, and as far as official CanLit was concerned our book world was a matriarchy. Robert Kroetsch wrote a novel narrated by a woman. Matt Cohen stopped writing experimental fiction and began a series of realist family novels. The children of European immigrants started telling *their* story, in detailed referential prose and verse.

The refraining from writing as writing was a source of despair for those few critics who saw more sociology than literature in thematic criticism, and the fiction or drama or poetry that seemed to be written with thematic criticism in mind. Here is what those critics, and some of the readers, could hope for: that the writers would get tired of the history made popular by the events of 1967, or become hostile toward it; and that some women would decide that their story had been told as much as the standard (and let us say patriarchal) forms could tell it.

In recent times it looks as if their hopes may be realized. Canadian novelists are finding reasons to deconstruct history and thus invent their own version of the post-colonial postmodern. See the fictions of Kroetsch, Michael Ondaatje, Jack Hodgins, etc. And a growing wave of not-necessarily-young women, led by poets who sometimes write fictions, are saying that they can do something to or without history, even that ubiquitous Herstory.

2.

It is no wonder that the most respected voice of the female avant-garde is Nicole Brossard. She has grown up on some margins, and sought out as many others as she could find. She is, not only as a person but always as a writer, a woman, a French-speaking Quebecker (who sometimes uses English titles for her books), a lesbian, a single parent, and a poststructuralist. Thus she knows that she needs language to save herself from disappearing entirely, and that she must question every syllable and every grapheme of any language anyone is prompted to offer her. Her books are not stories or poems, but texts, or textes, and texture, not picture, is her métier. Realism, in the sense that one tries to recount a given reality, is never in the question. No mining of one's life for narrative resources.

Brossard edited an anthology called *les stratégies du réel* (1979), which was her first significant gesture to English-speaking Canada, a book in both Canadian languages, filled with avant-garde Quebec writing. It was co-published by her press, La Nouvelle Barre du Jour, and the Coach House Press, the most important publisher of postmodern writing in English Canada.

For Nicole Brossard the text is always in the hands of the reader. It is filled with gaps, white spaces. Her first collected poems were called *Le centre blanc* (1970). If for the architectural novelists such as Henry

James and his followers the long fiction was erectile, for Brossard it is textile. Text means something woven, something the abandoned and thus freed Penelope can do. Brossard's sentences and lines are complicated with the kind of knots heroic Odysseus lived his story to escape. Brossard's reader is not to be persuaded, not impressed with the story of some narrator's youth; she is invited to contribute to the text, to write in the white, to prolong the fiction, to defer an ending. "Prolong fiction, *in reality,* I look at things straight in the eye," Brossard says in a piece called "The Face She Makes" (1978, 41).

Ernest Hemingway once said that he was not saddened by tragedy because he knew that all our stories end with death. He was the master of the fictional ending, of closure. He wrote the last page of *A Farewell to Arms* forty-three times. Brossard is a Wittgensteinian. She knows that only games truly end, some after an endgame. But the contestant's favourite word is "another?"

Here are the last two sections of Brossard's recursive fiction *A Book* (1970) — note that she stops before reaching the number 100:

98

The words are yours.

99

The game is over. The book too. The manuscript is no more. O.R., Dominique, Mathieu, Dominique C. and Henri continue on. Time passes slowly, so slowly. Someone is reading. And gently closes the object.

If that "someone" is Brossard the "object" is a manuscript. If that someone is the reader the object is a book, but not *A Book,* because while a book is now closed, *A Book* is part of a new combination of which the reader is another part. For the person of whom the reader is a part, *A Book* can now be experienced as integral subjectivity. The ostensibly male reader becomes aware of his bisexuality because of his, not just the book's, intertextuality.

This is not a case, as with a referential story, of "identifying" with a "character." In Brossard's writings there is a good deal of confusion between characters and something the words call "the text." In a sex scene Brossard is likely, as she does in *French Kiss* (1974), to advise: "unbutton the text and prod it to get rid of inhibitions in a narrator who changes them to make them fit a personal desire for prolonging pleasure. . . ." (65).

In reading the texts of Nicole Brossard the reader is always feeling insecure because the referent floats away, often beyond her peripheral vision; but the reader is also feeling welcome, a sister at least, as if she is expected to join in the production, the composition. And why not? "we learn to read together after all," says the text of *Turn of a Pang*

(1976, 50).

The writers of Quebec, their land surrounded by a continent of English-speakers, know that it is in language that they will find their difference. The women writers of Quebec know that even that language, while it was created by women, was arranged in an authorized syntax by men. To find *their* difference the Quebec women, having no other written language, had to investigate the possibility of a syntax, of a *number* of syntaxes, of syntaxonomies. Nicole Brossard is the most prominent of those Quebecoises, but she is a sister, a supporter of many others, including Louky Bersianik, France Théoret, Danielle Fournier, Madeleine Gagnon, Yolande Villemaire, and the bilingual Montreal writer, Gail Scott.

3.

I mentioned that Nicole Brossard reached out to English Canada in 1979. It is curious, and gratifying, that when writing becomes reflexive and the writers theoretical about their language, writers begin to meet across linguistic "barriers." Notoriously in Canada, our two literatures have tended to be parallel rather than intertextual. Nowhere is this more true than during a time of anecdotal realism, especially when it is related to nationalism. Our Story is no more than "their story." But once a woman begins to interrogate the conventions of the language and literature bequeathed to her by her patriarchs, she has something in common with the other woman who is interrogating "hers." They have, perhaps, a communolect.

Nowadays there is some mutual curiosity being expressed between male writers of Quebec and English Canada; but it is nowhere near as significant as the exchanges between the not-necessarily-young women writers. A great deal of their mutuality is fostered by the pancontinental *Women and Words/Les Femmes et Les Mots*, a 1980s organization that manifests its power and potential in national conferences, anthologies, and regional activities. Nowhere is the union seen more hopefully than in the collaboration between Nicole Brossard and Daphne Marlatt.

Daphne Marlatt, like Brossard, is a writer who has always shown no easy acceptance of the boundary between verse and prose. She is the first woman who comes to mind when one is asked to think about the avant-garde in English Canadian writing. Like Brossard she is the mother of one child, and is among other things a lesbian writer. She was, at the beginning of her career in the sixties, the lone female voice among the *Tish* poets of Vancouver, the language-centered avantgardists to whom the origin of the postmodern in Canadian poetry is usually traced. She was involved in difference a decade earlier than that, when as a girl she moved from the Malay Peninsula to the west coast of Canada.

From the beginning of her career Marlatt's texts have been what we
have come to call writerly rather than readerly. They have also been
characterized by their recursiveness. The prose-poetry of her most
famous book, *Steveston* (1974), does not labour to describe that
Japanese-Canadian fishing town at the mouth of the great Fraser River.
It resembles the flowing and tide-reversed water the community lives
on, as in this paragraph from "Sun & Moon thru the Japanese
Fishermen's Hospital (1898-1942)":

> We've come to where, what, changes at the heart: this General
> Ward, white a, widow's mouth (sea glinting just offshore), a
> mother's hole? We've come to generations, generation, Steveston,
> at the heart: our death is gathering (salmon) just offshore, as,
> back there in this ghostly place we have (somehow) entered (where?)
> you turn & rise, gently, into me.
> (1984, 74)

A story, a work of descriptive realism, says: there, that's over, and
now you have this book instead; the young sensitive girl grew up and
died into authorhood, and now when you read you collaborate in the
death of the author so that the book's story can live. The characters in
a story by Jane Rule should "come to life," and when they do they live
in a world that is a "mirror" held up to the world. You cannot look at
both in the same glance.

But a mirror can show only a world already in place. A photograph
mirrors a place already gone. Writing such as that of Daphne Marlatt's
is not interested in replacement. Neither is it interested in detachment,
the favoured attitude of the realist. It desires and hungers and feeds. It
is made by a writer who wants to be in it and to have it in her (a fish
drinking). In a little piece about *Steveston*, Marlatt wrote: "The line
had to do with taking a deep breath — deep enough to in-spire a world,
that is, giving back out what I took in." Not to tell Our Story, or her
story, or a story. "In the deepest sense of it I wrote to be, I wrote for
Steveston to be, here now & myself here now in it. The world I was
writing was & is a world I in the company of everyone could continue
to live in: creation, goes on being created as writing enacts it" (1979,
316).

The world going out again, after being inside a woman's body, goes
out in the form of warm breath made into words. The body is female,
and the words are problematizing: the woman speaking senses that the
words are "normally" ordered into or by male taxonomy and topology.

The writing of Margaret Atwood never considers this problem. Her
style is characterized by detached wit, ironic scorn, epigrammatic
comment that is generally thought to be distinctive of the masculine

temperament in discourse. Atwood practises feminist equivalence rather than feminist difference. Her approach to feminist writing is to appropriate the patriarchal forms. Marlatt looks for difference, but she is not entirely recusant. Like Brossard, she knows that she has to use the given language, and that given, that she has to look for its unstable parts, for the crannies, where the female image shows, for the spaces that have not been filled and overwritten. In *How Hug a Stone* (1983) she speaks of the search for a way to redeem "ourselves, our 'selves' our inheritance of words. wanting to make us new again: to speak what isn't spoken, even with the old words."

The book's narrative is the search for the origin of motherness, told by a mother going to England to find her own mother's ghost, to look among ruins of stone and runes of the Mother tongue for a living source, not something simply defined as the matrix of a murdered god. She comes to this paragraph, which follows immediately on the passage cited above:

> although there are stories about her, versions
> of history that are versions of her, & though
> she comes in many guises she is not a
> person, she is what we come through to
> & what we come out of, ground & source.
> the space after the colon, the pause (between
> the words) of all possible relation. (73)

Yeats had said: "All imaginable relations may arise between a man and his God" (*A Vision*). The erectile verb there probably distinguishes old father Yeats's intent from Marlatt's. Yeats saw ghosts bringing him images for his language. For Marlatt the language is the body of the goddess; or rather the absences presented by the language are.

Over the past few decades we have been scorned by writers and readers who do not like to hear poems talking about the language. Their notion is that language is a device used to speak about reality, a code for reference, even a tool with which to exert control. It is to be tested against the things in the real world, otherwise nameless. It should guide us to them and then disappear. But language is the world in which a writer such as Daphne Marlatt, or anyone, lives. We learned to read together, after all, as soon as we saw our mother smile. Someone had to teach us to learn separateness from the world; to erect an I.

In the past few years we have been fortunate to hear Nicole Brossard and Daphne Marlatt reading together. They have been collaborating in the Feminine, translating and traducing from the original French and English. Not filling the gap, but prolonging it, making a we of *oui*. Or as Marlatt wrote it back in *Steveston*, "ɇyes" (1974, 51).

4.

A poet new in the eighties, Lola Lemire Tostevin, has been doing such collaboration herself. Brought up among French-Canadian families in an English-Canadian environment, she developed not so much on a margin as between overlapping margins. Her titles are *Color of Her Speech* (1982), *Gyno-Text* (1983) and *Double Standards* (1985). The poems are made of both languages (with their difference in gendering gestures) and woven of interlinguistic puns, a great advantage to the recursive attention:

a
different
tongue
to
pen
a
trait

le
trait
d'union

(1983, n.p.)

A trade union places a good check on man-age-meant, one is invited to say, for instance; so that tradition must be a history of invention, not an inpenetrable canon.

So you see, there is still reference here, but it is reference first to other words, and then to whatever is called up from the remainder of the world. One might argue that such language-centered poetry calls up much more "content" than does anecdotal poetry, because it touches first on so many suggested (and supplied by the composing reader) signifiers.

• • •

Easy-to-read middlebrow poetry is not going away. There are enough newspaper reviewers, ambitious small presses, and impressionable school teachers around to keep anecdotal poetry and mimetic fiction in production. New versions of Our Story keep showing up — in Canada lately we have had surges of "work" poetry and immigrant anthologies. Simplistic responses to women's issues have inflated and hurried the reputations of numerous female poets with lines to lay down about growing up on the farm or being the uprooted daughter in an Italo-Canadian family.

But the language women are showing up more and more. The fresh critics coming out of university graduate schools with their worn books by Kristeva, Irigaray and Cixous (and Bahktin, Derrida and Lyotard) are predominantly women. More than half of the generative post-thematic criticism in the country is already being produced by women, from inside and outside the universities. The poets first, and then the fiction writers, such as Gail Scott and Paulette Jiles, are declaring their difference in practice, not only in experience.

The anecdotal writers repeat an error pointed out by William Carlos Williams in 1948. He said that too many post-Einstein poets tried to describe a relativistic world and universe by the means of Euclidean-metered verse. Writers such as Brossard and Marlatt say that they cannot truly and fully speak of their experiential difference in a practice that is borrowed from stable Apollonian poetics. Nor can they rely on some kind of noetic mining of their subjective resources. They understand Julia Kristeva's picture of the relationship among language, text and writer: "In calling the text a practice we must not forget that it is a new practice, radically different from the mechanistic practice of a null and void, atomistic subject who refuses to acknowledge that he is a subject of language" (1984, 210).

There is a heartening number of newer not-necessarily-young poets in Canada, both women and men, who understand that relationship. Diana Hartog is the author of two books of poetry, the more recent one called *Candy from Strangers* (1986). Here is a little piece she calls "Doing Time":

The Chambered Nautilus shimmers platinum on the sill, its
glorious shoulders hunched. The shell's chambers revolve on an
innermost room — reached through a tiny crawl-space, an addition to the addition built last spring. Yet no debris has been left
by workmen, no sawdust or nuggets of molten lead. The ceiling is low and vaulted, a creamy porcelain rubbed smooth by
the inmate's habit of rocking back and forth. Crouched, he
presses his face to his hands, as if meaning to offer his head — So
heavy! — to the first person who knocks. It's here the dead water
is stored, later to be jettisoned by the shell to propel itself, *in
extremis*, in the mode that Art Pepper improvised on the sax: his
features raw, ecstatic, as he blew and threw the last facts known
to him away. (28)

Art Pepper there, far from stasis, in-spires the world, perhaps, in the sense that Daphne Marlatt suggested, not imposing his subjectivity on the referent, but blowing out what came in, and giving himself up in a hoped but unplanned moment, met with skill.

I will leave this little tentative survey with a quotation from Sharon Thesen, the west-coast composer of three books of poetry in the eighties. Thesen's verse is suffused with desire (a word that looks as if it should implicate the disappearance of the patriarch); it names, while failing to embrace, the "objects" of the erotic surround. And it admits regret for all those emoluments that women muses and women poetesses were persuaded to believe in; it admits them *while* refusing them. This little poem from *Holding the Pose* (1983) might make a nice emblem for a collection of contemporary women writers in Canada:

PRAXIS

Unable to imagine a future,
imagine a future better
than now, us creatures
weeping *in the abattoir*
only make noise & do
not transform a single fact.
So stop crying. Get up. Go out. Leap
the mossy garden wall
the steel fence or whatever
the case may be & crash
through painted arcadias,
fragments of bliss & roses
decorating your fists. (26)

1987

WORKS CITED

Brossard, Nicole. "The Face She Makes." Trans. Josee M. LeBlond. *Room of One's Own*, IV, 1-2 (1978): 39-43.

_____. *A Book*. Trans. by Larry Shouldice. Toronto: Coach House, 1976.

_____. *French Kiss*. Trans. by Patricia Claxton. Toronto: Coach House, 1986.

_____. *Turn of a Pang*. Trans. by Patricia Claxton. Toronto: Coach House, 1976.

Hartog, Diana. *Candy from Strangers*. Toronto: Coach House, 1986.

Kristeva, Julia. *Revolution in Poetic Language*. Trans. by Margaret Waller. With an Introduction by Leon S. Roudiez. New York: Columbia UP, 1984.

Lemire Tostevin, Lola. *Color of Her Speech*. Toronto: Coach House, 1982.

_____. *Gyno-Text*. Toronto: Underwhich, 1983.

_____. *Double Standards*. Edmonton: Longspoon, 1985.

Marlatt, Daphne. *Steveston*. Vancouver: Talonbooks, 1974.

_____. *Steveston*. Edmonton: Longspoon, 1984.

_____. "Long as in Time? Steveston." *The Long Poem Anthology*. Ed. by Michael Ondaatje. Toronto: Coach House, 1979.

_____. *How Hug a Stone*. Winnipeg: Turnstone, 1983.

Thesen, Sharon. *Holding the Pose*. Toronto: Coach House, 1983.

Munchmeyer and the Marys

I have always been more interested in Audrey Thomas's long fictions than in her short stories. Like Alice Munro and Margaret Atwood, she is a master of the modern short story, and like them she leaves a reader satisfied that the craft was water-tight and the trip both enjoyable and enlightening. By contrast her novels and novellas give the passenger a feeling of insecurity. Are there serious holes in the hull? Does the steersman know what he's doing? Are we lost?

I like Audrey Thomas's stories more than I like her long fictions, but I am more interested in the long fictions.

The most daring of her long fictions is *Blown Figures*, a radical rewriting of *Mrs. Blood*, itself an experiment in the use of a bifurcated narrator. In *Blown Figures* narration is replaced, its space usurped by a continuous collage of found information, visual fragments and overheard speech. If narration is what is made out of what the teller knows, and the reader is the one being given the knowledge, how can one have narration if it is the task of the reader to assemble rather than decode a text?

Margaret Atwood is a writer who does the expected, usually, and the sensible: that is, her novels are conventional in structure and quickly comfortable in form. When she wants to experiment with strange modes of address she does it in very short pieces such as those to be found in *Murder in the Dark*.

But Audrey Thomas always treats a story as something to tell, and a novel as something to make. That, too, makes sense. Not all her book-length works are unorthodox. *Songs My Mother Taught Me*, with its nostalgia and first-person recuperation of family life, is like one of Thomas's stories grown too long for a collection. But even *Munchmeyer* and *Prospero on the Island*, two long stories published together as a 150-page book, are odd enough in concept and execution to charm a decent reader and amuse a fellow writer.

• • •

Munchmeyer is a mock-Dantean tryptich told from a variety of points of view, about an aging English graduate student who becomes bored with his family and seeks an escape, hoping to find an environment in which he can become a serious fiction writer. *Prospero on the Island* is the purported diary of an ex-graduate student who has been given a temporary escape from her family, and is learning to live on an island while she works to make herself believe in herself as a serious writer of fiction. The book she is writing is *Munchmeyer*. But there is at least the possibility that the book that Munchmeyer is writing is *Munchmeyer*.

"I had more fun writing that book than any other book I've ever written," said Audrey Thomas in a discussion with me (26). *Munchmeyer* was fun because its author could exaggerate, invent, outrageously spoof Dante's structure, make a fool of her male character, let him make a fool of himself. The scary scenes are scary as a fright movie is, the audience trembling half from fear and half from laughter. The essential solemnity of mimetic realism is what we are taking a holiday from.

• • •

Thomas prefaces Munchmeyer's story with a quotation from the beginning of Dante's fifth canto in *The Inferno*. That is where one might find the carnal, those who abandoned the good light of reason and gave way to their carnal passions. Yet when Munchmeyer builds himself a writing room in his basement, it is to escape from his wife, who would rather couple than burn, rather rut than think. It is not that he misprizes the odd slap and tickle. It is just that he has always pictured himself as a career fiction writer, and domesticity is not part of that scenario.

His wife Martha, named by Thomas (or Munchmeyer) after the woman chastised by Jesus for overvaluing housework, is continually knitting sweaters, fatefully producing texts in which to swaddle her husband and three children. Munchmeyer, meanwhile, is a constipated author with a lot of excuses for his writer's block.

In his basement, hiding from the "Brobdingnagian" upstairs, he decides to write a diary, or a novel disguised as a diary, or a diary that he hopes will become a novel. Audrey Thomas has him start it on April Fool's Day, and put a date to only the first four entries. The rest is composed in short but undated entries. The first of these starts with interesting duplicity:

> And I write this as though it were a novel, in which I play the role of narrator, (*a*) because Martha thinks I'm writing a novel down here in my cellar, and thus it's easier not to make a slip; but (*b*) — and really what is most important — diaries scare me. From myself to myself — a kind of schizoid thing. (5)

Thomas is, I think, here having a well-earned laugh about the question that always comes up in discussion of her work — whether it is invented or "merely" transcribed from life.

Perhaps Munchmeyer's book is a diary, but if it is, it is the daybook of a dreamer. He depicts himself as an habitual fantasier of his own life, usually placing himself in standard old movie situations. In fact in the first entry of his diary he is a condemned man in his cell, tough-guying his interview with the death-house priest. Thus when he follows that entry with another written the same April 1, about his job, house, and marriage, the reader might be disposed to treating it too as fancy. The end of his book is also made of alternative scenes; and in the above-mentioned discussion the author said that as far as the reader is concerned "they're both fantasies."

To confuse matters more, in a passage in which he imagines someone's finding his diary, Munchmeyer says that he has disguised it as a novel in order to evade responsibility for the antisocial material. But that is a confession that any reader will find, and distrust. Fearful of public exposure, one does not (admit that he will) disguise the private as public writing. It is not a wad of purloined letters. Where is the "real" Munchmeyer? The book is fun to read, too, Thomas.

● ● ●

All graduate students who are becoming English professors are also trying to write novels, or to become novelists. Many of them fill their writings with allusions to the literature that professors have to teach and students have to study. Audrey Thomas did, and Munchmeyer does. Finding allusions to Dante and Heraclitus in the works of Eliot is part of being a graduate student. The graduate student then drops allusions to Dante and Heraclitus and Eliot into his writing and his life. Just about the time that the evening is stretched out against the sky like a patient etherized on a table, Munchmeyer finds the way down to his favourite beach and glimpses Beatrice.

She is a young hippie girl who comes by with lover and flute player, and gives Munchmeyer the usual drug-and-fashion-induced smile of the sixties counter-culture. Munchmeyer dubs her his Miracle Girl, and enrols her in his fantasies, as the ideal of freedom to counter Martha the reality principle. A little while later he allows a drifting party girl to substitute for his Beatrice, but cannot stay interested in her availability except as the quality of an idle fantasy figure.

Munchmeyer the cynic sees his marriage as his hell, but probably also intuits that his cynical lacklustre escapism provides for a hellish boredom in a hastily conceived personal comedy. Once with his hippie friend, tiresomely named Diana, he finds a coffin on the beach. "'I wonder if you can screw in a coffin?'" (21) says Diana. Realizing that that is what he has been doing at home, Munchmeyer spends the night in it, his fine and private place. "I see everything now as sign or symbol" (22), he confesses, but he is not a Malcolm Lowry character, only an academic gloss on one. He has worked easily to make his reader dismiss him as just another Munchmeyer.

Yet Part 1 ends as he comes back to his house after sending his family tearfully off for a visit to relatives in England. He sees a "kid-sized turd floating around" in the toilet bowl (25), and weeps until he has to sit weeping on the floor. No fun.

· · ·

According to the structure of this unhypostatic comedy, Part 2 should portray a purgatory, at least a purgation of a more-than-kid-sized turd. It begins after drunken Munchmeyer gives away his manuscript in a bar, walks back to a Kitsilano park, and loses consciousness. When he wakes he finds that he has lost his wallet, including all his identification, and his glasses, without which his world is little more than a coloured blur.

What follows is a hallucinatory series of paranoic adventures, in which the victim Munchmeyer resembles a mock-Lowry hero who has stumbled onto a Samuel Beckett set: "With his loss in vision he seemed to have suffered a loss in hearing, in locomotion — a general debilitation" (29). He feels like "an old man hunched against the wind" (29).

A young red-haired man with a mutilated hand appears, to taunt him, pretend to help him, and then lead him across town, into the grip of a dark man and a silent woman, to frighten him, to chase him around an empty Sunday department store in which the escalators are still running, the way up and the way down. The first young man has Audrey Thomas's red hair, and is a funny and scary Virgil for this trip, possibly psychedelic, as they used to say. A bad trip that is a lot more fun to read about than it would be to experience, and a lot more fun to read than the minutely-detailed ordinary.

Along the way, his myopic eyes find the name of the park erased. When he smells a bakery, his weird guide refutes his senses, and later accuses him of trying to enrol him in his fantasies. The red-haired man, who is called Pierre (a private joke for Thomas, one among many) by his associates (who have mutilated hands and talk in coded conspiracy language), claims to be leading Munchmeyer to an optician, but Munchmeyer knows that the latter does not exist. Thus transported steadily away from the reality principle, which had been represented by his sweater-knitting wife, Munchmeyer the captive daydreams about his early days with Martha.

In the middle of his ride, Munchmeyer falls asleep. "Dead to the world," says his guide. Thomas likes this business because she gets to make bad jokes, and to unroll some silly intrigue dialogue, as in the hide-and-seek at the store:

"Square three?"
"Square three." And the red-haired man beamed paternally at his friend.
"You know," he said thoughtfully, "if I were single . . . "
"What do you mean?"
"He's incredible! Absolutely incredible! Like finding a beautiful thing preserved in a rock or in peat."
"You're crazy." (45)

etc.

Munchmeyer, meanwhile, insists on his sanity and is thus removed from all this weirdness. He runs for his survival, and hides in the store's Mothers' Room. (All of Thomas's writing is about mothers and children.) It is there that he comes to the realization that "There are no victims!" and bolts for freedom. The reader is conditioned by now to expect that freedom is illusory, but Munchmeyer, in a section of the Ladies called the Mothers, has named his fear. He is afraid of being raped and then killed. He has done what men taking hallucinatory drug trips in the sixties were supposed to do — get in touch with the female inside him.

• • •

The story as allegory is not tidy. It is an awful mixture of Mack Sennet anarchy and mock Beckett agony. The reader easily remembers, and the essayist must remember to remember, that comedy is unruly, that part of the fun is in smashing things, including the desire for a tidy discussion of smashing. In the already cited interview, Thomas said: "It isn't really supposed to be a parody of the Divine Comedy, but it is in fact very comic in the other sense" (26).

Still, this Part 2 is written in the third person. That means that it is definitely not Munchmeyer's journal, that at least someone's writer's block is ended. Is it Munchmeyer's novel? Then why does he use his own name? What we do know is that it is Thomas's invention, something that nicely purges the custom of converting life's minutiae into realism.

Two pages before the end of Part 2 there is a break in the narrative. Just before the break the reader finds out that Munchmeyer has not escaped his terrorists after all, but that Munchmeyer falls asleep. Just after the break Munchmeyer is at his favourite beach, where the phantom Beatrice has been listening to his story of fright. and offers her opinion that it was a "bad trip," an interior reality. In other words, this non-victim has somehow made it all up. Then she finds his glasses and

wallet (clear observation and clear identity) and gives them to him.
"You're marvelous!" he says (50), and she disappears. He is left,
bespectacled but half-blind. The scary characters are gone, but this is
purgatory, nor is Munchmeyer out of it.

• • •

Part 3 is told in the third person, too, but in another voice, a plain voice
with a no-nonsense attitude. Most of the third part is told through
dialogue, and there is no fiddling with literary allusion or free-
associating parenthesis. This voice is wise to Munchmeyer, and says of
a "rather stupid virgin," for instance: "He had wanted to touch her so
much the noise of her chatter was simply a minor irritation" (74).

Part 3 has a title, "Resurrection: Mr. and Mrs. Lodestone." Munchmeyer has broken with his old home, to rent a suite upstairs in the
house of the Lodestones, a painter and his wife. The suite is even less a
paradise than the basement was hell. Looking out the window, he sees
a feckless student-driver and remembers Wolfe's recollection that
Goethe said that man is like a drunken beggar on horseback: "'The
important thing was that he was going somewhere'" (55). Lode means
journey, but stone suggests stasis. Munchmeyer sees himself as having
crossed the bar, as setting out on his great travel as a writer, but Thomas is an anti-Dante here. The way Munchmeyer sees it, he is out of
domesticity but able to observe it from above, "above that life, but not
completely removed from it. It was as though for a moment he saw little Mrs. Lodestone as another Martha, and the as yet unknown Mr.
Lodestone as himself, or himself-that-was" (55). The mature reader
knows that he is going to descend those stairs.

When he does he will be back where he began his April Fool story.
In the aforementioned interview I suggested that we are working with
base character rather than old-fashioned character development, and
Thomas said: "That's right, in the sense that the end of *Munchmeyer* is
the beginning; you're right back where he — you know the kind of
very maudlin journal he's keeping. You're right back again. It's a cir-
cular novel" (18).

Munchmeyer is a sucker for the image of Mrs. Lodestone with her
child, and takes a suite in her house because he is moved by the wel-
coming domestic touches in his rooms, yellow painted bed, stained
mattress, amateurishly-decorated rug. He will involve himself more
and more with Maria, his surrogate Martha. He will undergo the bap-
tism of baby pee. He even comes to identify with the baby: "He felt
protected and liked the peace of the room, and her obvious concern
rocked him gently back and forth" (72). Munchmeyer settles down in a
new domesticity, but this time as child again rather than husband and
father. He is free to enjoy the homey atmosphere, he thinks, while

making up fantasies about his new family and his cinematic adventures.

• • •

Then he meets the third Mary (*Mrs. Blood* is full of Marys, too) in Mavis. She is a naive and nubile student, whose family name is Marvell. Thus she replaces the Miracle Girl, replaces her or brings her to threatening domesticity. There is a hilarious scene in which Mavis's parents in the perfect suburb spring the trap, a huge roast lamb dinner with all the trimmings, all made by the girl's *own hands*. But.

But that scene follows a number of others that feature Munchmeyer's ability to recall and duplicate late-night movie scenarios with himself as hero or victim. Maybe this is all fantasy; or as Maria says in the second-to-last scene: "'I think you make all this stuff up. Or if you really do it, it's only so you can talk about it afterwards'" (86).

That second-to-last scene, and the last one, are alternative endings to Munchmeyer's dream. In one he comes home to a lonely Mrs. Lodestone and seduces her with a poem. In the other he is seduced into seducing her with a bottle of wine. (Student stuff.) Poetic or plain, each is probably another fantasy. Munchmeyer is probably still in the basement of his house. He may have written a short novel made of his fantasies about writing and women. He may not have gone anywhere. He may have daydreamed about writing and women to avoid both. It happens. There are many would-be novelists among people who slip from the second-best of studenthood to the second-best of teacherdom. Narration slides from dream into fantasy, as those black-and-white typewriter heroes fall back on their last defences against despair. It's funny, isnt it?

• • •

If Munchmeyer's city is a nightmare or at least the site of a bad trip, Miranda Archer's island, called Magdalena (another Mary, of course) is its opposite, a dream, a good place for a new home. Miranda the mother and writer has a grant, and spends the winter half of the year in a cottage on the island, writing her novella about Munchmeyer, and her diary about an academic painter on sabbatical. This figure, Alex MacKenzie, is the counter to Mr. Lodestone, the husband of Maria. While Munchmeyer promotes a fantasy about himself and Lodestone burning the midnight electricity in the lonely pursuit of art, Miranda finds her "Prospero" to be not a magician but a friendly sort who eases her introduction to the homey folk of her willing bucolic exile.

It is a brave new world with such pleasant people in it, bibulous grandpas, breastless women with British accents, earnest hippies. "My God," says Miranda, "people are marvelous" (99). Among the marvelous one need not seek a miracle girl or boy. On Prospero's island any marvel is possible. "Perhaps it was not off the swampy coastline of Florida, but along the Gulf of Georgia, that Ponce de Leon should have searched for the precious Fountain of Youth" (102). Rather such a fountain than "the flotsam and jetsam one often sees in the streets of Vancouver" (103).

As Miranda adds daily to her two books, life around her proceeds bountifully. Old folks are spry. There are children galore. Even her husband, who had seemed boring, seems now transformed on his weekend visits: "Friendship — Love — Friendship — it becomes a kind of arc or parabola. Something good has happened now. I wonder, will it last?" (105-106). Of course it will, as long as one remains Miranda on the island, not Munchmeyer, her latent side (each has a lot of children and a distant spouse). Miranda knows this, and when she is having trouble with a page of narration, she draws a contrast between her industrious self and the incandescent, fancy-generating non-starter:

> If I were Munchmeyer, sitting in this room on this small island, I'd have two tape-recorders going and be dictating into both of them alternately. (For I'd be working on two novels, at least, if not more.) I would have borrowed this place from my friends Tom and Maria ("Christ, man, I've just got to get away.") and I'd be drinking Scotch and scratching absentmindedly at my balls and wishing somebody would knock upon my door. Then maybe after a few more hours and a lot more Scotch I'd call up Vancouver.
>
> "Hello, Maria, is that you? Yeah. No, nothing's wrong. I was just wondering if there was any mail." (114)

Unlike the baffled Munchmeyer, Miranda finds writing easy, and is sometimes amazed to see how much she has written at a sitting. It is a gift.

All she has to do is to remember that she could be Munchmeyer, and that she, Miranda, could be Munchmeyer's Miracle Girl. He caught a glimpse of her on his secret beach, and then she disappeared with her fairy folk.

• • •

For the reader, the story of Munchmeyer's failure, especially with its tight structure, is more interesting to read than is the wandering diary of Miranda's success. But the reader remembers, in the midst of all these narrative conjurations about narrators, that it is Miranda Archer who writes Munchmeyer's story. It may look as if *Prospero* is the writer's diary of the time she takes to write *Munchmeyer*. A little reflection, whether on Jung's mirror or the bland surface of the sea between the island and the mainland, will result in the thought, at least, that *Munchmeyer* is the sub-text of *Prospero*. Every day Miranda writes away her nightmare and enjoys her day dream. Having begun her book in September, Miranda finishes it in April, just about the time that Munchmeyer's is foundering. The task is finished. It is one of spring's gifts, along with flowers around the cottage and a great bonanza fish from the sea. Volunteer parsley appears everywhere in the garden and outside it. "Who says I am not blessed?" asks the book-writer. Blossoms pop out above her head, promising "Edenlike apples from our arthritic apple trees" (155), this on April 23, birthdate of the first Prospero's author. The fountain of youth, indeed.

The year, says Miranda, has been a gift. She will polish it and keep it, as a medal, a talisman, a boon. She will keep Munchmeyer where he belongs, in her shadow. He who pretended to seek isolation and had to people it with companions to help him forget his youthful promises to himself, he will stay down there, not knowing which way is up. She has gone to an island and found herself surrounded by human beings she likes, people who send her happily to her lonely occupation as their creator.

There are two sides to every story, including the story of the still young parent who has always wanted to be a writer of fiction. She has read some college Dante and some college Shakespeare, the Inferno and the Tempest. The calm eye of the storm is the best viewpoint from which to see the fires within. Hell can be fun to write about, but for a place in which to set up your writing table you need a little heaven, or at least a little Eden. And you have to create it as you go.

1985

WORKS CITED

Bowering, George. "Songs and Wisdom: an interview with Audrey Thomas." *Open Letter,* "Three Vancouver Writers," Fourth Series, No. 3 (Spring 1979): 7-31.

Thomas, Audrey. *Munchmeyer and Prospero on the Island.* Indianapolis, New York: Bobbs-Merrill, 1971.

3

William Carlos Williams

The American Indian Medicine Man

(a simple tender essay about the poet who set me straight early)

1. The New World

America was native soil before the first generation of Europeans arrived there and began to chop down the trees and root up the bushes and plant European vegetables. Call those people who were part of the American continent Indians, and call those others white men, who tried to make a New England, New Holland, New France, Nueva España. William Carlos Williams says that a person may make a choice, and that he himself chooses to be an Indian because he finds "nowhere the open, free assertion save in the Indian" (*In the American Grain*). It is an esthetic choice and a socially-aware choice, and stands at the basis of the man's whole life and careers, the prime decision in his thought-out and lived-through concept of order. It is also an expression of Modernism, that artists in the twentieth century can choose rather than inherit a tradition.

So I take it that Williams's earliest important principle is that Americans should make art that is American, not transplanted European.

In 1925 New Directions published his book about that choice. It is called *In the American Grain*, and is a fusion of historiography and esthetics. Its heroes are notable for two qualities: (1) spiritual self-reliance despite indifference or betrayal by the crowd (Columbus, Aaron Burr); and (2) devotion to the potential in the New World (Champlain, Houston). Williams identifies with Daniel Boone, who keeps moving away from the spreading European enclaves and into the wilderness, surviving by adapting to American necessities, preferring the company of the natives to the crowding of the white men. But Boone did not try to become an Indian. He did not smear himself with war-paint. "There must be a new wedding," says Williams, and "Boone saw the truth of the Red Man, not an aberrant type, treacherous and anti-white to be feared and exterminated, but as a natural expression of the place, the Indian himself as 'right,' the flower of his world." Thus Boone took the Indian as his master, "Not for himself surely to be an Indian, though they eagerly sought to adopt him into their tribes, but the reverse: to be *himself* in a new world, Indianlike" (1956, 137-8).

The importance of that distinction may be perceived in

corresponding words that Williams wrote about the making of art. For instance, in one of his major poems, *The Desert Music*, the poet says that he wants:

> — to place myself (in
> my nature) beside nature
>
> — to imitate
> nature (for to copy nature would be a
>   shameful thing)
>   (1963, 111)

In America, no person, no artist, could place himself in nature unless he placed himself in an American nature. No great art would come from America till the artists grew their work from the American grain. (In *In the American Grain*, Williams is not bandying the term "America" in that vulgar usage that would equate it with the U.S.A.)

But it is not enough for the American artist to use America as a setting. Williams agrees with Poe that Poe is an indigenous New World writer, while Hawthorne is not, because Poe sought to express his *locus* by letting it into his style, the words, the making of the sentences. It is not hard to perceive that when Hawthorne allows someone of working caste to speak in his books, he seems to write like a tourist doing a curious travel piece. (Also note that Henry James, who went to live at Hastings, liked Hawthorne and thought Whitman no artist because the latter did not subdue the self.)

• • •

When Columbus arrived in the Indies he remarked the shapes of the strange trees. Williams believes that America differs from Europe by its shapes — of trees, of cities, most important for the writer, of the language. The American language was the hardest thing for Eliot to shake, and Pound never tried (though the *Pisan Cantos* show that he did not keep up with current argot). Williams keeps an honoured place in his writings for Noah Webster, H.L. Mencken, Gertrude Stein, people who expounded the American language. People express their entire culture through their languages, says Williams, and only through their languages. American writers will be great when they are linguistically true to their own experience, and will only then make something as definable and enduring as Irish, Spanish or French literature. He early came to the idea reached by linguists, that our experience is learned and transmitted and believed in only when we form language — thus the importance of the care for words and lines and sentences (prior to thought of "subject"), that will not falsify experience.

Williams opposes rigidity, generalization and propaganda because they blunt and falsify. He is in favour of particularity of place, of language and of structure, to clear the process of poem-making, to discover the whole. A poet would put it better: "If the doors of perception were cleansed every thing would appear to man as it is, infinite."

In the anthologists' favourite old Williams poem, "Tract," we then see that the poem is as much an early tract of esthetics as it is of ethical behaviour:

Here the reader should read "Tract."

The poem is both a prescription for local veracity and a demonstration of it.

2. The Details

Remember that Williams wrote *In the American Grain* during a time when many American writers were deserting the American experience, or getting to some distance wherefrom to criticize it. Eliot and Pound were imitating classical models. Hart Crane was using deliberately archaic language and prosody to try to paste an epic sense onto the surfaces of American materials. But after World War II, Williams, through his poetry and his words about poetry, was to become the greatest influence on serious American poetry, and by the sixties we could see that even the serious young British poets had taken Williams to be their most important teacher. Obviously there is more to Williams's esthetic than discovering an American language. Williams went on to apply his scrutiny and practice to these simple and famous principles:

American culture and American language for American artists.

Celebration of the local to achieve insight into the universal.

Precision of observation (no ideas but in things), even if rude and unpleasant.

Re-creation as opposed to description — a tireless application of Pound's borrowed edict: make it new.

Structure and form as the way to reality, all poetic "content" or "matter" being fantasy.

A new measure to put the lie to dreams of "free" verse.

For Williams as for Whitman, the New World is not simply the Americas. The New World is what awaits each pair of opening eyes (Williams delivered thousands of babies, new citizens of northern New Jersey), and the New World is what each poet's verse should set beside nature:

Getting through with the world —
I never tire of the mystery
of these streets: the three baskets

of dried flowers in the high

bar-room window, the gulls wheeling
above the factory, the dirty
snow — the humility of the snow that
silvers everything and is

trampled and lined with use — yet
falls again, the silent birds
on the still wires of the sky, the blur
of wings as they take off

together. The flags in the heavy
air move against a leaden
ground — the snow
pencilled with the stubble of old

weeds: I never tire of these sights
but refresh myself there
always for there is small holiness
to be found in braver things.

("Approach to a City"; 1965, 177)

In a world forever in flux, as the nineteenth-century American poet had it, a person cannot theorize reality — he has to recognize it in the details of the street that is flowing with him as he moves along it. In order to do that he has to see with eyes and poems eidetic, as the other nineteenth-century American poet had it.

In his introduction to his *Selected Essays*, Williams says this about the pieces there gathered (and how many good essays did not make the cut!): "I cannot vouch for the opinions offered, for they represent a span of years during which I do not pretend to have had any but those largely in flux." He goes on to say that "Time is a storm in which we are all lost. Only inside the convolutions of the storm itself shall we find our directions" (xv-xvi). Here is where Williams differs from Eliot. Eliot escapes or wishes to escape the storm in the refuge of church and castle. Williams examines the effects of the storm while being carried bodily by it, stethoscope in his smock pocket.

Put it even more simply: Eliot seeks the meaningful by transcending the local (making objective correlatives from his vantage point); Williams examines and worries the local precisely to take the scabs off the principles and emotions of the universal. But the emotions do not control. Mind controls the poem, "mind, which drives and selects among [emotions] as though they were a pack of trained hounds" (xiii).

But the emotions, like the ideas, are not the subject matter of the poems. In fact the matter is not subject. Williams works in a way quite similar to Hemingway's (though his people are less symbolic) — to be precise in presenting the perception and the things perceived, and to take such care with construction as to make the ideas and emotions arise in the reader's own consciousness, as in music, architecture, and other non-verbal arts:

> The day before I died
> I noticed the maple tree
> how its bark curled
> against the November blaze
>
> There was some work
> to do and three birds
> stepped awkwardly abreast
> upon the bare lawn
>
> (from "Tragic Detail"; 1965, 119)

Precision is the objective; the poet should with that aim seek to make it anew, not to step into the snare of poesy-worn words or words melted by jargon of any kind.

Making it (a)new is opposite to seeking to be correct. The new cannot be correct, hasnt time for that agreement, feels an impulse that makes old measurement false for now. Gertrude Stein said that the new in art appeared in part ugly to viewers. Williams said in "A Point for American Criticism" that "Joyce has broken through and drags his defects with him, a thing English criticism cannot tolerate" (*Selected Essays*, 85). One need only look at the pronouncements of F.R. Leavis to understand that. Williams is always interested in criticism. He thinks that criticism, like any other human language, should arise from its environment, including that art made of the writing to be criticized. "A descent to Freudian [add Aristotelian] expedients of classification is in a literary discussion a mark of defeat" (*Selected Essays*, "A Point for American Criticism," 85). As a critic Williams says that he can admire Eliot's virtuosity in his use of language, but that his "substance" is irrelevant to the New World. "We must invent, we must create out of the blankness about us, and we must do this by the use of new constructions" (*Selected Essays,* "Caviar and Bread Again," 103). It is pretty obvious that any greatness the United States has ever experienced has occurred because it has been a country of inventors. Through its inventors it became the technically most advanced country.

There is no ruse in using the metaphor just offered. Williams everywhere speaks of the artist's function as a socially-responsible one, the artist given the task of re-creating society. Thus his dislike for the Puritan ethic, his resistance against borrowed and irrelevant institutions. In his essay, "The Basis of Faith in Art," he talks about the usefulness of art. He brings Shelley's *Defence of Poetry* to mind when he says that "Poetry is a rival government always in opposition to its cruder replicas" (*Selected Essays*, 180). To make people see clearly and understand their own location is a good aim in art or political living. Williams carries much of the sense of the most American of philosophers, William James and John Dewey. "The basis [of art] is honesty in construction, that you can do certain things with the material and other things you cannot do. Therein lie all answers" (*Selected Essays*, 175). The words were spoken of architecture, and applied to poetry.

The artist, then, has a social responsibility. In Williams there is no art for art's sake, just as there is no "free" verse. We are all caught in sections of the same storm. Eliot seemed to be horrified by the changes seen in twentieth-century communities, and turned to the museums of culture. Williams's definition of culture is the act of lifting local details into an ordered and useful whole, expressed in art that is for that reason always different from official art and always changing, ever new, not simply novelty. Culture is in the act, not reposing in what is left as a record:

> It took a stroke to slow me up . . . finally I was almost incapable of reading, I had to read so carefully. In fact I had to learn to read — took instruction in reading from Hilda Yoder in New York, a specialist in correcting speech defects and public speaking. Twice a week for two months we went through the drill and it gave me confidence.
>
> (1958, 98)

3. The Imagination

I made that quotation because it shows the determination of an old man who still has the sense not to come in out of the storm. Art, says Dr Williams, is not the mirror held up to life; it is the life, transmitted to a tighter form. Without art there are no people, only such quasi-beings as party members, patriots, numbers in the genus *homo sapiens*, and so on. As a family doctor, Williams could have ceased to think of his work as art — he could have acted methodically and impersonally in his job of pulling newcomers into the cold air of earth. But one of his last published poems was an excited account and celebration of a working-class woman's vigorous baby. Probably at the moment of childbirth the doctor-poet can most clearly see the conjunction of life and art. "When a life approaches the conditions of art we have clement weather, when it recedes from them the weather is vile and tormented" (*Selected Essays*, "Against the Weather: A Study of the Artist," 206). So if there is a storm, the approximating of life and art is our best hope for something like refuge. For Williams, that means that as many as can should see life clearly, while making art not more rigid than fluid life. Thus he warns against the dangers of the *Divine Comedy*, that in trying to penetrate deeply into the spiritual truths of his order, Dante may have accepted too tight a prescribed order from outside his art. But he praises Dante for saving his art by attending to his own experience of language, moving away from the customary, authoritative, poetical Latin, into the Italian spoken by church-goers rather than the church. When Dante found the entrenched method for poetry insufficient to his real purposes, he left it aside. Williams says that that is the real care for culture, the real meaning of making it new. He says this for those legislators or poets who run slavishly to the verticle of received forms and sentiments: "Those who see it one way call it the defense of tradition. Others see tradition belied in that tradition once was new — now only a wall" ("Against the Weather," 204).

To enforce his point he uses the image of the American invention of open formation fighting that defeated the closed ranks of the British armies during the American war of independence. (Two centuries later the U.S. army found out that it was out of date in the guerrilla jungles of its own colonial wars.) The point of this image is that the individual soldiers were not seeking their own aims by their dispersal, but the aims of their society, in this case the rest of the army. It may be unfair to artists to be compared with soldiers, but the image serves a limited purpose, and has certainly been used by Gertrude Stein, and often enough in other cultures (as for instance by Hideo Kobayashi).

That great essay of 1939, "Against the Weather," is one of Williams's most important writings, because many of the ideas in the middle years of his thinking are there expressed. He discusses the threat to art and living culture that comes from false claims to order that is not order "discovered in its living character of today, but always an order imposed in the senseless image of yesterday — for a purpose of denial" (203). Thinking of the war in Spain, he mentions Chamberlain's keeping England out of it, the prime minister's error in choosing to think of the largely chimerical British Empire under the Tories rather than the defeat of the traditional British idea of liberty in Spain. Worse than that, says Williams, is the artist who sells out his art, because "his responsibility is the greatest" (212). Chamberlain was acting according to a symbol, the Empire, in order to evade the claim made by the thing symbolized. Williams says, especially to the poet, "No symbolism can be permitted to obscure the real purpose, to lift the world of the senses to the level of the imagination and so give it new currency" (213). That is what the classical epic strives to do, and what Williams's greatest poem, *Paterson*, is all about.

In Williams's terms, the imagination is the means by which a human being may find his place in the universe of flux, in the storm of time, because the imagination is itself capable of producing change. "It is the power of mutation which the mind possesses to rediscover the truth," and the "objective is an order," through whose resulting structure "the artist's permanence and effectiveness are proven" (213). These are tenuous principles. Williams's apt successor, Robert Creeley, offers a seemingly simple illustration:

> Looking to the sea, it is a line
> of unbroken mountains.
>
> It is the sky.
> It is the ground. There
> we live, on it.
>
> It is a mist
> now tangent to another
> quiet. Here the leaves
> come, there
> is the rock in evidence
>
> or evidence.
> What I come to do
> is partial, partially kept.
>
> ("The Innocence," 118)

Wishing to lift the world of the senses to the level of the imagination so figured, the artist provides a loyal opposition to forces such as the medieval church, which strove to keep the mysteries from the people, or certain poets' similar priestly decisions to cast a monopoly on the world of the imagination. If the imagination, however, be public, people may see the mutability of the truth. In political terms, Williams lauds Jefferson's notion that there should be a revolution every ten years. Not that a nation's desire for truth should be altered, but that the forms keep up with the changing exigencies. So in poetry, Williams inveighed against the sonnet, and also against anyone's hoping to adopt a Williams form for his norm. "How then can a man seriously speak of order when the most that he is doing is to impose a structural character taken over from the habits of the past upon his content?" (217) Take note: the near past is the past.

4. The Search for a Measure.

More and more, in the later years, Williams's discussion of order centered on his belief that truth is beauty, and that both are to be discovered in structure, that in order to make a good structure one must find a dependable measure, and that he may have found his way based on what he called the "variable foot" (see the famous letter to Richard Eberhart, May 23, 1954). I have dealt particularly with these questions in my other essay on Dr Williams, "Dance to a Measure," and will not go into all that detail here.*

The first important document of this late period is the 1948 address given at the university of Washington, and called "The Poem as a Field of Action." The paper gives a description of the discoveries that went into the composing of Williams's great books, *Journey to Love* and *The Desert Music*, and formed the basis for the most important developments in poetry and poetics by Americans and Canadians since that time.

As the title suggests, the talk concentrated on the poem as a dynamic event, as process of discovery even more than communication — mutual discovery by the poet and the listener. Williams allows that many poets in modern America have welcomed new subject matter into their poems while failing to allow changes in structure; that is where they have not been in touch with the really changing real. The subject matter of a poem is always made up, the dream that only corresponds to actual objects and events. It is in the structure that the poet may confront the real, at least the reality his own voice and rhythms make. Furthermore, that reality is not, can not be, fixed. No two people breathe alike. No person's rhythmic responses are at all times and stages consistent. Hence to strive toward the real a poet must learn to measure, to see how he measures up, not to impose, not to try to measure out his life, but to *take* its measure. "The only reality that we can know is MEASURE" (*Selected Essays*, 283). Or as Williams concludes *Paterson V*:

> The measure intervenes, to measure is all we know,
> a choice among the measures . .
> the measured dance
>
> "unless the scent of a rose
> startle us anew"
>
> Equally laughable
> is to assume to know nothing, a
> chess game
> massively, "materially," compounded!
>
> Yo ho! ta ho!

---

*See the essay that follows. *Editor's note.*

We know nothing and can know nothing
                    but
the dance, to dance to a measure
contrapuntally,
          Satyrically, the tragic foot.
                    (278)

As the materials of a society change, so does the structure. In his Seattle paper Williams speaks of the irony in the fact that poets were speaking of the theory of relativity, without seeing that it applies to their composition. If relativity applies to anything in the universe it must perforce apply to everything. "Our prosodic values should rightly be seen as only relatively true" (*Selected Essays*, 286). When our poets begin to devote themselves to the subject materials of their poems, they have come to the end of their poetic means. (Speaking of fiction, Robert Kroetsch would say, "The minute you ask answerable questions, you're beat as a novelist" (38).)

So where can the poet go to make his discoveries? Williams does not deviate. The poet should go to the land of speech. If he is an American, to American speech as it is different from British or textbook speech. (It was sad a few years ago to see the young British poets in the middle of their mimeograph revolution, choosing Williams as a source, only to write lyrics by copying his lingo.) In any case, he should go first to his own speech, and that of others he hears in that first cause of his culture. (Charles Olson and Robert Duncan were to follow that lead further, referring to the work of linguistic studies of the American language more fully than Williams did in his attention to Mencken.) While the academics swallow the tapeworm of a poet's work in relation to his forebears, the poet should attend to language sources as he hears them.

Remember that Dr Williams's talk about his new measure was delivered when he was in his late sixties and early seventies, when most of the younger poets had retired during the Eisenhower-Eden years into the academy-welcomed neo-augustan boredom so deadeningly characterized by things like Christopher Fry's verse drama. In Cid Corman's magazine *Origin*, in 1954, Williams said: "Most poems I see today are concerned with what they are *saying*, how profound they have been given to be. So true is this that those who write them have forgotten to make poems at all of them" (195). See the anthologies put together by Donald Hall.

There are forces at work to dim and falsify experience (parties that generalize, propaganda that rigidifies, jargon that distorts or deadens), and their attack is on the language — so the artist has a responsibility in human affairs. In terms of the culture we go to the artists to tell us of our past, searching endlessly for one more line of Sappho. Present-day poets should keep that in mind when they compose. With this social function in mind, the artist cannot resort to art for its own sake, nor to what is called committed art or academic art — no secret cabals. In his medical life, Dr Williams was a general practitioner and baby doctor rather than theorist or research doctor. More than that, he deliberately chose to be a doctor when he could have been just a man of letters. He wanted to hear the language spoken, and people tell their doctor things they wouldnt tell their own families.

John Malcolm Brinnin simplifies Dr Williams's poetic aims quite well: "to devise the poetic structure that will formalize experience without deforming it; to let the beat of speech determine the measure; to rinse the language of ornament and encrustation; to be scrupulously selective but to allow for accident and impingement" (7).

One of the results is that the poem becomes active on the page, the poem as a field of action there, with reader engaged to follow the mind in the act of perception, thus opened to perception himself, not to relax under a recalling mind's estimation of experience. If you know you have miles to go before you sleep you are already half-asleep. Reading the poem can become an existential activity, or at least a dynamic one. Here is the simplest possible example of what I mean, an early poem with Imagist echoes:

As the cat
climbed over
the top of

the jamcloset
first the right
forefoot

carefully
then the hind
stepped down

into the pit of
the empty
flowerpot

("Poem"; 1951, 340)

Or here is one of my favourites from the post-*Paterson* period, a beautifully rimed and cadenced example of what Philip Whalen likely meant when he called a poem the graph of a mind moving:

According to Brueghel
when Icarus fell

it was spring

a farmer was ploughing
his field
the whole pageantry

of the year was
awake tingling
near

the edge of the sea
concerned
with itself

sweating in the sun
that melted
the wings' wax

unsignificantly
off the coast
there was

a splash quite unnoticed
this was
Icarus drowning

(1963, 4)

There is no doubt that this sounds like common spoken American, but
it is so carefully selected and measured both in its sounds and its
rhythms as to be beautifully formal, on the edge of song, yet not
rhythmically boring as are so many forgettable quatrains from American and Canadian college anthologies and university quarterlies. And
the endless supply of small press anecdotalism.

Attending to speech, and to the possibilities of chance and change,
Williams avoids the trap of achieved attitudes that brings the end of
the poet's writing, such as that of T.S. Eliot, who stopped that he might
not repeat himself. Williams does not have to worry about repetition
— one of his last poems was about Yuri Gagarin's first steps on the
new ocean of space.

Similarly, the poem need not develop in discursive consequence; it
may be a field of action, presenting blocks of perception as in a
Cezanne landscape, or a walk past a row of show windows in an American city. As the city has its own changing order, so will the poem, the
reader being left with an accumulation of intelligence not gained in a
logically linear arrangement. The element of chance, immanent
change, can be more than spoken about, as "theme" — if it is important
to a poet's sense of order as inspiration to the poem, it surely has its

place in the structure of the poem, where the artist confronts or communicates reality.

Dr Williams's supreme working of these ideas can be found in *Paterson*, with its metaphor of man/city/mind confronting the intricacies of subject and form in the twentieth century. In nature itself there are no beginnings and ends except birth and death, which are of themselves meaningless, according to Dr Williams. That is why the artist should not copy nature, but rather imitate it. There is flux as the main law, but there are also an apple, a flower, a man, a work of art.

Take the statue of a woman, says Williams — it is senseless to make a statue one would mistake for a real woman; the secret lies in the marble of it, what the imagination may do with it to add to the fact of the woman, to place it in nature as another work, not to make a feeble copy of nature's work. The secret is to *act* as nature does, not to stick mirrors up in front of trees. The poem as a field, of action. Not to try to be an Indian if you are not, but to be yourself in a New World, Indian-like.

Many people think that the Indians lost America. William Carlos Williams's lifetime of work gives hope to us in the New World that there are still eyes and ears among the trees.

1967

WORKS CITED

Brinnin, John Malcolm. *William Carlos William.* University of Minnesota Pamphlets on American Writers, no. 24. Minneapolis: University of Minnesota P., 1963.

Creeley, Robert. *The Collected Poems of Robert Creeley 1945-1975.* Berkeley, Los Angeles: University of California P., 1982.

Kroetsch, Robert. "Contemporary Standards in the Canadian Novel." *Open Letter,* "Robert Kroetsch: Essays," Fifth Series, No. 4 (Spring 1983): 37-45.

Williams, William Carlos. *I Wanted to Write a Poem: The Autobiography of the Works of a Poet.* Reported and edited by Edith Heal. New York: New Directions, 1958.

———. *In the American Grain.* New York: New Directions, 1956.

———. *The Desert Music and Other Poems.* New York: Random, 1954.

———. *The Collected Later Poems.* London: MacGibbon & Kee, 1965.

———. *Pictures from Brueghel and other poems.* London: MacGibbon & Kee, 1963.

_____. "On Measure — Statement for Cid Corman." *Origin XII* (1954): 194-7.

_____. *The Collected Earlier Poems*. New York: New Directions, 1951.

_____. *Paterson*. New York: New Directions, 1963.

_____. *Selected Essays*. New York: Random, 1954.

Dance to a Measure

Some words about form in the poetry of William Carlos Williams

Everything should be as simple as it can be,
    but not simpler.
                    — Albert Einstein

If William Carlos Williams had been given to cognitively pondering the evidence of existence, he might have said, to begin, "I measure; therefore I am." He said many times that the only reality we can know is measure, and in the closing moments of *Paterson*:

The measure intervenes, to measure is all we know,
    a choice among the measures . .
        the measured dance (239)

So to measure is to take one's bearings, for the first time continually, as it may well be. To avoid being lost or deluded into thinking that one's presence alone defines one's location. To measure is to see every thing present, including difference, to gauge the thing and the distance between things. A boy doesnt run a stick along a picket fence for the noise only.

Williams always relates the shapes of art with the surrounding social culture; this is obvious. Where the traditionalist poet will use a new vocabulary made possible by the work of Albert Einstein but still speak in metrics familiar to contemporaries of Queen Victoria, Williams will ask that poetic form, its utterance, reflect what Einstein has done to the rest of the universe. We learned to accept relativity over absolutism in every phase of our living, till beauty came to be nearly synonymous with appropriateness — the beautiful lines of the space rocket even before they were flown, without a nose-cone ring of gargoyles.

So too the poem. By finding its own physical rather than literary movement, the poem could take us to new areas of sensibility cleared by scientific thinking. Aesthetics is mated with physics, said Williams (making an egalitarian variation of a remark by Whitman); we should be prepared for relativity in all knowledge. The poet no less than the scientist expands his experience by measuring:

our prosodic values should rightly be seen as only relatively true.
Einstein had the speed of light as a constant — his only constant —
What have we? Perhaps our concept of musical time. . . .
              (*Selected Essays,* "The Poem as a Field of Action," 1954, 286)

So Williams's "variable foot" steps at a pace that can be measured, but
not metered, in a dance rather than a march.
    The variable foot responds to the present sense of relativity, plus the
hankering after a constant. It is sensitive to the pauses and intonations
in the poet's speech, as no convention of metrical consistency can be:

Outside
              outside myself
                            there is a world,
he rumbled, subject to my incursions
— a world
                       (to me) at rest,
                                     which I approach
concretely —
                       (from *Paterson* II, 57)

The variable foot will allow no preconceived pattern outside of the single timing syllable or rest. The beauty is that this kind of measuring is
the constant that lifts the language of speech to the form of poetry —
common speech arranged in an uncommon order, Williams called it.
(So the poet can write about any occasion that interests him; he doesnt
have to rely on subjects that will by their nature and usage sustain the
height of poetic utterance.)
    The poet concerned with taking his bearings vocally continues to
measure between objects when the word-phrase is an object, or seems
to be one. The space between phrases, no less than the phrases, is
significant in linguistic measurement. In poetry this break is syntactic
as it is rhythmic; it projects the way a poet's mind tends to measure his
world; it produces the cadence of his expression. It is here that the
artificial split between content and form begins to fail. Just as the
scientist no longer manages to distinguish between matter and energy,
so one who discusses the poem should not be hasty to distinguish
between form and content, especially in an art form whose content is
so difficult to define. In the tradition of Albert Einstein we see a gra-
dual acceptance of relativity in all aspects of poetry — in rhythm, in
rime, in all matters of prosody and diction.
    The acceptance of relativity brings with it a movement of the atten-
tion away from the species, the class, the category, to the particular, the
specificity of all things. So that when William Carlos Williams writes
of a red lily, he writes of the one in front of his eyes, not of the variety

of flower. The object of contemplation is seen in relation to its neighbour, not its far-flung family. Louis Zukofsky referred to Williams's procedure as "his Stein-ish definition of substance 'a this.' *This* is Williams' contribution to culture" (1981, 51). Seeking the particularity of all things is, of course, a big job. It entails discovering the world entirely in terms of one's own perceptions of all things. Hence Williams's continuous celebration of the perceptive act and the unspoken (usually) implication of revealed truth. It is quite the opposite from Ezra Pound's (CIV/n not a one-man job) going to the lessons of the Old Masters for aid in giving form to one's own needs. The body of a Williams poem depends on his (and the reader's) perception of an active situation as it exists in its seeming objectivity rather than historically, in relation to something greater than itself. Thus Williams stands before a famous painting hundred of years old and calculates:

> According to Brueghel
> when Icarus fell
> it was spring
>
> (1963, 4)
>
> • • •

Ranging beyond the act of perception and the sensing of the particular, the form of Williams's work as a whole seems to me to embody his attempt to find and define a moral and social order which people can accept, knowing they must accept it on completely personal terms. The poet, in writing about people, has to be aware that people live under principles that are universal, while at the same time each person lives by principles that are necessarily particular to him. Edward Sapir, writing from a sociological consciousness, sees people as beings defined by axes of culture and personality. Poetry has to express what a man senses of both kinds of principles. Ezra Pound gives primary attention to culture, or the universal; Williams to personality, or the particular.

In a search for form, T.S. Eliot goes to culture for props and shims with which to shore himself up, whereas Williams starts from his self and moves outward, making form as he goes, perceiving, adding, changing the view to meet occurrences:

> There is nothing in literature but change and change is mockery. I'll write whatever I damn please, whenever I damn please and as I damn please and it'll be good if the authentic spirit of change is on it. . . .
> It is in the continual and violent refreshing of the idea that love and good writing have their security.
> ("Prologue to *Kora in Hell*," 1954, #10; #20)

The notion of form to be found in continual change was not un-known to poets before Einstein. Walt Whitman came to it in the writing of *Leaves of Grass*. But in our century T.S. Eliot looked for order in recorded tradition. Robert Frost looked for it among the seeming constants of nature. Both made a withdrawal from the sufficient "this," a denial of the private experience and the idiosyncratic response, the very things asserted by Williams, the personal things that occur while a man measures. Those things show in the poetry — in the concrete imagery and the directness with which the images are brought into the poet's address; and conversely, the directness with which the poet places himself among the things of his world, not searching for an authority but for a commonality of human perceptions and responses. Meaning, if that is the goal, is to be bestowed by the potentialities in the perceptive act, and in the uniqueness of the thing or action perceived, as well as the particularity of self felt by the perceiver.

Order, if that is the goal, is the order found normally by a perceptive person, living, discovering, adding and sorting, able to sustain his equilibrium in the face of continual change. Form, in poetry, is the record of this finding of order, the shape of a life. The sounds the poet makes, his prosody and syntax, are his natural and aware responses to a sense of this order, and are a part of this order itself. Hence the poet's language is to be perceived, sharp as typing from a new ribbon; it is the way to find order in all experience, the parts of it to be seen as objects among experience, found in their own particularity:

Convivio

We forget sometimes that no matter what
our quarrels we are the same brotherhood:
the rain falling or the rain withheld,
— berated by women, barroom smells
or breath of Persian roses! our wealth
is words. And when we go down to defeat,
before the words, it is still within and
the concern of, first, the brotherhood.
Which should quiet us, warm and arm us
besides to attack, always attack — but to
reserve our worst blows for the enemy, those
who despise the word, flout it, stem,
leaves and root; the liars who decree laws
with no purpose other than to make a screen
of them for larceny, murder — for our
murder, we who salute the word and would
have it clean, full of sharp movement.

(1965, 209)

The opposite of particularity is abstraction, or classification, which destroys uniqueness to get its job done, and neutralizes perception. Hence Williams's attack on the drift toward categorization that started with the Greek thinkers and suffused all European thought — religion, ethics, science, history — to the present time, so that even now we are expected to feel a sense of relief when military theorists suggest that an H-bomb attack will kill only seventy million Americans rather than a hundred million as formerly thought. Hence too, his attack on rigidified systems laid on the construction of poetry.— for instance the infamous sonnet. It denies, says Williams in agreement with Ben Jonson before him, continual change and muffles particularity; and principally, it does not allow for a poetic response that would find direct correspondence with active stimuli. No one falls in love fourteen lines at a time. Or as Williams said, "I did not theorize directly when I was writing but went wherever the design forced me to go" (Letter to Henry Wells, *The Selected Letters*, 1957: 333). The river on its descent to the sea: the artist imitating nature. It is no conventional rhetorical trick, Williams's referring to the "stem, leaves and root" of the word.

"Let form take care of itself," he said in *I Wanted to Write a Poem* (73), and like a plant in its specific soil, so it will. The poet's job here is to sink roots, to know his immediate particulars, those normally obtainable to his curious self: in *Paterson*, his *locus*. Knowing as well as he can his local reality, the poet should make it his business "in the particular to discover the universal." In the *Autobiography* Williams quotes John Dewey: "The local is the only universal, upon that all art builds" (391). Thus *Paterson* the poem/city. T.S. Eliot once remarked that William Carlos Williams was a poet of some local reputation. Eliot's narrator lived in "Unreal City/ Under the brown fog of a winter dawn."

• • •

The plant, the city, the human being, any kind of organism, the poem, undergoes perpetual change; yet at the same time it is characterized by a unique shape. For the organism, order is process — the search for form *IS* form, the form. It is the poem, searching for language, that manages to imitate nature, the only palpable universal. An Aristotelean desire suggests that poetic form implies a beginning, a middle, and an end, and that this is the base for all that can be said about form in nature or in its imitation. But a humble eye looking at the water sees nothing ending. Only the eye can close. This is all admirably handled in the preface to *Paterson*.

What is a beginning, what is a middle, what is an end? The poet takes the position of a man standing beside a river. How to imagine, rooted to that spot, the beginning of this river, to imagine its end, when it is continuously there before him? It is no capitulation to accept the contextual non-ideal of organic form: form is the temporarily achieved, its shape, as the form of another human being is that shape to be seen and felt. William Carlos Williams (a name that suggests eclectic circularity) brought *Paterson* to a "close" in 1951, achieving a "finished" form, defined by the "ending" of Book IV, a seemingly stable number. But the dancer reconsidered, or could not stop, took one more step. Williams added book V in 1958. Does this action discard the notion of achieved form? No more so than a man's decision to grow a moustache, or amputate a toe.

The search for form, and its declaration: *there* is form. As a doctor Williams says that there is no final cure; as a poet he knows — this is his enduring strength — that human beings must find their identity in the pieces of things available to them where they live. If one measures that which he sees, if one measures his language to meet what he sees, one will be doing what he can in the world that Einstein has revealed to him. Excellence within unavoidable though fluctuating boundaries is the standard to be attempted: poetic form is tentative and relative:

How to begin to find a shape — to begin to begin again,
turning the inside out: to find one phrase that will
lie married beside another for delight .   ?
— seems beyond attainment .
                    (*Paterson*, III, 167)

How. The poet needs to renew the language. To perceive and to order content: that perceived into form, in a search for rest that will never end, simply because perception will never end. Zukofsky again: "The poet, no less than the scientist, works on the assumption that inert and live things and relations hold enough interest to keep him alive as part of nature" (7).

It is pretty clear that a writer's poetic form bears a direct relationship to his attitude toward nature and his place in nature. Simply: if he regards himself as the centre of his environment, he will write poems that show the master's control over his materials — the ideal of the conventional book reviewer in the daily press. Sometimes, particularly in the principal magazines operated by the enduring New Critics, the poem is a test and a display of intellectual and scholarly resources — of the poet and of the reader. The ability to control emotions, images, rhythms and so on becomes the test of a poet's form. Imitation of nature is forbidden; control of nature is insinuated.

A similar impulse led to eighteenth-century landscape gardening, or the equally unnatural iambic pentameter. Rhythmically, nature is defeated, or at least adumbrated, and rather than measuring his world, the artist meters it. He places trees in a line eighteen feet apart, or stresses in a line two syllables apart. Similarly he places himself in a line, this the great chain of being, in which he esconces himself high, but not too dangerously high — his egotism is guarded. It is with no felt shame, then, that mankind decides that everything is there for his use, just as he chooses to interpret his Genesis, and subdued by mankind if it should seem to challenge his dominance. So the Puritan expended a few centuries meeting the challenge of the American forest and asserting mastery over it. Except for those few who went before, leaving their kind behind, and entering among the trees.

But while man in his egocentricity can assert, he can never fully know — he should see that he can never be in complete control, for the simple reason that there are always certainties in nature's things (even himself) that he can never see. Why, then, should the major impulse not be toward discovery rather than control, measure rather than meter? Why should the artist be ashamed to make episodes and fragments, imitating nature, running ragtag and bobtail after nature? He is charming for that, and respectable. The pure scientist is not concerned with the journalist's idea of "harnessing" the atom — he wants to understand more about it. As meetings with new orders permit men to land rockets on other orbs in space, others should sweep aside men's determination to stick to previous ideas of artistic form. It seems to me that formalists react mainly out of fear, or at least a desire for security. They feel unsafe, as if they might be attacked from any quarter, if they dont see symmetry, or a sense of finality.

Similar people centuries ago went insane in the face of the possibility that the earth is not at the centre of the universe (as they had always metered things), or they dispatched anyone who said it is not. The modern scientist works with the functional notion that maybe knowledge is undelimitable, discovery forever continuous. So does the modern poet. The formalist closes all doors and windows to cut off the *possibility* of a draft. Taken to its logical extreme, his position would be on the barely near side of totalitarianism. William Carlos Williams makes it clear where he stands, when in a note preceding *Paterson* he says that his work is to be "a dispersal and a metamorphosis" (2). Form is, again, the search for form. "Virtue is wholly / in the effort to be virtuous."

But *Paterson* is not a poem written over a decade after World War II. As everyone who has read a fair part of the life's work knows,

Paterson was in the works for a long time before that. In fact, Williams's search for form is not only the theme of *Paterson*; it is the abiding impulse of his whole career as a poet. It is common knowledge that he began his writing at university as imitation not of nature but of earlier poetry, especially of Keats's. But the urge to act naturally was there early. In *I Wanted to Write a Poem* Williams recalls:

> Very early I began to question whether to rhyme and decided: No. I had to start with rhyme because Keats was my master, but from the first I used rhyme independently. I found I couldn't say what I had to say in rhyme. It got in my way. (14)

As to rhythm:

> The rhythmic unit decided the form of my poetry. When I came to the end of a rhythmic unit (not necessarily a sentence) I ended the line. The rhythmic unit was not measured by capitals at the beginning of a line or periods within the lines. I was trying for something. The rhythmic unit usually came to me in a lyrical outburst. I wanted it to look that way on a page. I didn't go in for long lines because of my nervous nature. I couldn't. The rhythmic pace was the pace of speech, an excited pace because I was excited when I wrote. I was discovering, pressed by some violent mood. The lines were short, *not* studied. Very frequently the first draft was the final draft by the time I reached the third book, *Al Que Quiere!* (15)

Many of the poems are indeed first drafts; many seem unfinished, like some paintings of the Modernist period. Some give little more than the sensation of seeing things (like bits of coloured glass in the rubbish behind a hospital) for the first time. Part of this is due to the fact that the doctor had to write in his moments (the measure intervening) stolen from his other vocation. Part is due to the doctor's refusal to improve on the facts — note his reference to his own "nature" in the passage above.

• • •

Ezra Pound, surely no enemy of studied art, was one of the first people to recognize Williams's sense of discovered form. In an essay about Williams in 1928, Pound quotes him: "All I do is to try to understand something in its natural colors and shapes" (390). Pound almost admits that to understand that way is the proper end of poetry — not to try to prove something from that understanding, not to fit it into any kind of habitual form of utterance. Not to improve on nature. In the following statement Pound is writing primarily about Williams's prose, but the same could be said about Williams's allegedly unfinished poems:

Art very possible *ought* to be the supreme achievement, the "accomplished"; but there is the other satisfactory effect, that of a man hurling himself at an indomitable chaos, and yanking and hauling as much of it as possible into some sort of order (or beauty), aware of it both as chaos and as potential. (396)

So "form" can be tiresome if the work carries nothing for the mind; the potential in the form of the poem can never be as great as the potential in the form (or chaos) of nature. Pound, though, isnt finished:

... plot, major form, or outline should be left to authors who feel some inner need for the same ... when put on ab exterior, they probably lead only to dullness, confusion or remplissage or the "falling between two stools." (398)

That is not to say, though, as some confused critics have said, that Williams turns his back, "anti-poetically," on all poetic form when he discards the form of Keats. The orderliness of poetry has always appealed to Williams, has always been the reason he wrote it: what other reason could there be, with any honour? More, he wanted an order that would be natural to himself, to the objects of his vision, and to the relations between himself and those objects.

Old orders, of other men and other claims, seemed foreign, restrictive. Williams decided, with characteristic simplicity, to give over his ego to the instruction he could get from the order of the world outside himself. Hence his association with the Imagists and the Objectivists. A large part of his pre-*Paterson* poems are about natural objects, often flowers. "I have always had a feeling of identity with nature, but not assertive," he said (1958, 21). Hence the flower he writes about takes on personality, as a neighbour would, and the poem tries to emerge as an organic piece of neighbourly living form:

I must tell you
this young tree
whose round and firm trunk
between the wet

pavement and the gutter
(where water
is trickling) rises
bodily

into the air with
one undulant
thrust half its height —

and then

dividing and waning
sending out
young branches on
all sides —

hung with cocoons
it thins
till nothing is left of it
but two

eccentric knotted
twigs
bending forward
hornlike at the top

("Young Sycamore"; 1951, 332)

Williams says, looking back on the period of that poetry:

> Whether it was a tree or a woman or a bird, the mood had to be
> translated into form. To get the line on paper. To make it euphoni-
> ous. To fit the words so that they went smoothly and still said
> exactly what I wanted to say. That was what I struggled for.
>
> (1958, 34-5)

So that as one object in nature is formed by association with its neighbours, one item in a poem — the word or the syllable — is formed by
association with the sounds of its neighbours. Any quibble about "true"
rime makes as much sense as a dispute about whether a certain tree
should have the same number of branches as the one illustrated in the
biology textbook.

But variety and singularity dont mean freedom, nor does their imitation mean free verse. Free verse, for a poet like Williams, is no more
possible than a "free" tree. (In fact the term "free verse" is now a kind
of paradox, though we remember that when it was coined it was coined
in French and it was meant relatively, in comparison with rigidly
metered and rimed poems.) No poet so much dedicated to imitation or
understanding of nature as is Williams can ever be free from nature's
order, any more than nature's other participants can.

The form of *Paterson* is defined by the river as it moves down the
mind to the sea; it is as natural as that. The process of writing a poem
is this: the poet recognizes his place as a part of nature in mutual
response with nature's other objects; he becomes aware of the natural
order operating in himself, including his habits of speech; he tries to be
faithful in his verse, first to his own order, then by extension to the

order of the world he lives in and writes of. This means that he will train himself best by writing of his own life and environs, and by investigating the rhythms and lines of natural objects such as birds, trees, and working people. Such is the training and the poetry of William Carlos Williams. The question of how to give order to his poems while responding to the unregimented rhythms of his own nature became a great concern, and Williams found an answer in his discovery of the variable foot:

> The foot not being fixed is only to be described as variable. If the foot itself is variable it allows order in so-called free verse. Thus the verse becomes not free at all but just simply variable, as all things in life properly are.
>
> (1958, 82)

The dance of life and the relative universe do not deny order; they simply insist on an order of their own, begun before human beings began expressing themselves. As *Paterson* seeks to embody and express Williams's idea of the "resemblance between the mind of modern man and the city," I would say that language is for the mind what characteristic activities of its parts are for the city. Williams in his poetry tries to make language capture the forms and movements in the city — or garden, or hospital ward — outside him, always trying for the not quite possible exact correspondence.

In writing of the world he must make beauty inhere in the words. Someone once said that Williams was the literary equivalent of a painter of the American "Ashcan School," who would say: look, isnt it beautiful in itself despite your associations? But he succeeds not just with the image; he does not merely present the verbo-visual idea of the ashcan, but rather another thing, the poem, with physical parts as useful and inherently as serviceably beautiful as those of the first object, the ashcan if you like.

Too many critics and anthologists of American poetry used to pass Williams off as a member of various short-lived literary movements; and in particular too much was made of Williams the Imagist or Williams the Objectivist. From the beginning, and in continuous development through all his work, he gave form to "content" by articulating his natural emotional responses, sometimes by subtle implication, as in *Spring and All*, sometimes in exclamations (which always make more immediate sense on recordings made by a poet than in the written score of the poems), as in that wonderful later poem "The Orchestra." This, after all, is the way a person measures out his life, with the response a human being makes on the strings of a cello, or with the dancer's feet.

While reading *I Wanted to Write a Poem*, I discovered that I had never more strongly sensed that I was listening to the actual intimate responses and reflections of an active poet or artist of any kind. It is this quality, this immediacy of sensitivity, more than image, or speech patter, or cadence or rhythm, that makes Williams's poetry so damned pleasurable, and at the same time such graceful art.

1968

WORKS CITED

Pound, Ezra. "Dr. Williams' Position." In *The Literary Essays of Ezra Pound*. Ed. T.S. Eliot. London: Faber, 1954.

Williams, William Carlos. *Selected Essays*. New York: New Directions, 1954.

_____. *The Collected Later Poems*. London: MacGibbon & Kee, 1965.

_____. *The Selected Letters of William Carlos Williams*. Ed. with an introduction by John C. Thirlwall. New York: McDowell, Obolensky, 1957.

_____. *I Wanted to Write a Poem: The Autobiography of the Works of a Poet*. Reported and edited by Edith Heal. New York: New Directions, 1958.

_____. *The Autobiography of William Carlos Williams*. New York: New Directions, 1951.

Zukofsky, Louis. *Prepositions: The Collected Critical Essays of Louis Zukofsky*. Expanded Edition. Berkeley, Los Angeles, London: University of California P., 1981.

How I Hear *Howl*

Moreover
thou hast taken
thy sons and thy daughters
whom thou hast borne unto me,
and these hast thou sacrificed
unto them to be devoured.

Is this of thy whoredoms
a small matter
that thou hast slain my children,
and delivered them
to cause them to pass through
the fire for them?

Ezekiel, xvi, 20-21.

(Poetry is still a vocal art. In the following impression of Allen Ginsberg's poem I will refer not so much to the printed versions as to his spoken version on the Fantasy LP 7005, *Howl and Other Poems*.)

1.

I dont know how useful it is to relate a present-day poet to earlier poets, but I know that it is commonly done, and that it can be done here. Allen Ginsberg's sources are well acknowledged or scrutinized by the critics and other interested parties. William Carlos Williams, Walt Whitman, Blake, Shelley, Christopher Smart, the poets of the Old Testament.

Once in *The Village Voice* (August 26, 1959) there was an article by Allen Ginsberg called "Poetry, Violence, and the Trembling Lambs." Therein he made observations in slightly uncharacteristic regular sentences, that placed him as a modern Romantic, as one who professes much of what the English Romantics professed, holding those truths in mind for the present day, this one in 1965 (1987) or later:

Recent history is the record of a vast conspiracy to impose one level of mechanical consciousness on mankind and exterminate all manifestations of that unique part of human sentience identical in all men, which the individual shares with his Creator. (1)

Then speaking of some hopeful contemporaries, he says that they:

> have had the luck and courage and fate to glimpse something new
> through the crack in mass consciousness; they have been exposed to
> some insight into their own nature, . . . the nature of God.

Blake had said:

> For Mercy Pity Peace and Love
> Is God our father dear:
> And Mercy Pity Peace and Love
> Is Man his child and care.
>
> (from "The Divine Image"; 30)

For Ginsberg as for Blake the idea of God in a context other than the
nature of human beings at their best is meaningless; and this spirit,
Mercy, Pity, Peace and Love, is dangerous and beautiful opponent to
what Ginsberg calls the "mechanical consciousness," psychic successor to the Dark Satanic Mills inveighed against by Blake.

(At this point the reader should listen to "Sunflower Sutra.")

Similarly, Shelley, the man who was ejected from university for
demanding atheism, and was subsequently referred to as "pervert and
anti-Christ," put his religion this way, speaking to the West Wind:

> Make me thy lyre, even as the forest is:
> What if my leaves are falling like its own!
> The tumult of thy mighty harmonies
>
> Will take from both a deep, autumnal tone,
> Sweet though in sadness. Be thou, Spirit fierce,
> My spirit! Be thou me, impetuous one!
>
> (1977, 223)

In the face of great mechanistic war-centred threats playing on
people's fears and suspicions, to dehumanize them, in fact, the pro-
phetic words of Blake, Shelley and Ginsberg might seem at least
optimistic, as they express their hope that the love that people's souls
are mutually capable of can serve to withstand and defeat the murderous impulses let loose in the world. Beat poetry, and the surge of
spiritual optimism it gave voice to, made a remarkable answering
shout of Aw Shut Up! to the delicate pessimism in post-Eliotic verse
that had dominated the American academy and American anthologies
in the forties and fifties.

The reputation of Eliot himself experienced a steady decline after
World War II, and old greybeard Walt Whitman began to peer out from

behind his many flourishing leaves of grass. It is no wonder that Ginsberg turned to Whitman's all-inclusive barbaric yawp of optimism as well as to the visionary exaltation of Shelley and Blake. Whitman sang:

O to make the most jubilant song!
Full of music — full of manhood, womanhood, infancy!
Full of common employments — full of grain and trees.

O for the voices of animals — O for the swiftness and balance of fishes!
O for the dropping of raindrops in a song!
O for the sunshine and motion of waves in a song!

O for the joy of my spirit — it is uncaged — it darts like lightning!
(from "A Song of Joys"; 323)

Ginsberg was happy to regard himself as the natural American son of Walt Whitman; like him he came eagerly out of the suspect industrial country of New Jersey, and took America and then the girdled earth as his scene, likewise containing multitudes. But the son knows a significant and painful difference wrought upon his country. Whereas Whitman could celebrate with exuberance in the conviction that he shared his expansive freedom as a part of all the hopeful American kosmos, Ginsberg knew quite early that his allegiance and association had to be with what partisans could term the real America. He had to say what the little countries constantly invaded by the U.S. military always say, that they love Americans and hate their rulers. The dream of the real America, a pocket of resistance enduring within a continent taken over by a commercial army of occupation. (Blake wrote about a version of such events in England, in his two poems called "Holy Thursday.") Ginsberg's "America" is a strangely comic place, comic in its attempts to be sinister, rather ineptly powerful:

(The reader should listen to "America.")

But Ginsberg's idea of the state of the nation is not always so indulgent. Another time he asks this unsettling question:

Deviants from the mass sexual stereotype, quietists, those who will not work for money, or fib and make arms for hire, or join armies in murder and threat, those who wish to loaf, think, rest in visions, act beautifully on their own, speak truthfully in public, inspired by Democracy — what is their psychic fate now in America? An America, the greater portion of whose economy is yoked to mental and mechanical preparations for war? . . .
    When will we discover an America that will not deny its own God? Who takes up arms, money, police, and a million hands to

murder the consciousness of God? Who spits in the beautiful face of
Poetry which sings of the Glory of God and weeps in the dust of the
world? (8)

Whoever they are, they include the academic-slick poets — the ones
who live on universities AND turn out "safe" rehashes of tepid verse
turned out by *their* professors, praise the proper people in the university quarterly book reviews, join organizations, and wait till it's *their*
turn for a Guggenheim. [It was my turn for a Guggenheim 1965 —
A.G.] That is: William Meredith at one end and John (New Yorker)
Updike at the other. A good example is John Ciardi, a curiously tough
member of the safe school, a *Saturday Review* editor who exhibits a
hardness and selectivity that are foreign to the Romantic poet. Those
qualities are conducive to closure. Ciardi has actually professed a lik-
ing for Robert Frost, and more peculiar, a belief that Frost is a major
poet still. Ciardi speaks indulgently, like a permissive but sarcastic
adult, and characterizes the Beats as literary children, an idea that
might not insult Blake, nor, I venture, Ginsberg. Finally, Ciardi passes
the Beats off as an "unwashed eccentricity." Something like the tourist
lady from the Milwaukee inter-faith council who could not *bear* the
odor of Palestine.

This is, of course, the famous Establishment's traditional reaction to
the visionary poet. Blake was punished by his mother for seeing a
vision of the archangel Michael in a field. Yet his mother professed to
being a Christian. When Shelley began publishing his poems, the
Establishment pitied his wife for being forced to live with an intellectual pervert. When Ginsberg was at Columbia University he studied
under Lionel Trilling and Carl Van Doren, learning about Poetry in the
approved genteel fashion, and learning to turn out charming verse so
constrained that it looked as if it would some day qualify for a Donald
Hall anthology. Then one night the young poet had a "beatific
illumination . . . during which I'd heard Blake's ancient voice and saw
the universe unfold in my brain." After this point student Ginsberg
wrote a new poetry, not a poetry that would seek to tell of reality, but a
poetry that would *make* reality, unconstrained by any non-poetical
notions of "taste" or "control" — and he showed some to his mentors at
Columbia. Pooh, they said, feeling as if they had just lost a hopeful
youth, that's not poetry, it's hopeless raving. Shortly thereafter, the
story goes, Ginsberg was expelled from the university for inscribing
"Fuck the Jews" on a dirty window. [The story is not accurate. — A.G.]
But why would he do that? wondered the university officials while
they were throwing him out. That bafflement has characterized the
academy ever since; and the solution has always been the same — if
something is impossible to understand, reject it in case it is dangerous,

or a put-on. Other people with a similar idea are the government and the police — hence the banning of books, burning of books, and police raids on cafes and nightclubs and theatres.

Ginsberg's reply to those actions was the only one a poet and pacifist should make: "Who denies the music of the spheres denies poetry, denies man, and spits on Blake, Shelley, Christ and Buddha." Christ was spat upon in his passion. So were Allen Ginsberg and, for instance, Martin Luther King Jr. But each of them replied with gentility. That gentility is the spirit that one notices emanating from the poet. If there is something to approximate the centrality of Whitman's everlasting optimism and gaiety, it is Ginsberg's openness and love, always offered. (A strange thing to talk about in a literary essay.) His poems do not express hatred toward anyone. Even in his most famous early poem *Howl* he does not attack the America that destroys the best minds of his generation. Instead he expresses love for the victims of Moloch, especially as they are symbolized by Carl Solomon in the madhouse, a lately consigned Kit Smart, the eighteenth-century poet who dared to ask people to come to God outside the official church.

(Here the reader should hear Part III of *Howl*.)

2. HOWL

The central image of *Howl* is the "robot skullface of Moloch," the mechanical monolith that eats the children of America. The original Moloch was just as fearful, though geographically more specific. This was the lingering Canaanite god that appealed to the wives of the original Solomon, and earlier to the followers of Moses. He was figured as a giant stone statue with arms held out and fierce flames burning all round him. It was the practice of religious women to worship Moloch by casting their children into the arms of the statue and watching them burn alive, held by that mockery of care. So Ginsberg's image of a present-day monster, as much more terrible as the Empire State Building is taller than an ancient Hebrew statue.

(Here the reader should hear Part II of *Howl*.
Then listen to the whole poem.)

Depending on whether one is for or against Moloch, the sacrifice can mean two things. A ravenous murder of children by their self-interested parents and society, or a chance for the children to purify themselves through flames and torture and death. The latter strikes close to the Christian way to paradise, past what Ginsberg calls "the starry dynamo in the machinery of night." All through the poem heaven and eternity are in sight, are being called upon; or are being bitterly regretted, so that a cynical second best stands as ironic refuge from the world of present Moloch. In a haunting parallel to the sermon on the Mount, Ginsberg says not that "theirs shall be the kingdom of heaven," but "their heads shall be crowned with laurel in oblivion."

Christ, remember, went on to say: "Blessed are ye, when men shall revile you, and persecute you, and shall say all manner of evil against you falsely, for my sake. Rejoice, and be exceeding glad: for so persecuted they the prophets which were before you."

These are the people seen by Ginsberg in the first broad scene of his poem: "I saw the best minds of my generation destroyed. . . ." In seeing them, he has his eyes open wide, perhaps three of them, and his mind open outward, opening with long torrential lines rolled out together on an axle of sound, the words propelling one another, as in the rime and consonant-leading of this:

> who chained themselves to subways for the endless ride from Battery to holy Bronx on benzedrine until the noise of wheels and children brought them down shuddering mouth-wracked and battered bleak of brain all drained of brilliance in the drear light of Zoo

But woe betide the scholar person who says that a person does not have time to see precise truth when he is lipping off this way. Let me say that the great poet comes to truth/world through the sounds he picks out of it. So I will mention some things I hear in Part I of *Howl*, and I say that in his rapid setting down, Ginsberg was in the happy poet's place where the true sounds of the galaxy are joined by true sightings, and the poet's pen is hard-pressed to get the most he can down, in frantic pursuit.

Here I return to the "vast conspiracy to impose one level of mechanical consciousness on mankind," and the means by which the Occupation does this. The agents of the Occupation wield their control by controlling money, time, machines, institutional education, and all the public means of communication.

Ginsberg goes underground against the tyranny of Time, finding some refuge in the consciousness of eternity that is sanctuary for artists and religious martyrs, where Shadrach and associates really walked while Nebuchadnezzar thought he had them in his Moloch furnace. So Ginsberg's martyrs are "burning for the ancient heavenly connection to the starry dynamo in the machinery of night," antithesis, maybe, to the machinery operated by the social state.

Ginsberg itemizes the staggering true story of his martyrs, who cower, get busted, purgatorize their bodies, see lightning in their brains that illuminates "all the motionless world of Time." He is interested in motion, soul's motion, emotion, something to break through the motionless world of Time: Standard Time, Time Magazine, Time payments, There's a Time for Everything. The face of Moloch is a clock. The martyrs sit for hours waiting doom-crack, talking continuously for seventy hours, disgorging in total recall for Biblical seven days and nights. Section I of *Howl* displays portraits of people the poet knows, caught in the eye of Time.

Finally, in one great gesture of revolt, they throw their watches off the roof, "to cast their ballot for Eternity outside of Time, & alarm clocks fell on their heads every day for the next decade." Imagine it with your sense of touch. The insurgents, now, demonstrate, and the Occupation answers by dropping bombs, clocks, the terrible measure of bombs for a decade, the weapon of Time. In retaliation the insurgents smash "phonograph records of nostalgic European 1930s German jazz" — captured Time broken loose in the smashing, the motionless world liberated for a second of Eternity; but in Eternity a second is all Eternity, and thus a significant blow can be struck against the duly invested authorities.

The insurgents keep active, barrelling "down the highways of the past," and driving cross-country in seventy-two hours of time, looking for Eternity in the motion, a vision of Eternity, a hope. They make a raid on Denver, defy Death and Time for a moment, only to be blocked again, to go away again, "to find out the time." To try again in a bombed-out cathedral where their hope, "the soul illuminated its hair for a second," but a second away from Eternity, where the soul should be; a second in Eternity is all Eternity, but shown in Time it is only a second.

Carl Solomon, hero of the poem, is torn from the cathedral and thrown into the madhouse, into the "total animal soup of time," where he still dreams freedom, making "incarnate gaps in Time & Space." He is, as Allen Ginsberg is, "putting down here what might be left to say in time come after death," for a time after Time, for Eternity, one would think, when the cities will be destroyed, when Moloch will fall on his back. In the world, hope; in poetry, prophecy — this from Solomon, from Ginsberg, from each martyr, each "madman bum and angel beat in Time."

At the same time the martyrs demonstrate against the other oppressions, money and academy, prisons where not criminals but children are locked up, bent, warped, trained to pass themselves through the sacrifice fires of Moloch. Ginsberg gives a clue to what *Life* magazine called the "Beat mystique" when he first presents the insurgents as "poverty and tatters and hollow-eyed," scorners of semi-official advice: "Clothes make the man. Physical fitness keeps America strong." These were the fifties.

To the academy's control of the developing brain Ginsberg opposes direct vision, religious, hallucinatory, a flash of light, what happens in that revealed second of Eternity. So the insurgents "bared their brains to heaven," seeing "Blake-light tragedy among the scholars of war." Here is personal Ginsberg biography, as everyone must know by now, and apt — Blake is anathema to the scholar's approach; he does not fit the syllabus, he baffles the overconscious mind, and professors have historically dismissed him or tried to make him something he is not — politician, patriot, moron. So the young insurgents, in one another's arms a lot of the time, preferring their semi-Blakean visions, are like him "expelled from the academies for crazy & publishing obscene odes on the windows of the skull." Strange tough variation on Petrarchan image, and more interesting than bad advice to the Jews.

"Crazy" still, and making archetypal protest, they leave the university and burn their money (the "heterosexual dollar"), which is not only a plain-fact crime against the American state, but an insult to the treasury as sure as that other insult to the academy's programs of lassitude: "who studied Plotinus Poe St. John of the Cross telepathy and bop kaballa because the cosmos instinctively vibrated at their feet in Kansas."

A clear sight of *Howl*, you see, needs not interpretation, needs only listening ear, maybe rearrangement by the mind that remembers qualitatively. That is, I am sure that the Gysin/Burroughs cut-up suggestion would work here — the objects, the nouns, speak out. All words are becoming nouns. Grouped together, they speak out.

The martyrs, insurgents, wanderers now, seek out visionary Indian angels, insulting the professor at Columbia Berkeley Reed Iowa State University. [No, ever courteous. — A.G.] [Actually, I meant that the prof would be insulted that they went to the visionary instead of him. — G.B.] The visionary Indian angel is not caught in motionless Time; if he were he would not be around, alive this century. The wanderers throw Dada potato salad at CCNY lecturers on Dadaism, making moment of gooey vision in sordid program of a hard soul trying to intellectualize, footnote, chapter heading, discourse, organize the slippery — itself, the lecture, hopeless Dada that can only invite and be pointed out by a handful of white edibles on vest front. Organic communication for a second.

As opposed to mechanistic control of machine and communication. "Excuse me. I think my telephone's tapped by the FBI." "Then use instant spirit semaphor, or like jazz."

I think that the first part of *Howl* deals largely with that major concern of writers of the fifties — anxiety about communication. The heroes of the poem are broken and punished and trained for sacrifice through the control centre's hold on the machinery of contact. When they become insurgents it is because they have instinctively, religiously sought communication that transcends the machine.

So they drag themselves down long straight communication streets, the city's way to Harlems, looking for a visionary connection. It is only under the communication El that they can bare their brains, looking for the heavenly fix. They get busted at communication Mexican border for transporting grass illumination — the machines work better in the dark. They wander in a maze of blind streets looking for heaven lightning to transport them impossibly to "Poles of Canada and Paterson." They jolt along in communication subways, tunnelling away from brilliance in that above-board undergound machine. They return and return to the big American Whitmanic successful communication Brooklyn Bridge, and finally leap off, into dirty waters that go nowhere but down. In their prisons they wait for the light that cracked the gloom of Peter and Simon. The tune machine in the background is trapped mechanical singer of this age, seen by Ginsberg as "hydrogen jukebox," through which the crack of doom will be communicated. [1965 Rock Roll "Eve of Destruction" on jukeboxes. — A.G.]

The railroad in the nineteenth century (Whitman) pushed west to the Pacific, opening the continent and closing it too. The railroad was the communication network that made America big and was supposed to make America great. Now Ginsberg's heroes "wandered around and around at midnight in the railroad yard wondering where to go, and went, leaving no broken hearts." They are lost in America's communication centre, outsiders, not even able to participate in the grand design as does Pauline of the Perils, who at least knew what was going to happen as she lay there trussed to the Union Pacific tracks. The vibrations along the rails were news.

Through the streets of New York, Idaho, blitz purgatory, deep in subway tubes, on bridges, they are lost where people should find. They sit cold in "boxcars boxcars boxcars," racketting through unknown snows of farmland America, prisoners of the long train in the night. Better to be inside something timeless, the volcanoes of Mexico, for instance, volcanoes that are ancient and revered; they reach for the sky, but they have deep holes in them, where gods can enter or exit the earth. In America del norte the volcanoes thin out, and they are not all that supernatural. To the Yanqui they are noted for their size, or their names as national monuments, objects of our Time. "To converse about America and Eternity, a hopeless task," Ginsberg says.

I want to say something about every phrase in the poem: they all arrest one, they exfoliate. But it can not be done, and should not be done anyway. Let me touch finger to some, let the reader stop to regard more slowly where she will.

For instance: you *know* where Ginsberg is and where the control centre is, and who is doing what with the means of communication, when you hear that the martyrs "howled on their knees in the subway." In the fifties people on the subways must have thought of people in the forties in cattle cars. Who has not dreamed the "horrors of Third Avenue iron dreams"? But even in the shadow of the great communication machines the insurgents arise betimes to construct their own holy machines of worship, to reach beyond the steel sky, these "who sat in boxes breathing in the darkness under the bridge, and rose up to build harpsichords in their lofts . . . rocking and rolling over lofty incantations," doomed songs of freedom. Their songs are drowned out by the Orwell "radio of hypnotism" in the end. But outside Time there is no end. There is a place to reach. So the martyrs reach, and they try to communicate in their own underground networks, each attempting:

> to recreate the syntax and measure of poor human   prose and stand
> before you speechless and intelligent   and shaking with shame,
> rejected yet confessing out   the soul to conform to the rhythm of
> thought in his   naked and endless head.

This is the gentle defiant enemy of Moloch. In Part II of *Howl*, Ginsberg howls his defiance as his fathers carry him toward the fire and the gleamy eye, the final torture and death at the hands of the monster lurking throughout Part I, where he is seen in concrete, stone, lead, iron and ugly flames. In Part II Ginsberg starts by asking: "What sphinx of cement and aluminum bashed open their skulls and ate up their brains and imagination?" Formally, the poet is remembering the first line of Part I, the image of the best minds of his generation destroyed (as Pound saw his contemporaries destroyed by the empires' WWI), here eaten out of bashed-open skulls.

At the Chicago reading (on the Fantasy recording) the poet begins Part II with a suddenly deliberate pace, after the high flight that ended Part I. (He is now in a small radio studio rather than in public.) By the time the fifteenth and last line of Part II is reached, there is an exciting tension in the voice, great emotion mixed of pain and defiance. He confronts Moloch, maybe a second before his own brains are to be slurped down.

As Part I was one long exhausting sentence, Part II is the natural series of noun clusters and exclamations that come from the throat of a son about to be sacrificed, the outcry that has little time. When there is little time and no place for decorum, the noun comes out: "Moloch! Solitude! Filth! Ugliness! Ashcans and unobtainable dollars!" Here Ginsberg strips his statement to essentials: "Moloch whose mind is pure machinery! . . . "

Ginsberg has switched from the survey of the American Occupation in Part I, to first-person confession and resistance. He rips through formal logic in presentation, to the naked communication available in words direct from the pained soul, as adjective gives up and becomes noun, and noun becomes adjective which is noun anyway: "Crazy in Moloch! Cocksucker in Moloch!" Rules of communication are removed entirely while the poem stays clear as falling rock, while it becomes a lesson. What a difference here from the abstract sludge of business jargon evasion ("due to circumstances beyond our corporate control, the cost efficiency factor destabilized and indicators suggest") . . . or evasive poetry language ("You would think the fury of aerial bombardment / Would rouse God to relent; the infinite spaces / Are still silent")!

Ginsberg's relentless clarity in the exclamations of Part II is the necessary saving heart of the poem.

"They broke their backs lifting Moloch to Heaven!" says Ginsberg of the martyrs, and he tells in four great powerful long lines then, the tragedy of the lost sold-out American dream gone down the choked-out American river, or again, "down on the rocks of Time!" — the treacherous killer of the drifted mind removed from Eternity's hope.

Part III is addressed to Carl Solomon. Now Ginsberg has passed "thru the fire to Moloch" (2 *Kings*, xxiii, 10). "I'm with you in Rockland," he says. Rockland is the name of the loony bin, but as rock land it is the metamorphosed America, rock being the material of Moloch, the mountain of American machine, the "incomprehensible prison" of Part II.

Carl Solomon is addressed as a crazed Jesus, the enemy of Canaanite Moloch. Now we are directed to think of the possibility of hope, resurrection, peace, direct ascent to heaven, the connection by way of soul to starry dynamo. This mad Jesus has murdered his twelve secretaries, cries that "the soul is innocent and immortal," and his soul will never be returned to its body "from its pilgrimage to a cross in the void." Carl Solomon (in the Old Testament the wives of Solomon betrayed him in their worship of Moloch) is a rebel Jesus, plotting against the "fascist national Golgotha," skullface Moloch again.

Ginsberg at last predicts victory for this sacrificial leader of the insurrection, saying that some kind of angels will reappear to "split the heavens of Long Island and resurrect your living human Jesus from the superhuman tomb." Resurrection will be the signal for revolution, the uprising of the sacrificial victims, accompanied by angelic bombardments by the souls' airplanes to counter the alarm clocks. The spoils are the remains of America and the tatters of the freedom with which Whitman tried to identify it.

Howl, one notices, is an ode and an elegy, forms one expects from a romantic poet intent on the triumph of human freedom. One hears the ode's third part as one hears the elegy's proclamation of hope. In the fifties Allen Ginsberg knew, cognizant of the social order and the condition of poetry, that we would have to start with hearing.

1966, 1971

WORKS CITED

Blake, William. *Blake's Poetry and Designs.* Ed. Mary Lynn Johnson and John E. Grant. A Norton Critical Edition. New York, London: W.W. Norton, 1979.

Ginsberg, Allen. *Howl and Other Poems.* Fantasy LP 7005.

____. "Poetry, Violence, and the Trembling Lambs." *The Village Voice*, August 26, 1959: 1, 8.

Shelley, Percy Bysshe. *"Ode to the West Wind."* The Poetical Works of Shelley. Cambridge ed. Ed. by Newell F. Ford. Boston: Houghton Mifflin, 1975.

Whitman, Walt. *Complete Poetry and Collected Prose.* New York: The Library of America, 1982.

4

Ondaatje Learning to Do

Most of the Canadian poets whose work I admire have been published at some time by Coach House Press, the poets' house that became habitable in the same year that its predecessor, Contact Press, closed its door. As a Vancouver writer I have been cheered for years by the fact that this fine press in the middle of Toronto's university district should publish the works of the best non-U poets from my bailiwick. I am thinking of a list of names that has grown surprisingly long, and includes Fred Wah, Daphne Marlatt, Lionel Kearns, Robert Hogg, Frank Davey, Dwight Gardiner, Sharon Thesen, and Gladys Hindmarch.

Sometimes we facetiously refer to Coach House Press as the Toronto arm of the West Coast movement, even citing the fact that bp Nichol and Victor Coleman have at various times lived in the Vancouver region. But Coach House is, we admit from time to time, there for reasons other than our own, and for poetry that stems from different traditions. David McFadden is there, not at all hip but the material that the hip love. D.G. Jones and Sheila Watson we enclose because of their interest in matters linguistic rather than thematic. There are the young Toronto poets who plunge into and out of the speedy multiface glistening of Toronto. And there is the peculiar case of Michael Ondaatje, most of whose books have been published or printed by Coach House.

The development of Ondaatje's poetry, from his early years in this country to the present, resembles the development of the main currents of Canadian verse over a period perhaps twice as long. Unlike the Vancouver poets with their advocacy of open-ended, process form, Ondaatje emerged from the school that believes the poem to be an artifact, something well-made and thus rescued from the chaos of contemporary world and mind. If the Vancouver poets might loosely be said to descend from Robert Duncan, and Victor Coleman from Louis Zukofsky, Ondaatje might be said to descend from Yeats and Stevens.

But over the course of his first fifteen years as a Canadian poet, Ondaatje came to seek a less British and more American poetic. Having come by way of England from colonial Ceylon, and once here through UEL universities to the Coach House Press, he had many skins to rub off. In his fourth book, *Rat Jelly* (1973), he arrived at a poem called "'The gate in his head'," and dedicated to Victor Coleman. It finished with a passage that may not open the gate but at least points to its location, that signals the way out and in:

My mind is pouring chaos
in nets onto the page.
A blind lover, dont know
what I love till I write it out.
And then from Gibson's your letter
with a blurred photograph of a gull.
Caught vision. The stunning white bird
an unclear stir.

And that is all this writing should be then.
The beautiful formed things caught at the wrong moment
so they are shapeless, awkward
moving to the clear. (62)

It is a departure, if not in form at least in intention, from his earlier predilection for preserving his objects in the amber of his directed emotions. In his poetry since 1973, and more so in his non-lyric works, we have seen him seeking the unrested form he requires, and the realization that it is in form that we present what we deem the real. All content is, as William Carlos Williams pointed out, dream; and while dream is interesting, it is interesting only when it is not volitional.

In his early poems, arresting as we knew them to be, Ondaatje had a habit of intensifying the world, of fashioning artifice, as I have said. In them we found steady images of brutality, especially of the suffering of beasts, as in the verse of Pat Lane. I was slow to respond favourably to the poems in *The Dainty Monsters* (1967), attractive as they might have seemed with all their violence, because they were, by the time I the reader got to them, over with; there was no mystery left, no labour for the reader, just puzzle or rue. No mystery for writer *or* reader, that is. Observe the lightbulb in "Gold and Black":

In the black Kim is turning
a geiger counter to this pillow.
She cracks me open like a lightbulb.
(1973, 12)

You see, black instead of dark, because it is emotionally more intense. Geiger counter, dangerous and scary because out of place in that context. And the simile: it is intended to set your teeth on edge. Really, I dont know what happened there, because the dream was not meant for me; it did not come up out of my funnel into the universal memory. On the other (left) hand, though, I clearly remember Ondaatje's Billy the

Kid sitting among the animals in a real unpainted barn.

On reading the first two books of lyrical poetry (though on reading the selected poems at the end of the decade I was to change my view to my gain) I saw the poems as anecdotal, really Canadian in that way, and considered them to be exercises written between sessions of work on Ondaatje's more serious and larger concerns, such as Billy and Bolden. The shorter pieces were poems for enjoyment, and I enjoyed them. They were, in my view, well cut and shaped, but not risky.

An exception was his famous poem about his father, "Letters & Other Worlds." It does take risks, and for most of its three pages it is a world rather than a picture of one. But at the last, in getting out, Ondaatje the son trips over a Figure of Speech which contains "blood screaming." That sort of thing the reader can only accept or reject as a *mot* performed by the author; he cannot experience it.

One consequence of fashioning ordered, unified, palpable poems is that one makes anthology numbers. A reader often re-encounters Ondaatje's poems, or thinks that he does. More than a usual number of them stand up well after an elapsed time as notable set-pieces, such as the snake poem, "Breaking Green," which ends with a flourish:

The head was narrower now.
He blocked our looks at it.
The death was his. He
folded the scarless body
and tossed it like a river into the grass.
(1973, 33)

The maiming and torture of animals is either an obsession or secure access to affect. He psyches it and we squirm if we are so bent, we death-dealing Canadians. One animal poem, "A bad taste," out-Rosenblatts Joe and out-Lanes Pat, but was wisely left out of the selected poems. It is about rats, Ondaatje's favourite animals. In the poem, which I too will leave in the book it lies in, the author is perverse as he must be, saddled, let us say, with that central metaphor. You will go and look it up. But I mean if the animals have dreams, as Margaret Atwood has said, we are their dreams.

Rat Jelly was an improvement on *The Dainty Monsters*, rather than an advance, for the most part. But it was and is that rare kind of collection nowadays, a book of poems to enjoy, not to be dislocated or awed by. The poems were, I suspect, among the last id-haunted remnants from an ex-English boyhood. The aforementioned poem addressed to Victor Coleman probably satisfies the essentially neo-Georgian literary people who make up the Eastern establishment, but the aim it announces, when totally realized, should turn them right off and thus conserve energy, and we will use the reserve to warm the house for the invited not the commanded muse.

On the cover of Michael Ondaatje's selected shorter poems, *There's a Trick with a Knife I'm Learning to Do* (1979), there is a photograph of a seated man using his *left* foot to throw knives around the body of a woman who looks like Dorothy Livesay. Whether or not that says anything about the course of Canadian poetry, it does suggest the nature of Ondaatje's wit: among other things (especially while we notice that the title of the book is nowhere to be found among the poems), the poet's "trick" is to use an edge that seems to miss its target, barely.

When Ondaatje, while learning, comes closest to his boundary, there is a great deal to admire in his performance of these left-footed poems. The later ones, in a section of the book called "Pig Glass (1973-1978)," are intent upon not quite that dislocation I looked for earlier, but a dislocating settlement, a resolute oddity. The last line of each poem sounds like your most adept friend's final smack of his hammer on his fifteen-story birdhouse, or the last knife thunking into the board above your own pate. Observe the ironic pastoral, "Farre Off":

> There are the poems of Campion I never saw till now
> and Wyatt who loved with the best
> and suddenly I want 16th century women
> round me devious political aware
> of step ladders to the king
>
> Tonight I am alone with dogs and lightning
> aroused by Wyatt's talk of women who step
> naked into his bedchamber
>
> Moonlight and barnlight constant
> lightning every second minute
> I have on my thin blue parka
> and walk behind the asses of the dogs
> who slide under the gate
> and sense cattle
> deep in the fields
>
> I look out into the dark pasture
> past where even the moonlight stops
>
> my eyes are against the ink of Campion (80)

Subtitled "Poems 1963-1978," the book is made up of Ondaatje's selections from *The Dainty Monsters* and *Rat Jelly*, plus thirty-five pages of "Pig Glass." We see just over a hundred pages of work of the lyric poet from the age of twenty to the age of thirty-five, a bracket that always seems interesting in the careers of Canadian poets.

That Ondaatje has always been interested in animals as figures is apparent from the three titles just mentioned (as well as his anthology, *The Broken Ark*, published originally in 1971 and reprinted in 1979 as *A Book of Beasts*). A later collection was nearly titled *Raccoon Lighting*. In his twenties he explored and exploited the violence implied in the confrontation between people and animals, but as I now read him, with a spectral uneasiness rather than the advantageous exposition of Pat Lane's lyrics. Lane tells us that man is naturally murderous toward his fellow beasts, but Ondaatje is interested in the experiential philosophy developing from a paradox pronounced early in his verse:

Deep in the fields
behind stiff dirt fern
nature breeds the unnatural.
(from "Early Morning, Kingston to Eananogue"; 1979, 5)

So did Ondaatje, especially in his first poems. Here is a typical example of his early predilection for the wry metamorphosing of the Anglo-American poets in the post-Eliot age, the sort of exterior design then found in the Donald Hall anthologies:

I have been seeing dragons again.
Last night, hunched on a beaver dam,
one clutched a body like a badly held cocktail;
his tail, keeping the beat of a waltz,
sent a morse of ripples to my canoe.
(from "Dragon"; 1979, 4)

That figuring was carved while Ondaatje was still a British immigrant student, at the Waspy English departments of Sherbrooke and Queen's. His poetic during that time might be characterized by a stanza from another poem:

I would freeze this moment
and in supreme patience
place pianos
and craggy black horses on a beach
and in immobilized time
attempt to reconstruct.
(from "Four Eyes"; 1979, 17)

But then came the association with the poets at the Coach House, and a poetics that espoused a non-Euclidean order. One need only compare the above passage with the later poem addressed to Victor Coleman, with its "blind lover" and the "caught vision." There is a concomitant change in the music, from deliberate manipulation to more subtle and patient rime. In "Pig Glass" there is a wonderful poem addressed to

Christopher Dewdney, a next-generation Coach House poet. It begins with a quotation from Dewdney: "Listen, it was so savage and brutal and powerful/that even though it happened out of the blue I/knew there was nothing arbitrary about it" (1979, 100). That message is obviously as important as the photograph that Coleman had sent from Gibson's.

So the younger Ondaatje's poems delivered a diction that was formalized, literary, or British; at least it signified an *elevation* of speech into printed language. But from the beginning the poet showed us a sure comprehension of what a line is, not just a length, not only a syntactic unit, but a necessary step in knowing and surprise. It is telling that when he comes to contemplating a painter's work, it is the work of Henri Rousseau, with its sharply defined wonderment. Thus, even while the subject is eerie or terrible, the words suggesting the man's observations of them are "exact," "exactness," "order" and "freeze."

In *Rat Jelly* there appear some family poems, with constructed metaphors; *i.e.*, what is this (thing, experience, feeling) like? It's like a _____. It is still a geocentric world, in which the poet's invention is the earth, albeit an unusually interesting one. But "Billboards," the opening of the selection from *Rat Jelly* in *Trick With a Knife*, seems deliberately to exhibit a promising progression of the poet's means, from fancy to phenomenological imagination. Its two pages end with this:

> Nowadays I somehow get the feeling
> I'm in a complex situation,
> one of several billboard posters
> blending in the rain.

> I am writing this with a pen my wife has used
> to write a letter to her first husband.
> On it is the smell of her hair.
> She must have placed it down between sentences
> and thought, and driven her fingers round her skull
> gathered the slightest smell of her head
> and brought it back to the pen.
>   (from "Billboards"; 1979, 35)

The last few lines, delivered not on stage but in dressing room, might seem to be tacked on, but they are really the emerging achievement of the poem. They hug to contours not their own.

Other poems, such as the oft-remembered "Notes for the legend of Salad Woman," enact wonderful images without the trace of academic super-structure, though perhaps a little Laytonic exaggeration, and lots of robust humour. The last is a feature of Ondaatje's writing that deserves an extended study. There are, in *Rat Jelly*, still some laconic poems about men's mistreatment of wild animals, as well as the poet's amused admiration for his dogs. But Ondaatje is still there looking for a magically charged world, a world with Margaret Atwood's immanent peril and Gwendolyn MacEwen's legerdemainous nature. "Burning Hills," an important piece, suggests on the other hand the self-referential narrative put to such good use in Ondaatje's most important books, *The Collected Works of Billy the Kid* and *Coming through Slaughter*:

There is one picture that fuses the 5 summers.
Eight of them are leaning against a wall
arms around each other
looking into the camera and the sun
trying to smile at the unseen adult photographer
trying against the glare to look 21 and confident.
The summer and friendship will last forever.
Except one who was eating an apple. That was him
oblivious to the significance of the moment.
Now he hungers to have that arm around the next shoulder.
The wretched apple is fresh and white.
　　　　　　　　　　(from "Burning Hills"; 1979, 58)

"Pig Glass" is a collection of lyrics that benefit from the practice of *Billy* and *Slaughter*, partaking of their concern with the ironies inherent in the act of composition, the acknowledgement that a writer who participates in motion cannot "freeze" a scene for the universal literary museum. In "Country Night" the poet notes the liveliness of the unseen creatures of the farmhouse while people are abed. He finishes by saying, "All night the truth happens." A pretty clear statement of the poetic. But when is he composing this? During the continuous present of the poem's night-time verbs, or out of bed in the daytime? Is this poem truth, that is, and is that last line from it?

The poems in "Pig Glass" are as the previous lyrics are, usually one page filled, a regularity suggesting that the author is working on a contract, as both entertainers (see title, *There's a Trick with a Knife I'm Learning to Do*) and bridegrooms (see cover photograph) do. The last section sports some travel-to-roots poems, some family poems, but most important, some departures from the regular observing occasional poem, in the direction of his peculiar pamphlet from Nairn Press, *Elimination Dance* (Later collected in *Secular Love*). There is, for example, "Sweet like a Crow," two pages of outrageous similes, in which the addressed one's voice is "Like a crow swimming in milk,/ like a nose being hit by a mango," *etc.* And there is "Pure Memory," the non-sequential meditations on Chris Dewdney, and there is the poem of Sally Chisum's recollections of Billy the Kid thirty-seven years later, the heartening evidence that Ondaatje does not consider *Billy* to be entirely artifact, over and closed. These were all good signs that Ondaatje was bringing to his shorter verse the engaging fabrication seen in his longer works: that the nature of invention had met and bested the culture of mastery.

Already, by the mid-seventies, Michael Ondaatje was a poet who was making art that was like the best of Canadian poetry. As a novelist he was making stuff most of our respected writers did not begin to dream of. As a fiction writer he was already superior; as a poet he had learned how to be one of our best.

1981

WORKS CITED

Ondaatje, Michael. *Rat Jelly.* Toronto: Coach House, 1973.

_____. *There's a Trick with a Knife I'm Learning to Do. Poems 1963-1978.* Toronto: McClelland & Stewart, 1979.

Stone Hammer Narrative

This will be a narrative of my reading of the "Stone Hammer Poem." How do you read a Kroetsch, I wondered. Robert Kroetsch and Eli Mandel said that "Stone Hammer Poem" is the beginning of the never-ending ledger of Kroetsch's poetic thinking. A ledger is both ongoing in aim and something we archivists look back into when it is done. Then we seem to see it going on as it did. A seed catalog is hopeful, future-oriented in two ways. A reader looks forward to the arrival of the seeds, and then to the growing of the seeds. First he will hope that the plants will look like the pictures; then he will forget the pictures because the plants are here. Unlike a ledger or a seed catalog, a stone hammer does not resemble a book. But it is the beginning of one. So I looked at the book.

Field Notes it said on the cover. How do I do that? I can field a pop-up pretty well, and a grounder as long as it isnt hit right at me. I can field questions if I am cornered or paid. But how do you field notes? It does make sense for an ongoing *oeuvre* to start with a verb. (Are those "feeled" notes, asked my ear. No, that would be felt notes, I said. Oh, notes written with a felt pen, hard to erase. Kroetsch is always erasing, I said. That is how he gets things done. "I fall back on paradox again," he said in a printed interview with Margaret Laurence. Why doesnt he use a computer, then? With a computer you replace when you modify. When he erases he doesnt replace, I said. You can see the old words. It's called a palimpsest by an archaeologist.)

"Stone Hammer Poem" is not itself a long poem, but it is written in the form of a long poem, as Kroetsch sees it, and I want to begin, silly me, at the beginning.

1.

The first line demonstrates a stone in the present, here.

The second line reaches into the past to show that the stone is, now, a hammer, or was.

The third line begins ambiguously. Is it a hammer made of stone, or is it a hammer that hammers stone? If the latter, is it logically self-destructive? As if his mind desires to get out of that conundrum, the speaker, whom we will eventually recognize as the poet, demonstrates a maul, which is usually made of wood, thus suggesting its temporality. Its relationship to L. *molere* is shared by meal from a mill, a kind of prairie economics.

It is the colour. That is its essence, its meaning?

Of all the qualities of bone, it is its colour. But then the poet undoes that "is" with a "no," showing his determination to get this observation right, and the unlikelihood of that. This is at least the second erasure of the poem. By erasing one gets back to the nothing of beginning, but not really, because the erasure is something, a history of the poem's making. That is the narrative of an alternative to narrative, an attack on the demonstrative.

"Bone is the colour" is an absurd remark. On top of that, bones are bleached of colour.

This seventh line makes the phrase rime with "Black is the colour of my true love's hair."

The end of the second stanza is the end of the sentence. A period means that the writer has settled on a statement, or something like a statement, you philosophers. So far he has told us what colour the object is, but he has not mentioned a colour. But he has confused us about whether he's looking at stone, something that was around before bones, or a hammer, something that arrived after bones.

Line eight adds skin to bones. Here we have an article rather than a demonstration, and the article loops (as Eli Mandel would like it) rather than subtracting, another method for the poem.

Then at the moment we find that we are dealing with loops as things, they are subtracted; but a new article is promised.

But that hand, a thing mainly of skin and bones, is subtracted the moment it arrives. Take away a hand, and a hammer is only a stone. Wary by now of this Indian giver, we are promised another article.

A buffalo's skull. We know that the buffalo is the chief western symbol of something gone. However we have at least its skull, bone with the skin gone.

The poet takes that away too, though, in a line that illustrates the writer's predicament or method here. The first word, "is," announces being, but the second word, "gone," denies it. The line, furthermore, mockingly resembles the first line of the poem, and calls into question that line's apparent demonstration of solidity.

But the first line of the fourth stanza, four being a number suggestive of wholeness, declares the definite beingness of the article in question.

Further, we see that it is not just a random stone but one turned into a resemblance, presumably by hands and a hammerer of stone, so that it is like the skull, presumably of the gone buffalo. This is an artificial quality, not just a colour. This is like a poem, suggesting illogical but likely connections. The head bone's connected to the hand stone.

Then the buffalo is gone again, and a child is born; something new. But given the age of the stone, something long gone. But "a child" is an invention, of the poem-shaper, of the gone stone-shaper.

When you write about a poem by Robert Kroetsch, you find yourself saying "but" a lot, or trying to find a way not to say it.)

So this first section of the poem is a western Canadian reconstruction of Keats's ode on an old urn; an act that Keats's poem suggested someone meditate and perform. We infer a succession all the way from sylvan historian to prairie archaeologist, a code transmitted from ditty to Dawe.

2.

The first line of section two releases the tight loops of the prosody and lies out flat, another demonstration, that reduces the poetical bone stone to a holder-down of papers on a probably wooden desk. Kroetsch you know is playing a game with us. In his next poem he plays that old small town game in which you are inveigled to answer the question the verse asks only so that the reciter can pinch you at the end. Here he is playing rock, paper, scissors, and you know what he is doing to the poem with his scissors. But you also know what the rock can do to his scissors (and the hand that holds them).

We hear Eliot's self-reflexive rime in the second stanza. In his begining was his end in both the world and the poem. "Where I begin/ this poem" is ambiguously at the paperweight and on this desk. The obligation of paper is a weight to such a poet, and the reason for his desire to add further subtractions.

But really, he does begin for us in this poem. Now we find out that this poem "was." This whole section will demonstrate the identification of poem and hammer.

Oh it was, was it? Either the poem was founded on a wheatfield, or the maul was found in the Canadian grain that will be, was, pounded into meal.

Now the wheatfield where they were found is lost, like the buffalo that used to be where it was. The prairie, we're told in so many narratives, is a "where" of loss. But now (parenthetically) the hammer was lost too. It was found lost. It turned up missing. It was included out.

Add the poem to that finding and losing. Go back to the title and see that "Stone Hammer Poem" are three nouns, like "Rock Paper Scissors," a game of continuous breaking, covering and cutting.

It is usually paper that is cut in this game, but if a poem is a stone, here the it is cut to a function. Is that a good description of a Kroetsch poem? I dont think so. We will subtract that.

This stone was. It was both cut to a function, shaped like a little-thinking head, and was.

Now it is not. The sentence is abandoned, lost, for a parenthesis unclosed, lost like a wheatfield. How do you grow a poem that is like a seed cast away, founded not? The poem-wielding hand is all right, but it is, like the skinless skull-hammer, gone, dashed, to the seemingly infertile ground —

3.

A colour does show up now, colour of age, not of a child's skull but of an aging man's head, two heads here. The poem is filling with heads and skulls, bone heads, stone hammer heads.

In the second line of the third section we apprehend that our syntax that brought us hammerer of stone was right, as we now get mauler of pemmican, a future meal (in the past, of course, though in the present reading of the poem).

For the second stanza the poet is trying to make a story of loss (and delight of finding), but even in this he has to subtract by adding the word "or," a softer way of saying his earlier "no." The poet, maybe from old habit, maybe indulging a little of the archaeologist's romanticism, attempts narrative, and employs a lot of liquid consonants, speculative tongue on the ceiling of his mouth. But he can not bring any story to a period now; that bit of punctuation left him as soon as he tried to picture Indian life. The ends of his lines rather say or . . . in . . . or . . . in . . . or. Or means other, which in this case might suggest out. The poet's mind is alternating, as if he cannot get narrative into gear, or as if he does not want to, as if he wants to continue rather than arrive at his stop. (Later the sad Phoenician or the silent poet will simply alternate "and" with "but.")

So "in" and "or" could continue as long as one can imagine Indians losing things, and so an end-stop might be posited a million years from now. That settled, if that is our word, we go backward a million posited years.

But first we are told that the hammer, which we were first urged "is," is now a million, the most liquid of numbers. Even if the poet did manage to tell its story, it would be one story in a million, not much of a case for narration. It even seems silly to speak of years, but what else can a man at a desk do while looking at a stone? A hand may have shaped the stone, but the hand, like Keats's potter's hand, held a shape imposed by the material it was holding. Lives are like that, too.

The stone is a stone, and does not care to distinguish between liquids, slough water or blood. Only paper, covering rock, wins that game. And this paperweight is on top.

The poet (in a Kroetsch poem as in a Romantic poem there is always a persona we call the poet) has identified stone with poem, shaper with shaper. Shape-changing, in the Indian world Kroetsch likes so much, is a kind of limited magic. The language, a respectful poet knows, is a million years older than the hand that wrote a poem or

4.

Thus the stone, no matter that one or two or three people think it is theirs, will fall from a travois or desk and be simply a stone again, as it has been for a million years. A narrator is, as the old old language leaves it, someone who knows, who has the knowledge. He can even pass it on, he thinks. Sometimes he thinks he can copyright a poem he has shaped. Sometimes old lost poems are found again, and sometimes they just become part of the ground of language again.

In section four, the poet, far from his prairie patronymy, returns from speculation to plainer looking. He demonstrates this stone maul.

He says that it was found. Isnt finding in the past tense a funny idea? But the poet is not intent on that. He has come back from the unfinishable, and thinks he can end a sentence with a period.

But that "in" his Indian speculation had so much trouble with comes back to erase the period, and do some damage to the "found." No wonder the liquids have given way now to fricatives.

If the period has gone, the stone was in the field. If not, the grandfather was in the field. If we do not quite know but have some findings that seem to promise knowing, and further down the road we are to be narrating what we know, we make field notes.

A field is and means flat, like paper under a weight. It means and is plane, and what we get out of that we explain.

What did the proprietary grandfather do in his field of vision? He thought. The stone-owning poet is thinking too; yes, thought is his. But we know that language, the earth of thought, has been around so long that it can not be his but only thought to be his.

Thought was the poet's father's too; no more than the earth was, of course.

And the poet's father thought was his grandfather's, words passed down from skull to skull. If we trace the personal pronoun back three generations or a million years, we arrive at a thinking stone, and if we come back to where we are, in our heads now, we come to a stone poem, obdurate and shaping, and sometime sooner or later to be lost. So much for that.

One whose father and grandfather were thought is not likely to be much more solid than that. So much for that that.

5.

It is a stone, the poet insists, as if that word we generally apply to mean solid thereness is in question. If the stone's being can be questioned, what of the poem only named for a stone?

In time, too, he insists on its ontogeny. It is either old as the previous one, or as old as the single remaining one, an insult to logic made to insist beyond hyperbole.

From the mooted future we go to the far past, the last Ice Age. Ice, though an earlier shaper of the stone, and though then enormous, is nevertheless ice, whose function is to flow and melt, to retreat eventually, and in retreating to nourish the ephemeral life it has seemed enemy to, at least obstacle to. This means that recreating and retreating are more alike than simply their words; and the poem's advancing from ice age through time, suggests that all retreating here will be recreating.

Kroetsch, we see throughout the poem, uses his notation to the advantage that his words, gerunds and others, do double duty, acting as more than one part of speech. Here the retreating for a few lines appears as both noun and adjective.

One also notices that the rime with recreating nudges us toward considering the other word to be re-treating, something a Kroetsch poem is never loathe to do. Retreat, then, is something different from loss.

Thus finding is something different from advance. Advance was a political word on the prairie, while loss was a literary word. A stone was an obstacle to the plow's advance, and reason for a farmer's loss, at least of time. In old photographs and naturalist fictions the prairie farmers have stony faces.

The poet's syntax retreats now, and parenthesis blooms, useless flowers bloom, flowers with Indian names grow whiter than bones. They speak, however falteringly, of natural cycles, putting forth a small image of the longer cycles of ice and stone, and the first appearance of straight lined things such as a wire fence. Someone thinks the field that used to be under an ice field is his.

The poem puts out definite articles at the ends of its lines, looking for things to plant in our hearing, settling for a beginning of uncultured berries, scant meals where there was retreating.

The pemmican replaces the buffalo, but winter, the recorded voice of the ice's age, will not let the pemmican remain a noun for longer than four syllables.

The rrrr sound of the first ripping stanza has been replaced by the windy /w/ of the second stanza, and in that whiteness there is no comma or period anyone can see, neither you nor I.

6.

Section six greets us with another demonstration, a returning one. The poet is trying to rewrite section four. He goes into the narrator's past tense. The storyteller thinks he has his punctuation back, a point to make; thus the first few lines do not lack for punch.

The plow, old Germanic word, breaks into the poem at last, recent ground-shaper stopped in its path, perhaps crosswise on the path of the gone ice, crossing perhaps the invisibled path of a non-scoring travois or buffalo.

Here the various sounds made back in the throat attend the work on the earth, where the German man now is, the late Christianized pagan resolved to the one God. But when Indian's earth stops this man he curses his faith, announcing that his God is not on this earth but in his own retreat.

Still the virgin soil of the American poem has now been visited by the European word for deity. God is in his heaven (or the heavenly field one thinks is his?), all's right with the world. That is how the various properties are arranged. So the plowman curses.

In this place the infragrammar of the poem becomes hard to ascertain. We know only that the poet goes into a flurry of erasures, by parenthesis and misleading self-contradiction. The first definite article leads to a question of definition followed by a negative.

The not finding of the maul did not of course occur here; otherwise the Indian would have found it, or not lost it in the first, uh, place.

But the next stanza speaks of finding the maul, and then finding it cursed. Yet we know that that happens in the stone's future, the poet's putative past that he is presenting in our reading now, or just a few seconds ago, happens when the poet's grandfather curses or cursed it. This way old Indian and old German meet in their curses, and Kroetsch meets Al Purdy, who had archaeological poet cursing as he unscrewed a screw screwed in by a pioneer of a previous century in a Purdy poem. (In a section of *Seed Catalogue*, you will remember, Kroetsch and Purdy carouse together in a restaurant atop a huge screw towering over Edmonton.)

Now the poet allows narrative to retreat as he flags his lines with question marks. He is the poet who does not know. He asks whether the Indian cursed, having just reported that he did. Even the confounded narrative is erased. So what is written on the palimpsest now? A second question — did the Indian try to curse? Our third question is:

what could stop his cursing, or was what could stop a curse something like what could stop a plow? In its retreat, did the ice leave booby traps?

Go back, says the poet. Doing that, we see that the line connects to the previous one. But it is also what we are trying to do. And let me tell you, I cursed a few times, trying to plow through this poem.

What happened is usually what the narrator is confidently telling us. What happens is luck, means luck. With all this losing and finding, this happening, we should be with a hammer on the happy hunting grounds.

I have to, says the poet — happen, curse, go back? I want, he says — not the voice of narration. Then when he finally gets to a verb, it becomes not final, as he makes the negative in parenthesis. That could make it appositive, not knowing being another name for knowing; or a second self-correcting voice, the one that a line earlier substituted desire for compulsion, the voice that here prefers mystery to chronicle, prefers the stone to the history of the stone.

The last line of this section carries, with its caps, as much force as the grandfather's oath. It is a shouted interrogative, the kind of thing one utters when one despairs of an answer. A non-cursing prairie farmer, if there is such a thing, might yell WHY ME? A poet with a desk writes what this one writes. A critic or teacher or student wonders, too.

7.

The news in this little section we already know, or think we do. So what is it doing here? Does it present more than the poet's resting from speculation, and tidying what he sees in front of him on his desk?

There is a nice ambiguity of grammar as elsewhere in the poem. If the poem is the stone, then this that we are reading is only words, notes about the poem, and these words I am spending are notes on notes, dust perhaps. Or if the poem is the stone, it lies by its own weight and we have no Indian's stone at all. Of course we dont.

If we take the copula verb to present simple high-school metaphor, then logic leads us to see the poem as tool, for making meal, for instance. I dont know whether I like that. In any case the stone is shaped like the stone, poem like maul.

I do like the poet's semi-erasure, during which high-school metaphor ("is the stone") is reduced to high-school simile ("like the stone").

Recall that when the poet offers a fully confident sentence he is likely to seem less ready for a period next time.

But while we are at such a short rest, let's say something else about these numbered sections of the poem. They are not progressive narration; three is not schemed to lead us into four. In a little piece called "Taking the Risk," Kroetsch wrote down "Begin: each morning (ab ovo) from the egg." One perceives his method clearly in a poem such as "Sketches of a Lemon," in which each section is a new attempt to get at that object of contemplation, and at the passive mind prepared for penetration by the act. Here the connections between numbered parts are made not by consequence but by resemblance. In a serial poem the numbers are like the dates given to days. One day follows another not because the waker wills it. The poet making the poem remembers earlier parts of the poem, but he is not busy developing them — he is busy writing the stone on his desk today. I would like to give you this stone, says the non-narrative poet, but all I can give you is this poem. That's his mistake.

Jack Spicer wrote in one of his letters to "Lorca": "I would like to make poems out of real objects. The lemon to be a lemon that the reader could cut or squeeze or taste — a real lemon like a newspaper in a collage is a real newspaper." Now that sounds like simile, but I'll bet it isnt.

8.

The truth is that no poet can give you the object of his affection; he can not even give you a poem. The poem is not his to give in the first place. But here is the fiction we agree to: we said "Goethe's *Faust*" only after Goethe disposed of it. The possessive follows the poem's release. Various contemplative religios, including western Indians, hold that true ownership of something, from stone to soul, transpires only when one gives it away. Poetry is potlatch.

Now the field is, announces the poet, as if it had not been till now. As if taking a stone from Alberta is like placing a jar in Tennessee.

But the sentence is determined to proceed, as if it is not going to slow down for erasure, for the poet who uses both ends of his pencil, true tool. The field is his because he gave it, retaining the poem he took out of it for a keepsake? The parenthetical price rubs out the gift, and hence the ownership, and we are back where we began, at the desk.

The field of this poem will be strewn with pronouns taking the place of nouns, another retreat, as we see the ground changing hands, from proper and unshaping nominatives to the third-person would-be narrator, who finally washes his hands of the whole thing. It will also be trod by sons, from the Queen's red children to the last-mentioned disburser of real estate and words.

"Genealogy is a primary version of narrative," wrote Kroetsch in "Beyond Nationalism: a Prologue" (83).

Unable to sustain narrative in these terms, the poet tries history, tries the network of consequence history is supposed to put in place. So Indian, Queen, and CPR. But history becomes family history, and history is eventually sold off by the prodigal who would rather tell than till. The grandfather's curse, as happens so often in western Canadian poetry, now lies on the page rather than on the once familiar ground.

9.

So it makes sense that now the poet's new first word, while it is still "this," is no longer a demonstrative adjective but a demonstrative pronoun. It points not toward the referent but toward the poem itself. It is, as they say, self-referential. It plays with the immediate future of the next stanza rather than the feckless work of the past.

It also addresses "you." If you are "I," you are the second person of the poem, in its field of vision. The poem is being given to you (for a price).

Why wont it surprise you that the poet's grandfather lost the stone maul? Because everyone else till then did? More important: why does the poet tell you something he thinks will not surprise you?

We know that the grandfather was the first to give the field with a curse rather than a price in parenthesis. I will admit that I was not surprised to hear that he was not interested in something shaped for a language that preceded his on the scene. And I know as well as you do that the poet's laconic revelation is humourous.

As far as his grandfather was concerned, this was another field stone, to be boated away and piled with the rest, to be collected and ignored, not isolated and contemplated. The poet, tempted often by the material in his ana, retrieves from his field not stone but notes, another gram, more weight. (Or a ditty of many tones?)

10.

So much for losing, giving, selling; so much gone, retreated, left. But we are trained, no matter if the poet hovers with an eraser, to think of poems as something kept, as Yeats did, saved from the chaos of life; or the words kept after the poet has chipped and hammered at the first rude shape.

Here the poet unashamedly permits himself narration and punctuation, as he saves the poem from the fate of ice, offers the fate of found-again stone. The poem stretches out, this section taking a whole page. Each paragraph ends with a period. The signals are of substance and decision. The feeling is of addition.

It begins with the poet's father, parent-thetically retired, retreated a little, to the yard around the farm house. He grew raspberries where the saskatoons and chokecherries used to bloom. He dug in his potato patch (notice how many of the lines are coming to resemble sentences or at least clauses), soil from which all stones have to be gone. The morning glass of wine does not make the poem ceremonial but familiar, personal. We see an individual seen by another individual. The latter, narrating, wants to bring the story from chronicle into myth. "He was lonesome," he says, normal for a retired Alberta farmer, "for death," kind of sententious, considering that we are looking at the regular first generation Canadian dad.

But when the phrase is used a second time, it begins a grammar for this part of the poem — it goes: he was lonesome, he was lonesome, he found the stone, he kept it.

First, he was lonesome for his work as remembered by his senses, for heat, smell, hum, and weight. The weight of a wrench in his pocket suggests something different from the weight of the dismembered Indian tool on the poet's papers. The retired farmer does not have the leisure of contemplation but the discomfort of memory.

Second, he was lonesome for his family as remembered by his flesh, for the prairie farmer's most intimate loss, for people felt too close for names, now under the earth or behind a desk. Absent means "not is," not "is not," but "not is." "Is" is the obsessed verb of the poem, and "is" means breathes. The hot wind, smell of horses, and distant hum of a threshing machine had all been brought on the breath of the earth, and are now absent.

As a retired man will often do, he had eyes to see value in what had once been an obstacle. He located in the sense of found the stone maul weight, and then he located in the sense of put it (the stone maul) in an otherwise empty raspberry basket. In both the found stanza and the kept stanza his son the poet represented his deliberate locating, by following preposition with preposition — there.

This retreating man gleaned the older maul and kept it like fruit, or associated it with the hand-crafted basket, an association that is in one way like its earlier putative association with rawhide loops, but in another way not. The basket on the railing is a little museum. The tool is a keepsake for the retiree with no crescent in his pocket. Crescent means growing, an unretired farmer's occupation. Even rockpiles cease to grow when the plowman retires to his porch to mull over his life.

11.

"In the poems we write towards cosmologies that cannot be (thank heavens) located," wrote Kroetsch in his essay on the Canadian long poem, "For Play and Entrance" (97).

Section eleven of "Stone Hammer Poem" is a resolution, and the ending of the poem. That is, it brings to a completion the change in the poem that began with the more firm narratogeny of the latter parts. It makes sentences with prosodic weight; and it fashions parallels or allusions to the preceding section. It ties the poem securely with loops, or at least puts it in a basket, though there are more secure places than a porch railing, or even a windy room.

In *The Crow Journals*, a bit of poem says:

I look at my hands.
They are no longer my own.
They have become my father's
hands. (52)

I keep it, says the poet now, and we are tipped off that the poem is now not so much serial, but laced together, this section to the last. Even the parentheses in this section tamp the poem down rather than scratching away its surface. The ice age is so far gone that the ground seems no longer in an interim condition, but settled. Even the desk, says this grammatical conservative, is stone, solid.

But very subtly the poet undercuts his accomplishment in bringing the poem at least into equilibrium. It is only sometimes that the implement is brought into usefulness, and only when the wind finds its way to the poet's desk; and what a use for a storied maul. Any old object, or new, can be used for such a simple job when such a need arises, infrequent as the white blossoms along a wire fence.

Very subtly. The word "smelling" is revealed by the syntax here to be what it properly is, a verb done by the poet rather than a condition of the object. Like his father he is lonesome, so he mimes in his place his father's missings, hot wind, smelling, memory. But having retreated further, he imagines further back. There is no unimagined scent, just as for Keats there was no unimagined tone from the urn.

For this poet the stone is a muse's tool that teases him further than the cycles of the ice ages, all the way to the dying sun, past Robert Frost's fire and ice metaphysic, to the most universal of seasons. "It is poetic, according to Kroetsch, by virtue of the way the mind working here transforms narrative into myth," said Sherman Paul in his article, "Serial Poems from Canada" (112).

The stone, given that cosmic field, is made of an original element, as was the buffalo blood, as is the poet himself. Sometimes the archaeologist stops looking at the losses that are his occupation, and writes, field notes, not for this stone hammer but for that.

That is, if you are properly hearing the poem you hear THAT at the end the poet is addressing the stone hammer, and telling it how large the subject and audience are. Stone and notes (and tones, yes) are only little, but everything is made of them.

1984

WORKS CITED

Kroetsch, Robert. "Beyond Nationalism: a Prologue." *Open Letter*, "Robert Kroetsch: Essays", Fifth Series, No. 4 (Spring 1983): 83-89.

_____. *Field Notes*. Don Mills, Ontario: General, 1981.

_____. "For Play and Entrance: the Contemporary Canadian Long Poem." *Open Letter*, Fifth Series, No. 4 (Spring 1983): 91-110.

_____. *The Crow Journals*. Edmonton: NeWest, 1980.

Paul, Sherman. "Serial Poems from Canada." A review of *The Long Poem Anthology* ed. by Michael Ondaatje. *North Dakota Quarterly*, 50, 2 (1982): 108-118.

bpNichol on the Train

A few years back some Canadian writers, Pierre Berton and others, published a spate of books on the great railroads of Canada, reminding us of the vital role they played in our history. In the years just before and after 1967, Canadian history became important to Canadian authors, especially the playwrights. There was a lot to be made out of Canadian history, including money, including Canada Council money.

In the hands of poets history tends to become myth, so I decided to spend some time in the libraries and collect poems about the Canadian railroads, to see whether the historians were right about the importance of the Last Spike to the "Canadian imagination." Of course we all know about E.J. Pratt's poem, though some of us argue about Pratt's attitude toward the businessmen and politicians who made whatever they could make while the gandy-dancers were swinging the company's hammers. But just how pervasive, I wondered, was the theme of the railroad in Canadian verse?

I found a lot of train poems, spanning a century from Pauline Johnson's image of locomotives as greyhounds racing across the west, to Gordon Lightfoot's railroad trilogy. I also found out some things. For instance, French-speaking Quebec poets have hardly ever written railroad poems, probably because the run to the ocean is not part of *their* history. Women poets very seldom write about the trains, not even to diminish them as Emily Dickinson did. Most interesting, to me, was the observation that during the latter years of the nineteenth century, when the heroic steel was joining us coast to coast, or rather coasts to Montreal and Toronto, the poets were not celebrating the event. Their favourite mode of travel seems to have been the birchbark canoe.

But when the jet airliners started zipping businessmen and politicians and Canada Council writers from city to city, and the railways went into decline, our poets stepped out of their courier-de-bois canoes and began to write prolifically about the train. It became a symbol, a myth, a setting, a controlling metaphor, sometimes even a character. Given the obvious mechanical difference between a train and a plane, it is hardly surprising that the trans-continental train-trip has become such a common subject at a time in which, as our literary commentators ceaselessly point out, the long poem has emerged as a prominent

Canadian literary form.

• • •

It comes as no surprise that the leading train poet is bpNichol. His first train poem was published in 1967. More importantly, his parents were railroad people. Apart from some sound poems and visual poems, his work has been largely in the long poem. He lives in Toronto, but his family is scattered across the west from Manitoba to Victoria. He travels a lot, as a poet and as a Nichol. Over the whole of his adult life much of that travel has been in long train trips. While he travels he writes. His journals are also journeys. His first book of non-concrete poems was titled *JOURNEYING & the returns*. For us, for bpNichol and us, the returns are the poems.

That book is made of several sequences, composed between 1963 and 1966. The third one is called "Ancient Maps of the Real World." On its first page the word "trans-continental" appears for the first time in Nichol's poetry. The poem is rich with references to elements of the natural world, earth, water, leaves, sun, air. Among them the young author looks cautiously for meaning: "what myth / lies there?" More significantly, he gives himself up to the motion of things:

> sun goes
> from east to west
>
> eyes & train follow

and so does the poem. Here is the faith or instinct that will not so much guide as allow his later train poems.

The train travels through much of Nichol's poetry from then on, partly because Nichol is such a restless and popular poet that he is often on the move. A long sequence called *Monotones*, written between 1967 and 1970, and published in 1971, dips into memories, many of them of trains, to make meditations. Nichol's major work, the many-volumed *Martyrology*, often mentions train travel. The invocation to Book III, uttered when the poet was realizing that this poem was companion to the longest journey a mortal can take, is offered to the poet's railroading father, and to his and to his:

> bless this poem
> this road that i have taken

The poet's life is made up of journeying and the returns. Two of the longest railroad poems are "Trans-Continental," published in *love: a book of remembrances* (1974), and *continental trance*, published in 1982, later to be seen as part of *Martyrology*, Book VI.

• • •

"Trans-Continental" is made of forty-nine short sections, and a trip from Toronto to Vancouver, March 13-16, 1971. As in the rest of a group called "Love poems," at least half the nouns are simply lower-case letters ("a drainage ditch/ an o"), love letters, perhaps. The text proceeds somewhere along the strip of taxonomy between naming of things and naming of the references themselves. The train ride is a short chapter in bpNichol's career of finding the alphabet and its cunning life in the phenomenal world. There the letters are foregrounded, are figures in the ground, momentary glyphs, part of the ground (or sky) itself.

So one reader is more than tempted to suppose that they are letters the concrete traveller at the window sees in his three and a half days, picks out, of the passing natural scene, from clouds, for example, from trees, fields, mountains, from a snowball splattered against the transparent glass ("a d in a cloudbank / an r by a sea") ("an l in a pool of pepsi"). As Heraclitus might have predicted, the letters are always becoming other letters.

A common letter in lyric poetry is I or lately i, and in this poem it does not take us long to remark its ambiguous being. It is one of the letters strewn like the others over the white space, but it also sits up straight as a subject in a sentence, or at least a sentence fragment. The others are usually objects, in noun clusters. bpNichol is a name and also a phenomenon in the world, a person. He is trying in winter-spring of 1971 to collapse the space between the operands of reference and their targets. If we sincerely believe that a word made of letters can "stand for" an object made of its parts, why should we not be able to make that reach in the opposite direction?

Or, wonders the same reader, is this all nonsense, a gratifying formula to replace fled understanding?

We all have experiences with letters, and have used them singly rather than simply as parts of words. So we look for similar uses by the poet. We cannot help wondering whether the letters are the initials of things; or of towns:

hornpayne to armstrong
h to a

If we have taken train trips we remember seeing lots of disphonetic letters, on poles, on the sides of freight cars, on sheds. They are messages to people who work on trains, but to the passengers they are only things. Even to the son of a railroading man, they are things now, love-letters from an illiterate world.

• • •

The brain of a poet like bpNichol is as much animated toward composition by letters as by mute unwritten objects. Composition means putting things side by side, which is the way to make words out of letters, and also the basic proposal of metonymy. Metaphor, on the other hand, puts things behind and in front. A train trip is metonymic, a periplum, and so is the alphabet, no matter what its sequence. A long train trip is of course periphrasis, no matter how straight the rails. Nichol's body travels along the track, but his mind goes round and round. If he sees a sign that says "est" (sec. 5) it may be a distinction from "ouest," but it will suggest being as in is, as well as a superlative, and maybe even a notorious western therapy-trip. We also know that Nichol, seeing "est" and "ouest," will wonder what kind of comment the Canadian rail managers are making in this kind of distinction: est ou est.

Thus Nichol makes his reader remain alert to his smallest moves, and that alertness is more important than the consequences of any wrong guesses. If you guess wrong, what have you done but find the delight the poet has been delighting in? I will give an example from section 6. After introducing the question of est-ouest, the poem says:

> this many miles from home
> r becomes everything

Reading eastward (if the poem is laid out like a map) you may find reverything. Reading westward from the word's r, you find reve, dream in a language recently introduced. A dream, for the traditional westward traveller, is hope. But on this track hope is the name of a town near the end of the line:

> later there is hope
> or lessness
> perhaps you dream

Thus one's train of thought is trained to disassemble a bpNichol poem as it is put together, and the poet does not mind that at all — in fact that is the subject of the art. That is the drawing of love, the disappearing of distance. Knowing what we know, we think, by the time we get to section 7, we see that Nichol has interested himself in suffixes. So "ness," he says, a noun suffix; "ing," he says, a verb suffix; and "ly," he ends up saying, an adverb suffix in its proper place.

Among those suffixes, this couplet appears:

> a rocking motion
> a creaking sound

and we can see how much, given Nichol's delight in looking inside words, he can do with what starts as a pair of noun phrases one would expect to accompany a train ride. The previous attention to suffixes suggests that for a moment we separate these from the roots, as the poem has been doing. We are left for a moment with two verbs, and do not have to be told that one is a motion, one a sound. As we did not have to be told, we suspect the telling, and then we think of nouns, rock and creek, thus going from the moving train to the geography it moves and sounds through. Now we have a verb, the train, moving through a noun, the land; we have reference and referent, if you like, because we know it is really a mind, or a sensibility moving through material (or as Shelley had it in "Mont Blanc," the other way round), especially if we substitute poem for ride, as Nichol will remind us to do. We have, to remember Nichol's favourite rock, Gertrude Stein, a continuous present, the train on which Einstein's relativistic passenger is justified in believing that he is sitting still, but which is in constant movement, as Heraclitus told us all, like a creek we can not step into twice.

None of this is unprepared by the poem. The poem is not there to dissolve once the language becomes real; each piece of it, each letter

resembles nothing more than
resembling

inging

(Here, when you read again, even nothing, no noun, comes participally, in the present tense.)

• • •

The same reader or any other can read each speck of the poem over and over this way, and writing about it, can write for days and days, longer than any continental trip. Turning his writing into an essay on the poem, he will leave most of his notes behind, shunt a whole baggage car of them. Reading the poem again, he will say oh oh from time to time, and often ho ho, gauging the track just passed, but more is already coming, some of it back there already toward the vanishing point, the disappeared period, some of it around the next bend: all at once, love letters like presents, blessings.

As a poet, Nichol is an old section hand. In section 20 here he imitates his mother load, Gertrude Stein:

bless this
i did say
yes yes yes
i did say i did say
bless this yes
bless this yes
bless yes yes

We remember that blessing was also associated with his father, in *Martyrology* Book III: "bless this poem / this road that i have taken."

He is not saying bless as if he were bestowing blessings as if he were a god of poetry. If he were a god he would not be taking the train. He is asking for blessings, and he is thanking, as a grateful person might say bless you to a rescuer. To bless means, originally, to sanctify with blood. Readers of Nichol will know that for him the words and letters are themselves sanctified, are saints, martyrs. Martyrs bleed, and hearts beat. Nichol's favourite letter, he has often said, is H, or h. In "Trans-Continental" it usually falls when the word "heart" or the organ itself could be expected. In section 30 a kind of country and western song (in regard to this kind of poem we should, I suppose, write c & w) is going through:

just another just another

broken heart
half-hearted dream

just another h another h another t

Between that h and that t there is an ear we can see but never hear. An h, like an r, is called a consonant, but is really a vowel, because each is made only with air passing through.

In any case, the letters in the word "heart" seem to be falling around one's attention more and more as the poem proceeds. Its e seems often to suggest Ellie, the woman at the core of Nichol's poetry. Blessing from the heart is a continuous response to the given, and that is why this is a love poem. It is a train of thanks for the present. The letters rain from the sky, released by a lucky stroke. Nichol's poem of response has to be self-referential; but unlike the witty self-referentiality of others, self-referentiality in the poetry of bpNichol *is always bound to emotion*, a referentiality to heart's feeling, suggesting that words and being are one, a sustaining breath, a susurous bee-ing:

a longing for flesh
a flash of long

a lingering look
a languid mood

an l in a pool of pepsi

a cola
an a

(A curious coincidence. At this point in the writing of this essay I reached my daily quota of words and went to the backlog of magazines

that arrived while I was out of the country. In *Brick* 23, the Winter
1985 number, I found a letter bpNichol wrote to Mary Ellen Solt in
1973. Here is a paragraph:

> the other thing that happened was a sudden integration of my
> breath line poetry (my belief in sound) and my literal obsession with
> the single letter & what it contains as element of word, as sound
> unit, & in terms of its own history (vis-a-vis Alfred Kallir *Sign &
> Design*) i had in my comic strip drawings frequently included
> letters floating in the sky or simply standing in the middle of the
> landscape   since "Frames" had shown me i could replace things
> with the names of things & still retain the power i suddenly realized
> that i could simply include the single letters in my poems   in this
> case the name & the thing were the same   the alphabet is runic   i
> began to write the *Love Poems* climaxing in a long 49 section poem
> not included here titled "Trans-Continental"   love poems because
> they expressed my feelings about the alphabet   celebrated my wed-
> ding to it (i wax romantic but its true — the burst of feeling when i
> wrote them was incredible) (19)

Feelings are likely to become clearer, or can at least be explored
more fully on a train trip, the traveller freed from daily chores and dis-
tracting telephone. At the same time the wheels click and the poles
flick by, the sitter sits long in the same position and lets himself enjoy

a trance state
a continental trance

— not exactly, as the cascading letters land on the poem's pages, a
train of thought. Maybe a train of Thoth. A trance-porting. A future
title.

The later poem will rest on these words: "an ending / in itself /
unending" (1982, 41). Approaching the Pacific in this earlier poem, we
hear "a new beginning / an ending." Section 49, the last (was the poet
awake forty-nine hours on the trip?), starts: "final finale," the second
word made by a final e as the train nears what used to be called Termi-
nal City. The last line of the poem is: "g t" — probably not goodbye
Toronto, more likely grand tour, or as we say out here, great trip.
Goodbye, train. Thank you for the book.

• • •

The journeying of "Trans-Continental" is followed a decade later by
the returns of *continental trance*, but as Gertrude Stein said (and is
quoted by Nichol at the beginning of the poem), "we cannot retrace our
steps." In the first poem the voyage is from Toronto to Vancouver, in
the second from Vancouver to Toronto. Although phrases from the

earlier poem come to melodize the later one, there are significant differences other than direction. Among the most important is that the poet is now wed to Ellie rather than to the letters of the alphabet. On this trip she is with him on the train and in the poem, and she has their next issue inside her.

The reader knows all this early because the poem is more conventionally narrative than its predecessor. It is at times anecdotal. It begins with a scenario: the poet and his pregnant wife are leaving Vancouver on the train for Toronto, at eight p.m. of July 27, 1981. With him he will carry memories of his trainman father and his mother; it is going to be a family story in a familiar language. The lines in which it will be told will be a good deal longer. There will not be a shower of discreet letters. Even the CN logo, the poet notices as he gets onto the train, has been erased.

By the time the poem gets to its second section, we know that we have a much more garrulous poet now, one who obligingly explains that the poem will tell a story, but that the latter will not go the way he had anticipated because the train is taking an alternate route at the beginning of its passage. Thus the "argument" of the poem is introduced early: the train trip, like a life, may be anecdotal and accumulative, but though one knows what is at the end, one will be transported in ways accidental and unplanned.

The poet is ten years older than the groom of the alphabet who had ridden the "Trans-Continental" to the coast. He is at an age during which one sees his life as drama rather than lyric. Close to dear life and undelivered life, he knows something about death. The rumour of death will, as the poem rolls eastward, become a pervasive suggestion made by many of the images.

Perhaps it is there in the first five lines of the poem:

minus the ALL ABOARD
minus my father waving
minus the CN logo
minus my mother waving
minus seventeen years of my life

He is not off to university to begin everything now — everything began quite a while ago. Minus nostalgia, he is daily adding experience to his life, images to his lifetime's poem. As he does so, days are subtracted from his life's quota, as here on the train-trip miles are subtracted from the total distance home. No wonder this train or poem he rides is called a "mixed metaphor."

Death and life. In 1981 bpNichol or "the poet" was halfway through the conventional allotment of years. Though their unborn child is taking this trip with them, so is the memory of their earlier child, who did not survive its passage. Mortality is real. Much of the poem deals with that lesson. First we learn to do our adding, then we have to learn our minuses: "as we will vanish / despite the wish to carry on immortal."

The message that he has to vanish just as everything else does is, for the poet, necessarily found in the structure of the poem. This he lets himself and us know in characteristic Nicholese: "you too, Nicky." He is punning on the name of the Japanese long poem favoured by poets such as Basho. There are at least three things about *utanikki* that I find interesting here (leaving aside the fact that it usually embeds *haiku* in nests of poetic prose). *Utanikki* are diary writings, usually associated with a long journey, or with family matters, both of which Nichol offers in *continental trance*. (Slyly Nichol mentions "the japanese family talking / words i don't know" among his fellow passengers.) In addition they make one continuously aware of the flow of time — as little images of life are blinked open, their immanent vanishing is noted.

Early in the poem the subject of death appears casual and coincidental:

The old guy who spoke to the porter just now said:
"my wife wanted to take this trip
before she takes her heavenly trip"

my grandma, 96, earlier today said:
"i don't think i wanta stay around too many more"

Ellie's sitting across from me
reading Peter Dickinson's *One Foot In The Grave*

& in the first draft of this poem i wrote:
"minus these coincidences
what is the world trying to tell me?"

But soon the sense of disappearance is seen to be the truth that ties personal mortality to the social condition. After a page of railroad reminiscence we suddenly get this, by mis-direction:

random information intrudes each time i ride these rails
maybe for the last time
headline in that Vancouver paper
GOVERNMENT AXES TRANS-CONTINENTAL LINE
    THRU JASPER
part of my memory disappears
1500 jobs & a slice of history

From time to time, as the poem passes through ancient geography, the poet reaches for history. Realizing that he "won't be here" when "that

leaning tree" falls, he spreads the knowledge of his husbandly age from
"Pacific Ocean to the Great Lakes / middle passage the explorers
dreamed of / died for...." This leads him to the awful realization:
"God my life ends / years before this poem possibly can."

So forget the "final finale / definite end end" of "Trans-Continental."
One's life, one learns in middle age, when there are parents *and* children, is a little middle of history. One does not have to control the beginning (which was a rerouting anyway), and one does not have to
imagine an ending. They will be taking on passengers after you've got
off.

· · ·

That is perhaps the neatest irony of the contemporary long poem —
that we see more vanishings and we see them sooner than people did in
earlier centuries, and therefore are freed from the logic of ending (or
grandly beginning) our poems. Where the *utanikki* and the *haiku* inside
them were informed by death and constant change, our poems are
informed by vanishings and quick change. Our poets are quick change
artists.

So we do not have to know it all as a Dante or Chaucer or early
Pound would seem to do. In *continental trance* bpNichol speaks of
"things i have knowledge of but cannot account for," and he is not
referring to metaphysical experiences. They are "insistent instances,"
or "random information," something like a movie film, Gertrude
Stein's analogy for her writing, "discrete frames in / a continuous
flow," which would also describe the picture windows in a moving
train. Pieces of life as sure as death, they persuade the rider that "none
of us can escape these details." The poem, then, moves not toward a
conclusion or a transcendence, but as a part somewhere in the ongoing
middle of the *Martyrology*, through a "flux logic." On the VIA rails, it
is a "linear narrative of random sequential thots," provoked by "the
given."

As the *utanikki* alternates between prose and poetry, this poem,
steadily putting miles between itself and Asia, alternates between
observed phenomena (outside and inside the train) and the still/moving
author's musings, on time, on death, on the poetics that unashamedly
operate in the conducting of a life as readily as a poem. This poem is
as self-referential as "Trans-Continental," but for different reasons.
Often the poem says "this poem" or "these words," and that seems odd.
It is as if the poem were demonstrating a poem, and that is not
reflexive. If it were reflexive the poem would say "myself." But it is
self-referential, in the way that a singer might say "this boy wants you
back again."

That is a thought that one might not bother developing here, but it is worth remembering for another time. Let us take the easy way, whereby we take the poem's comments on poetry-making to be thought by the poet himself. As voices of other passengers are recorded from time to time, so do at least two voices speak in the ruminations. One that is accused of butting in on the prime one turns out to be a bringer of good advice. It is the anti-nostalgic voice that seeks also to urge indeterminacy, inconclusiveness. It asks:

why the need to resolve parameters?

why not the rush of
the asymetrical
arhythmic
world?

why not the y *not* the z
in the unwritten alphabets ahead?

In the last two lines it proposes questions rather than conclusions, and counsels (or pleads for) suspension of resolution. (One might compare Robert Kroetsch's essay on the long poem, "For Play and Entrance.") Z is an ending only, the mark of zero. Who would look for a summing-up of a poem whose first word is "minus"?

Similarly, Nichol's guest voice (now) persuades him that he does not like the "symbol," or only as a sound instrument, "as accent to the basic drum / of consciousness," nor does he like simile "except as entrance to / a pataphysical reality," a Continental entrance in this case, back through the west opened up. His voice says that he prefers the play of words, and again we see that for Nichol oblique poetics serve and invite emotion, "the moment when the feelings focus / absolutely."

So there is another kind of alternation in this poem: there are plenty of relaxed observations of detail, in which a reader does not look for bpNichol's usual half-hid tricks, but now and then there are the *Martyrology* japes, performed by the ministering spirits, st. utter and st. ate. Usually the details are told in narrational sentence fragments, like those of Michael Ondaatje, and the poetics are dis-played; but for perhaps the first time in his writing, sobered by time and mortality, Nichol makes prosy comments on life, offers wisdom as if he were an elder. He will say "this is how the world is," and tell us; he will observe that some phenomenon is "like life." He seems to be practising up to be a father.

Among his observations is one that is ambiguous, maybe chilling, maybe only instructive. Geophysical patterns that prove illusory as the train and the eyes looking from it get nearer are "rimes that disappear as you draw closer to their sense." Does this mean that one gives up delight as one gets older and wiser, or is it further instruction to bend to closely revealed phenomena and let one's cherished order fade? Is that what rerouting haply brings? The ambiguity remains when the words say

> vanishing
> & nothing visible
> except a vast shining

A vast shining is emptiness, void of detail, of mortal darkness; but it is probably the place the saints return to.

• • •

The saints, familiar to readers of the *Martyrology*, visit after a routing delay in Winnipeg, where the young Nichol first looked up and heard them. He refers to them as not a literary device but "a vice i keep returning to." They are not the traditional bringers of inspiration, exactly:

> so many years spent talking with you
> a willed hallucination
> more than continental
> a kind of lifelong trance

That is a pretty good characterization of Nichol's ongoing poem, as well. Sometimes it is a rebus, sometimes a series of imagist verses, but always a journal, an *écriture* cognate with waking life. Because the "trance" is willed but the language encountered thereby is not, rime and coincidence lead to instructive narration. Coincidence is ironically permitted by the acceptance of the asymmetrical and the arhythmic.

One keeps one's eyes open and whatever is outside comes in. If the reader has ever had the travelling experience designated on page 33 of *continental trance*, he has caught a flick of the poet's first experience, and it is not a simple celebration of nature:

> the flickering light thru the trees
> sets up an echo in my brain
> petit mal
> makes me want to puke

> but the trees
> so clustered
> a bird could walk the branches
> a thousand miles or more

> it is a map of consciousness
> what the light yields disgorges
> perceived thru a pattern of branches

the birds fly free of

In the middle of his life the poet passes through a thick wood, but in Northern Ontario there is no Virgil to give up time and half of eternity showing him the afterlife. The best this sleeper's car can offer is more imagery, of dark and flickering light. After the sun goes down the clouds hide the stars and there is only a locomotive's eye, only a

dim flicker of light
visible suddenly across the lake
before the train takes us round the bend
into the illusory dark

bpNichol may not like the "symbol" much, but he is stuck with it. He bought the tickets.

That kind of symbol does not lead the death-conscious poet to thoughts of prayer, however. That is done by his first love, the seraphs of the alphabet. This happens in a nowhere place called Hornpayne, which also appeared briefly in "Trans-Continental." Nichol probably likes it because its name both starts with H and offers a good pun for the poet's vocation. There in Hornpayne, the story goes, Mr and Mrs Nichol can see most of a sign on the side of a decrepit building. What they see is OTHING. What Mr Nichol might have said in a poem ten years earlier is "o thing!" What he and Mrs Nichol see when they get closer, and rime gives way to sense, is CLOTHING. What the poet had fancied he might have the luck to see was NOTHING. He compares the "boarded up & broken" store to his lifelong wish for the clothing of belief, and then voices a purportedly hopeless prayer anyway:

the name of death is "NOTHING"
the name of after-death is "NOTHING"
accept Lord Mother/Father
the briefness of this life you've granted
this bliss

Bliss means lightning if you are fond of words, a lucky stroke. Accidents are the relatives of coincidence. Mis-reading is creation.

No thing. The poem approaching its destination is still minus-sing. The images and rumours of death become more numerous. It is a "construct of a conscious mind / governed by the inevitable end-rime / time." Though the poem has "a consciousness of its own mortality," the train racing to Toronto, its poet discounts personal loss. He invokes the name of Homer, who also wrote a poem about a man going home, and hints at the common theory that there was no single author of the story, that it was a poem made by many, a nation's epic by "a community of speakers." Yes,

i's a lie
dispenses illusions of plot

biography when geography's the clue
locale & history of the clear "you"

Not personal odyssean destination, but destiny of a nation.

• • •

The first stanza of *continental trance* tells of giving up a plan for the narrative because rerouting began immediately. Now not just intention but all personal proprietorship is gone. Early in the morning of August 2, 1981 the Nichols detrain, but other people, poets among them, will be sitting behind those windows tomorrow.

Before he alights the last words the poet sees on a wall are I WANTED TO BE AN ANARCHIST. The two ANs remind at least one reader of the two earlier nots: "why *not* the y not the z . . . ?"

"An," says Nichol to take it home, "ending / in itself / unending."

"Trans-Continental" was a poem about a turning point in life, an epithalamium celebrating his wedding with the beautiful letters. *continental trance* is the first poem of middle-age, when one becomes father and leaves "i" behind, celebrates not a wedding to come, but honours a marriage newly recognized. The *utanikki* does not sing about the response to country one passes through and eyes; it is the voice of the land speaking in phrases from whatever mouths it can find mature enough and still alive.

1985

WORKS CITED

Nichol, bp. *Journeying & the returns*. Toronto: Coach House, 1967.

———. *The Martyrology*. Books 3 and 4. Toronto: Coach House, 1976.

———. *love: a book of remembrances*. Vancouver: Talonbooks, 1974.

———. *continental trance*. Lantzville, B.C.: Oolichan, 1982.

———. "A Letter to Mary Ellen Solt." *Brick 23* (Winter 1985): 18-19.

The End of the Line

I guess I take the page for a fetish as much as the average reader does. I smell books, I'll rub the paper on my cheek, I snap the sheet's edge with my thumb. I seldom taste the surface, but I have been known to do so. I do like to get up close — I go to bed with as many books as I can. Up close — in the 1970s, as my writing turned to prose, I returned to composing with a pen, on lined paper.

But when I write verse it may not run off at the mouth as prose does. Notation of the line prevents that. One returns; there is the versus. The poem keeps returning from the verge, to the place where the poet is now, line by line, though he keeps going toward, in *its* direction. My little dog runs ahead of me and comes back to my feet, then off she goes again. I am I, in a poem, because my little dog knows I am there, hoping she is faithful. She can turn, and turn, and yet go on, and turn again.

Even in the middle of mixed metaphors, it means as much to come back as it does to go forward, and in composing a poem, one knows that it is for meaning, or rather because of meaning, that one stops, however shortly. The majority of poems one finds in magazines are trifles not worth rereading. They are likewise arrangements of words that seem to benefit not at all from their line-notation. One asks: why stop a line at all and begin anew unless such break in the flow means something? Here is, for observation, a little poem I found in a Canadian magazine in 1976:

black-winged birds
ride
the swells of grain.

the rain
scatters
across the sky

forcing
waves of wind
down
on the flatlands,
serving trays

gray in the rain.

I walk
between
the raindrops

slipping gently
around
my shoulders.

it is here
my ancestry
shows

Here.

mud under fingernails
grain
galloping south-west
rising
on black soil.

It is true that this is an insignificant descriptive poem, but it is also typical of what is to be found in the average well-produced-because-Canada-Council-supported Canadian poetry magazine.

For the life of me, I cant figure out why "slipping gently," for instance, should be considered a line, or why "around" or why "my shoulders" should be considered a line. In fact, if one does read the poem with any observation of the cadence suggested graphologically, one winds up with a silly mock-dramatic rhythm not unlike the popular burlesques of the old Hollywood Dracula: I want / to drink / your blood.

On the other hand we have Mr William Wordsworth, a practitioner of five-beat metrics, who knew that rime is not without reason, and knew too that the end of the line is not just sister to another mister. In "Lines Composed a Few Miles above Tintern Abbey," 1798, he says:

                    And I have felt
A presence that disturbs me with the joy
Of elevated thoughts; a sense sublime
Of something far more deeply interfused,
Whose dwelling is the light of setting suns,
And the round ocean and the living air,
And the blue sky, and in the mind of man:
A motion and a spirit, that impels
All thinking things, all objects of all thought,
And rolls through all things. Therefore am I still

A lover of the meadows and the woods.
And mountains. . . .

(ll. 93-104)

I am thinking of that phrase that hangs on the edge: "Therefore am I still," and of the sentence beginning "Therefore am I still / A lover." Earlier in the poem Wordsworth recalled with rue his earlier days, when he naturally imitated nature, "When like a roe / I bounded o'er the mountains, by the sides / Of the deep rivers, and the lonely streams, / Wherever nature led," thus resembling "these hedge-rows, hardly hedge-rows, little lines / Of sportive wood run wild." Now a learned and tempted priest of nature, he argues that he does not bound o'er the landscape, yet retains a thinking adult's love for the natural scene, his mind like spirit animating it. By tapping that word "still" at the end of his aforementioned line, he marvellously allows more than regular attention to the change and the continuance of his love. Change and continuance — that is a nice use for the turn and return of the line's end.

• • •

William Butler Yeats is a wonderful instructor in line-making and line-ending. The four octaves of "Sailing to Byzantium" end-rime in this pattern: *ababab cc*, and the *cc* of the fourth stanza rimes with the *cc* of the second stanza. (Yeats's wit lurks throughout, so that his *cc* makes the initials of his closing couplet.) When one finds in the work of an ordinary poet a strict end-rime, one expects some weakening of the sentence in the service of that structure. But Yeats is a great poet, and his work exhibits the riches gathered by his weave of sentence and line. I will cite three examples from "Sailing to Byzantium," each of which, like the Wordsworthian example, reveals form as thought.

Two (and more) appear in the first octave:

That is no country for old men. The young
In one another's arms, birds in the trees
— Those dying generations — at their song,
The salmon-falls, the mackerel-crowded seas,
Fish, flesh, or fowl, commend all summer long
Whatever is begotten, born, and dies.
Caught in that sensual music all neglect
Monuments of unageing intellect.

The phrase "The young" is a very short ending to line one, and the subject of a long sentence to follow. Its function in the sentence will emerge on reading that is made to come second to its function as completion of the line; and that order is created by the ending of the line. Among other school children we were taught that a sentence is "a complete thought." Well, all thoughts are complete thoughts, and they are also parts, hence uncompleted, of longer thoughts. So with the line of verse, anticipating its turn. "That is no country for old men. The young [!]" is a "complete" emotional outbursting; and in the prose writings of many poets the line is spoken of as the measure of emotion. Charles Olson gave the line to the individual heart and the syllable to tribal mind. In Yeats, it might be said, the line speaks emotion and the sentence thought.

My second example is to be found in the couplet, where because of the line-ending (the pause will depend on the reading habits of the reader) we hear "neglect" first as a noun, and that it is "caught in that sensual music" that beguiles the young. Then the next line tells us that "neglect" is a verb, and that the beguiled young have no time for mind or eternity. It is not that the second reading replaces the first — that would be impossible. We have both readings, and thus the density that Yeats's secretary, Ezra Pound, ascribed to good poetry.

The third example is a matter of the bond between rhythm and emotion. The first two lines of the second octave are unremittingly iambic:

An aged man is but a paltry thing,
A tattered coat upon a stick, unless

— imitation of resigned self-pity, and end with that word "unless" (that is, more), which is easy to rise slightly upon and follow with a suspension that is . . . (bang! bang!) followed by two spondees of joy:

Soul clap its hands and sing, and louder sing

They are the first two beats of the music of transcendence that Yeats is arguing for. The poem is about goodbye and hello, and he tells us with the line's end and the beginning of the line. Turn, return.

William Carlos Williams is a poet who, like Wordsworth before him, felt the need to draw attention to the active voice as the source for poetry. Wordsworth spoke of poetry as an overflowing of spontaneous emotion recollected in tranquillity. Everybody remembers that, but few also remember that Wordsworth went on to say: " . . . till, by a species of reaction, the tranquillity gradually disappears, and an emotion, kindred to that which was before the subject of contemplation, is gradually produced, and does itself actually exist in the mind" (740). Now, Williams is not usually thought of as contemplative — no poet who fills his poems with exclamation marks will be thought to have written after quietude. In fact, Williams used to pull his car to the side of the road to his patient's house, or delay his next clinic patient's entrance, in order to jot down a poem on his Rx pad. But no prescriptions, those.

The poems sought to sound not like descriptions, either, of the important moment/occasion, but like re-creations (re-actions, said Wordsworth) of them, re-present-ations of them. Observe the beginning of a poem from *Spring and All*, in which the subject is the coming into "the new world naked":

By the road to the contagious hospital
under the surge of the blue
mottled clouds driven from the
northeast — a cold wind. . . .
                    (1951, 241)

Most anecdotists and a lot of poets would have told of the "clouds driven from the northeast," but I always picture Dr Williams wetting his finger and pointing it toward the sky, or at least stopping to get it right — which he does for us with his re-created pause.

A few lines later he lowers his gaze to the nearby ground, and with him we observe "all along the road the reddish / purplish, forked, upstanding" flora. It is as if the viewer were to say that the stuff was reddish — well, really more like purplish. So the poem is not a description of a landscape, but a record of the actual voice of the percipient being on the scene. Image by itself is pretty boring, and generally received with passivity. The fetching line, though, brings the image home, through the transparent eye, to the place in which it belongs.

Margaret Avison, who gives the image into the service of the spirit, said:

Nobody stuffs the world in at your eyes.
The optic heart must venture: a jail-break
And re-creation.
                    ("Snow," 27)

Where line-break is a jail-break, the doors of perception are invitingly open. Lift your lids and sound out this following Avison poem; see how the reading eye is exercised, and notice at the same time where the inner eye goes, how quickly from telephoto to wide-angle, measuring, as Dr Williams said, between the objects:

The beauty of the unused
      (the wheatear among birds, or
        stonechat)
    the unused in houses (as a
      portion of low roof swept by the
          buttery leaves of a pear tree
          where a manx cat is
          discovered — just now — blinking his
          sunned Arctic sea-eyes in the

```
             sun-play)
        the beauty of the
          unused in one I know, of
          excellent indolence
          from season into
             skywide wintering
        should be
        confidently, as it is
        copious and new into the morning,
        celebrated.
                                    (1966, 99)
```

That poem is called "Unspeakable," but it certainly shows one how to speak its lines.

I suppose that generally the line and its breakage represent or record the meeting of self and other, writer and universe, maybe body and mind. If the heartbeat (personal consciousness), as Robert Duncan suggests, impels the line to continue pulsing forward, the mind (shared consciousness) interjects a suspension and a return. It edits. One encounters wit where the line ends and will begin. The heart, an involuntary muscle, says go forward, continue, my little dog. The language bank of rime and wit says wait, come back a second, what did you say, have you considered the ambiguity of your path? The heart knows nothing of mixed emotions (though it lives unknowingly too in mixed metaphors), but shared mind can read the meaning in the former's irregular murmur.

It was to illustrate such doubleness of desire and awareness that I wrote a little envoy to one of my books. It is of course always with distaste that one contemplates quoting oneself, but during the times between sittings here before this essay, when I have thought about it, I have remembered this little poem's intent. It is called "To You & You," and is meant as instruction on how to read one person and his poems, especially by lending ear to his notation — meant to be proof that emotional disclosure is made by intervention of the mind to end a line:

Keeping everything
at its proper distance

the story, split, of
my life.

I want you
so much
to look at my
ending.

Dont try to
understand, try to
stand
in the high wind

I make passing you
& reaching out
to hold you
off

(1974)

Poetry is not for consumption; bread is. When I was a kid two slices of bread and some peanut butter suggested the end jam meant in my world. On the other foot, the bread-line should not return. The poem's line does, perhaps at a dog trot. And out it goes again, a tongue with a human mind for a leash.

1981

WORKS CITED

Avison, Margaret. *The Dumbfounding*. New York: Norton, 1966.

_____. *Winter Sun, The Dumbfounding Poems 1940-66*. Toronto: McClelland & Stewart, 1982. Bowering, George. *In the Flesh*. Toronto: McClelland & Stewart, 1974.

Williams, William Carlos. *The Collected Earlier Poems*. London: MacGibbon & Kee, 1951.

_____. *Selected Poems*. New York: New Directions, 1969.

_____. *Imaginations*. Ed. with an Introduction by Webster Schott. New York: New Directions, 1970.

Wordsworth, William. *Poetical Works*. With Introduction and Notes. Ed. Thomas Hutchison. A new Edition, revised by Ernest de Selincourt. Oxford, London, New York: Oxford UP, 1978.

Yeats, W.B. "Sailing to Byzantium." In *The Collected Poems*. New York: Macmillan, 1955.

Author/Critic Index

George Bowering was born in the southern Okanagan Valley of British Columbia. He attended Victoria College, University of British Columbia, and the University of Western Ontario. Bowering has taught at the University of Calgary, Sir George Williams University, and Simon Fraser University, where he teaches now. Twice a Governor General's award winner, once for poetry in 1969 and for fiction in 1980, Bowering has lectured and presented papers at many universities in North America, Europe, and the Antipodes.